Apple Pro Training Series

Logic Pro 8 and Logic Express 8

David Nahmani

Apple
Certified

Apple Pro Training Series: Logic Pro 8 and Logic Express 8
David Nahmani
Copyright © 2008 by David Nahmani

Published by Peachpit Press. For information on Peachpit Press books, contact:

Peachpit Press
1249 Eighth Street
Berkeley, CA 94710
(510) 524-2178
Fax: (510) 524-2221
www.peachpit.com
To report errors, please send a note to errata@peachpit.com.
Peachpit Press is a division of Pearson Education.

Editors: Bob Lindstrom, Robyn Thomas
Series Editor: Nancy Peterson
Production Coordinator: Laurie Stewart, Happenstance Type-O-Rama
Technical Editors: Robert Brock, Bill Burgess, Justin Carlson
Copy Editor: Karen Seriguchi
Compositor: Chris Gillespie, Happenstance Type-O-Rama
Indexer: Valerie Perry
Cover Illustration: Kent Oberheu
Cover Production: Happenstance Type-O-Rama

ISBN 13: 978-0-321-50292-6
ISBN 10: 0-321-50292-2
9 8 7 6 5 4 3 2 1
Printed and bound in the United States of America

Acknowledgments First and foremost, a huge heartfelt thank you to my good friend Bill Burgess for his inspiring confidence. Bill, this book wouldn't have been possible without your respectful guidance.

Many grateful thanks to Patty Montesion for placing her trust in me and for offering her ongoing help and support.

Special thanks to my editorial team: Nancy Peterson, Bob Lindstrom, Karen Seriguchi, Robyn Thomas, Robert Brock, Bill Burgess, and Justin Carlson. Thank you also to David Dvorin for his advice and encouragement.

Thanks to the Apple Logic team for providing their insight: Bob Hunt, Jeff Taylor, Manfred Knauff, and Thorsten Adam.

My deepest gratitude to all the artists and producers who agreed to provide their Logic sessions for this book: Blumpy and Joe Hedges for the song "Mitral Valve Prolapse," Klayton from Celldweller for his remix "LVL-Home," and Myron for his song "Darkside."

Finally, very special thanks to all my students, to my fellow Logic trainers, to all the members of the Los Angeles Logic Pro User Group, and to all the good people on the Logic Pro Help forums for keeping the Logic user community alive by sharing their ideas and inspiration.

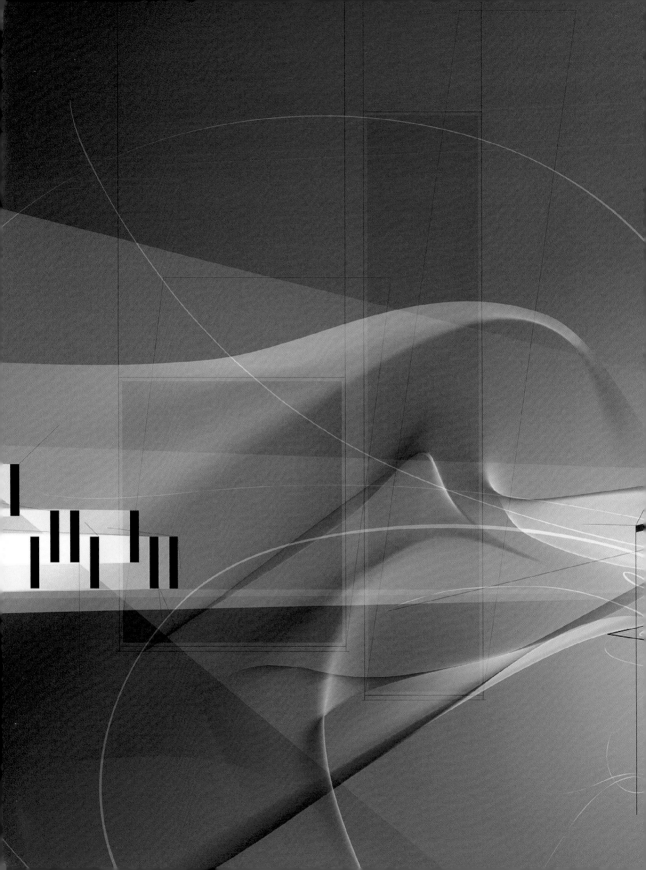

Contents at a Glance

Table of Contents

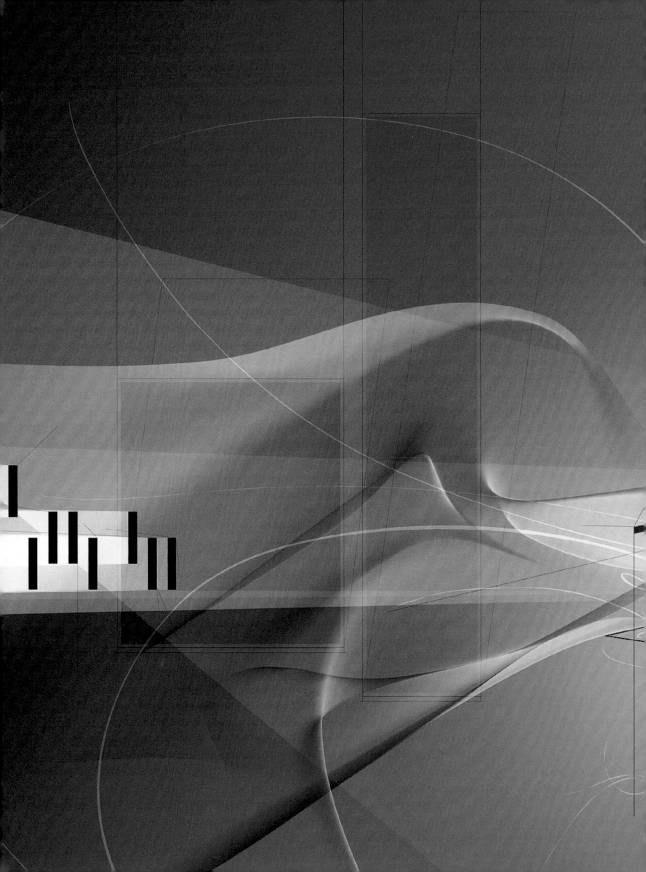

Getting Started

Welcome to the official Apple Pro Training Series course for Logic Pro 8 and Logic Express 8. This book—a comprehensive introduction to Logic Pro and Logic Express—uses real-world music and real-world exercises to teach you the many uses of this comprehensive composition application.

The Methodology

This is, first and foremost, a hands-on course. Every exercise is designed to enable professional-quality composing in Logic as quickly as possible. Each lesson builds on previous lessons to guide you through the program's functions and capabilities. If you are new to Logic, start at the beginning and progress through each lesson in order.

Course Structure

The book is designed to guide you through the music production process as it teaches Logic. The first lesson is an overview of the production process in Logic. You'll get familiar with the interface and the various ways to navigate a project while building a song from scratch using Apple Loops, then arranging, mixing, and exporting the song to an MP3 file. In the Recording and Editing section, you will go deeper into the stages of music production. You'll learn how to come up with the raw material that will be the building blocks of your musical project. The Producing section will show you how to take those building blocks and make sure their tempos match, then how to arrange and mix them into your final project. Finally, you'll learn the basics of scoring movies and become familiar with troubleshooting techniques to solve problems common to software composers.

The lessons are grouped into the following categories:

▶ Introduction to Logic: Lesson 1

▶ Building a Song: Lessons 2–7

▶ Arranging and Mixing: Lessons 8–10

▶ Other Topics: Lessons 11–12

Using the DVD Book Files

The *Apple Pro Training Series: Logic Pro 8 and Logic Express 8* DVD (included with the book) contains the project files you will use for each lesson, as well as media files that contain the audio and video content you will need for each exercise. After you transfer the files to your hard disk, each lesson will instruct you in the use of the project and media files.

Installing Logic

The exercises in this book require that you install Logic Studio along with all the Logic Studio Content included on the installer. To install Logic Studio, insert the first installation DVD in your computer, double-click the installer and follow the instructions until you reach the step Installation Type. Then make sure you select Logic Studio Content to get a solid checkmark in that checkbox, not a – (minus sign). Then continue following the installer's instructions to complete the installation.

NOTE ▶ If you have already installed Logic Studio but did not install all the content, you can run the installer again and choose to install only the Logic Studio Content.

Using Default Preferences

All the instructions and descriptions in this book assume you are using the default set of preferences (unless instructed to change them) and the default keyboard shortcuts installed with Logic. If you have changed some of your preferences or key commands, you may not get the same results described in the exercises. To make sure you can follow along with this book, it's best to revert to the initial set of Logic preferences before you start the lessons. Keep in mind that when you initialize your preferences, you will lose your custom settings, and later you may want to reset your favorite preferences manually.

1   From the main menu bar, choose Logic Pro > Preferences > Initialize All Except Key Commands.

LOGIC EXPRESS ▶ When instructed to choose an item from the *Logic Pro* menu, choose the same item from the *Logic Express* menu.

A confirmation message pops up.

2 Click Initialize.

Your preferences are initialized. To initialize your key commands you need to open the Key Commands window.

3 In the main menu bar, choose Logic Pro > Preferences > Key Commands.

The Key Commands window opens.

4 Click the Options pop-up menu and choose Presets > U.S. Standard (or if you have a laptop, Presets > U.S. MacBook).

5 Close the Key Commands window.

Screen Resolution

If you are using a small screen resolution, some of the project files may appear different on your screen than they do in the book. When you open a project, if you can't see the whole Arrange window, move the window until you can see the three window controls at the left of the title bar, and click the zoom button (the third button from the left) to make the window fit the screen.

When using a small screen resolution, you may also have to zoom or scroll more often than instructed in the book to perform some of the exercise steps. In some cases you may have to temporarily resize or close an area of the Arrange window to perform an action in another area.

Installing the Logic Lesson Files

On the DVD, you'll find a folder titled Logic 8_Files, which contains three subfolders: Lessons, Media, and Apple Loops for Logic Express Users. The first two folders contain the lessons and media files for this course. (See the section "Instruction for Logic Express Users" for an explanation of the third folder.) Make sure you keep these two folders together in the Logic 8_Files folder on your hard disk. If you do so, Logic should be able to maintain the original links between the lessons and media files.

1   Insert the *Logic Pro 8 and Logic Express 8* DVD into your DVD drive.

2   Drag the Logic 8_Files folder from the DVD to your desktop to copy it. The Media folder contains about 2.2 GB of media.

3   Wait for the "Copy" Progress indicator to close, and eject the DVD to make sure that you don't work with the files on the DVD, but with the files you copied on your desktop.

Each lesson will explain which files to open for that lesson's exercises.

Instructions for Logic Express Users

If you're using Logic Express 8, most of the instructions in this book are exactly the same as those for Logic Pro 8. When there are differences, you'll find a note in the exercises addressed specifically to Logic Express users. Keep in mind that Logic Express doesn't come with the same instruments, effects, and sound library as Logic Studio, and sometimes your screen may look different from the pictures in this book (for example you may see different settings in the Library, different Apple Loops in the Loops Browser, and different names on tracks and channel strips).

To install files from the *Logic Pro 8 and Logic Express 8* DVD, follow the instructions in the previous section and then install the additional Apple Loops as explained in the steps below.

> **NOTE** ▶ The additional Apple Loops for Logic Express Users were taken from the Remix Tools, Rhythm Section, and World Music Jam Packs, which come standard with Logic Studio. The loop Trip Hop Jungle Beat 01 was modified to use a GarageBand instrument available to Logic Express users and sounds different from the original Trip Hop Jungle Beat 01 included in the Remix Tools Jam Pack.

1   Open Logic Express.

The Templates dialog opens (if you have used Logic Express before, and a Logic project automatically opens, skip to step 4).

2   Click the Empty Project template.

An empty template opens, and a New Tracks dialog comes down from the Arrange window's title bar. Don't worry about the settings in that dialog; you just need to create at least one track (of any kind) to continue.

3   In the New Tracks dialog, click Create.

The dialog disappears and a track is created.

4   From the main menu bar, choose Window > Loop Browser.

The Loop Browser opens.

5   Close the main Arrange window underneath and keep only the Loop Browser open so you can see your desktop.

You may need to move the Loop Browser aside to see the Logic 8_Files folder on your desktop.

6   Double-click the Logic 8_Files folder on your desktop and double-click Apple Loops for Logic Express Users.

You should see a folder named "Drag to Loop Browser."

7   Drag the folder "Drag to Loop Browser" onto the Loop Browser window.

A green + (plus) sign appears at the mouse pointer, indicating that you can release the mouse button to install the Apple Loops.

When you release the mouse, an alert message pops up asking you if you want to move the loops to the Apple Loops folder.

8   Click Move to Loops Folder.

The Apple Loops are installed.

System Requirements

Before using *Apple Pro Training Series: Logic Pro 8 and Logic Express 8,* you should have a working knowledge of your Macintosh and the Mac OS X operating system. Make sure that you know how to use the mouse and standard menus and commands and also how to open, save, and close files. If you need to review these techniques, see the printed or online documentation included with your system.

▶   Mac computer with a 1.25 GHz or faster PowerPC G4 processor

▶   1 GB of RAM (2 GB or more is highly recommended)

▶   Display with 1024 x 768 resolution (1280 x 800 or higher is recommended)

▶   Mac OS X v10.4.9 or later

▶   QuickTime 7.2 or later

▶   DVD drive for installation

▶   PCI Express, ExpressCard/34, USB, or FireWire-based audio interface recommended

▶   USB musical keyboard (or suitable MIDI keyboard and interface) to play software instruments

▶   Low-latency multi-I/O audio interface highly recommended for audio recording

About the Apple Pro Training Series

Apple Pro Training Series: Logic Pro 8 and Logic Express 8 is part of the official training series for Apple Pro applications developed by experts in the field. The lessons are designed to let you learn at your own pace. If you're new to Logic, you'll learn the fundamental concepts and features you'll need to master the program. If you've been using Logic for a while, you'll find that this book covers most of the new features found in Logic 8.

Apple Pro Certification Program

The Apple Pro Training and Certification Program is designed to keep you at the forefront of Apple's digital media technology while giving you a competitive edge in today's ever-changing job market. Whether you're an editor, graphic designer, sound designer, special effects artist, or teacher, these training tools are meant to help you expand your skills.

Upon completing the course material in this book, you can become an Apple Pro by taking the certification exam at an Apple Authorized Training Center. Certification is offered in Final Cut Pro, DVD Studio Pro, Shake, and Logic Pro. Certification as an Apple Pro gives you official recognition of your knowledge of Apple's professional applications while allowing you to market yourself to employers and clients as a skilled, pro-level user of Apple products.

To find an Authorized Training Center near you, go to www.apple.com/software/pro/training.

For those who prefer to learn in an instructor-led setting, Apple also offers training courses at Apple Authorized Training Centers worldwide. These courses, which use the Apple Pro Training Series books as their curriculum, are taught by Apple Certified Trainers who balance concepts and lectures with hands-on labs and exercises. Apple Authorized Training Centers have been carefully selected and have met Apple's highest standards in all areas, including facilities, instructors, course delivery, and infrastructure. The goal of the program is to offer Apple customers, from beginners to the most seasoned professionals, the highest-quality training experience.

Resources

Apple Pro Training Series: Logic Pro 8 and Logic Express 8 is not intended as a comprehensive reference manual, nor does it replace the documentation that comes with the application. For comprehensive information about program features, refer to these resources:

► The *Logic Pro 8 User Manual*. Accessed through the Logic Help menu, the *User Manual* contains a complete description of all features. The other documents available in the Logic Help menu can be valuable resources as well.

► Apple's website: www.apple.com

► Logic Pro Help's website, an online community of Logic users moderated by David Nahmani: www.logicprohelp.com

Introduction to Logic

1

Time

Goals

This lesson takes approximately 90 minutes to complete.

Browse, preview, and use loops

Edit regions and create an arrangement

Navigate and zoom in the Arrange area

Use effect and software instrument plug-ins

Mix down and export to MP3

Make Music with Logic Now!

Let's get into the heart of the matter and start producing music immediately. In this lesson, you will go straight to the fun part of creating music with Logic—producing a grooving trip-hop song using loops—while gaining a global understanding of how you interact with the application and its library of loops, instruments, and effect plug-ins.

You will take an entire Logic project from start to finish. You will open an empty Logic template and build the song from scratch, using the Loop Browser to preview and add loops. Then you'll edit regions to build an arrangement, add effect plug-ins, mix, and export your song.

Opening Logic

You can open Logic by double-clicking the Logic icon in the application folder (Applications/ Logic Pro), double-clicking a Logic project file, or clicking the Logic icon in your Dock. To get started, you will add Logic to the Dock, making it easy to access. You will then open it and open an existing song file.

1 In the Finder, choose Go > Applications (or press Shift-Command-A).

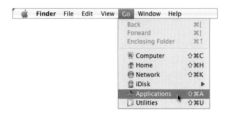

The Applications folder opens in a Finder window.

2 Drag the Logic application icon to your Dock.

> **TIP** You can type the first few letters of the application name (*lo* should be suffi- cient) to quickly select the application file. You can then press Command–Down Arrow to open the selected application.

Drag the Logic icon to the Dock.

3   In your Dock, click the Logic icon.

Logic starts, and after a moment the Templates dialog opens.

NOTE ▶ If you've already used Logic, the last project you worked on automatically opens when you open Logic. In the main menu bar, choose File > Close Project to close that project, then choose File > New to open the Templates dialog.

The left column displays several folders containing collections of templates. The first three collections—Explore, Compose, and Produce—contain factory templates installed with Logic.

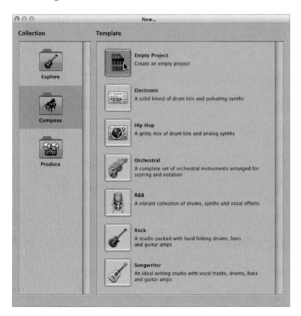

4   In the Collection column, click Compose.

All the templates from that collection appear in the right column.

The Empty Project template is available in all the collections, and it is the one you are going to use for this exercise.

5   Click Empty Project.

An empty template opens, and a New Tracks dialog comes down from the Arrange window's title bar. A Logic project always needs to have at least one track. For this exercise, the first track you will need is a software instrument track.

6   In the Number field, enter *1*. Select both the Software Instrument button and the Open Library checkbox.

7   Click Create.

A software instrument track is created, and the Media area opens on the right of the Arrange window, displaying the software instrument Library.

Until you manually save the project to a hard disk, it lives only in the computer's RAM, making it vulnerable to a power failure, a computer freeze or crash, or even a loss of notebook battery power. It is extremely important to regularly save your project as you progress.

8   Choose File > Save (or press Command-S).

Since this is the first time you're saving your project, a Save As dialog opens. Anytime you save a file on a computer, you have to provide:

▶   A filename

▶   A location on the hard disk where you want to save the file

9   In the Save As field, type your project name, *My New Day*. In the Where pop-up menu, choose Desktop (or press Command-D).

10 Click Save (or press Enter or Return).

> **NOTE ▶** Many desktop Logic users prefer the Enter key to the Return key because it is easier to reach, especially after entering a value from the numeric keypad. This book uses Enter as the final command in many steps, but the Return key works as well when confirming a dialog command or after entering a value in a parameter field.

Note that the new project name is now on the Arrange window's title bar.

You're already on your way with your Logic project by opening an empty template and creating a software instrument track.

When you open an empty template, Logic opens the Arrange window, which will be your main work area. In the next section, you will examine the Arrange window and its working areas.

Exploring the Interface

As you work in Logic, you will spend most of your time in the Arrange window. The Arrange window has six areas. Aside from the main Arrange area and the Transport bar, each area can be opened and closed, giving you quick access to most of the features you need.

> **NOTE ▶** By default, the Media or Lists area and the editing area (where you can open the Mixer or various editors) are closed. In the previous exercise, you selected Open Library when creating a new software instrument track, so the Library is open in the Media area.

Let's now open the editing area.

1 Click the Mixer button at the bottom of the Arrange window.

The Mixer is displayed below the Arrange area.

NOTE ▶ To resize the Editing area, position the mouse pointer between the Arrange area and the Editing area. The mouse pointer turns into a vertical double-arrow symbol, and you can drag vertically to resize the Editing area.

2   Examine the areas of the Logic interface.

The areas of the Arrange window are:

▶   Arrange area

▶   Editing area

▶   Toolbar

▶   Transport bar

▶   Inspector

▶   Media or Lists area

Notice that one of the areas has an illuminated title bar. The illuminated title bar indicates the area that has key focus (and responds to key commands). You can click the title bar or background of an area to give it key focus.

TIP▶ You can also press Tab and Shift-Tab to cycle the key focus forward and backward through the Arrange window areas.

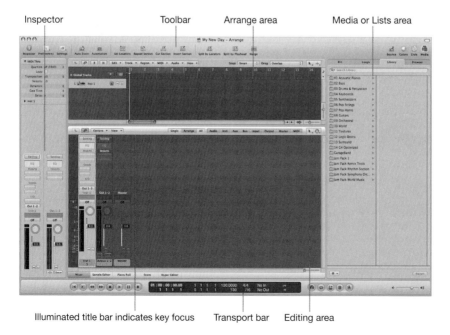

Inspector   Toolbar   Arrange area   Media or Lists area

Illuminated title bar indicates key focus   Transport bar   Editing area

Arrange Area The Arrange area is where the magic happens. It displays the tracks that make up your song. You build a song by arranging audio and MIDI regions on the tracks located below the Bar ruler.

Editing Area The editing area can display the Mixer or various editors that let you edit the contents of MIDI or audio regions.

Toolbar The customizable Toolbar provides quick one-button access to the features and settings you use the most.

Transport Bar The customizable Transport bar acts much like the controls of a CD player, offering transport buttons (Play, Record, Forward, Rewind, and others), information displays in the center (indicating the playhead position, tempo, time signature, and so on), and mode buttons (such as Cycle Mode and Metronome). For more information, see "Navigating the Project" later in this lesson.

Inspector The Inspector includes a contextual set of parameters. Its contents automatically update depending on the area in key focus, the selected region, and the selected track.

Media or Lists Area The Media or Lists area displays media files (such as audio files and plug-in settings) or lists of events (such as MIDI events and tempo changes).

Starting a Project with Apple Loops

In a moment, you'll learn more about navigating a project in the Logic interface, but you first need to fill out your project a bit. Using loops can be a great way to start. For the songwriter, loops can quickly provide inspiring rhythmic support, allowing you to focus on the chords and the melody. For the producer, they are a large resource of musical bits that can be layered with your tracks to add texture and interest.

The Apple Loops provided with Logic include professional recordings of top-shelf musicians along with software instrument settings designed by major sound designers. Since they are royalty free, you can use them for professional projects at no charge. In fact, as you become more familiar with Logic's collection of Apple Loops, don't be surprised if you start recognizing some of them on TV, on DVDs, or even in major movies.

> **LOGIC EXPRESS** ▶ If you haven't installed the Apple Loops from this book's DVD, be sure to install them before going further by following the steps in "Getting Started."

Browsing and Previewing Loops

To start building a song, you need to preview loops and decide which ones to use. The Loop Browser is the perfect tool for the job. It allows you to browse loops by instrument, genre, mood, and other attributes.

1   At the top of the Media area, click the Loops tab.

The Loop Browser opens.

Search field
Category button

2   In the Loop Browser, click the All Drums category button.

3   In the search field, enter *Trip Hop*, and press Enter.

The bottom part of the Loop Browser displays the Search Results list: all the drum loops that contain the text *Trip Hop* in their names. The first loop at the top of the Search Results list should be named **Trip Hop 70s Room Beat**.

LOGIC EXPRESS ▶ Only one loop, Trip Hop Jungle Beat 01, will show in the Search Results list.

4   In the Search Results list, click the first loop.

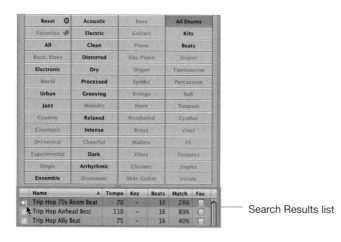

Search Results list

The loop's note icon turns into a speaker and you can hear the loop. The loop auto-matically plays at your project's tempo. Logic's default tempo for a new project is 120 bpm (beats per minute), which is way too fast for trip-hop! That explains why that loop's groove doesn't sound quite right. Now is a good time to adjust your song's tempo.

You can adjust any setting in the Transport bar display fields by dragging numbers up and down, or by double-clicking a value and entering a new one.

5 While the loop is playing, look at the Tempo display in the Transport bar. The default tempo is 120 bpm. Drag down the second digit (the *2* in 120) and listen to your loop get slower.

6 Drag the tempo digits to set your tempo to *70.0000* (bpm). Now it sounds like trip-hop!

Tempo display

TIP ▶ The tempo adjusts by whole increments of the digit you drag. Drag one of the digits on the right of the decimal point when you need more precision, and drag the first or second digit on the left of the decimal point for rough adjustments.

Now you can try directly entering a new tempo.

7 Double-click the Tempo display.

A text field appears.

8 In the text field, enter *73*, and press Enter.

The tempo is set to 73 bpm.

9 In the Loop Browser, click the next loop (or press Down Arrow).

The Loop Browser starts playing the next loop. You can press the Up Arrow and Down Arrow keys to listen to more loops until you find something you like.

LOGIC EXPRESS ▶ Since your system has only one loop with Trip Hop in its name, the Search List's selection won't advance and you won't hear any difference.

10   Click the currently playing loop.

The loop stops playing. Since you're about to drag loops into the Arrange area to build a song, close the Mixer to increase your workspace.

11   At the bottom of the Mixer, click the Mixer button.

The Mixer closes.

12   In the Loop Browser, scroll down through the alphabetical list of loops and click **Trip Hop Jungle Beat 01.**

That's a nice one! Let's use it for the song.

13   Drag the loop onto the Inst 1 track in the Arrange area, between the bar 1 and bar 2 grid lines.

The Inspector (the left area of the Arrange window) displays two channel strips: the selected Arrange track channel strip on the left, and the master output channel strip on the right. Logic automatically loads the necessary channel strip setting (the entire configuration of software instrument and effect plug-ins and their settings) to the selected Arrange track channel strip, and places the MIDI region containing the drum pattern on the track. The region snaps to the beginning of bar 1.

The channel strip setting name (2-Step Remix Overdrive) is displayed in the Channel Strip Settings menu. The track header displays the track icon and track name.

LOGIC EXPRESS ▶ The channel strip setting name is Dance Kit.

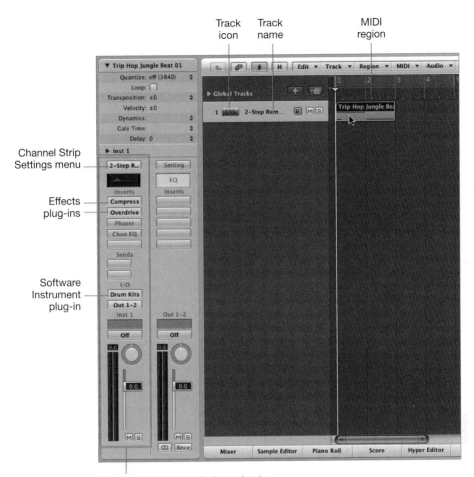

Selected Arrange track channel strip

MORE INFO ▶ In the Loop Browser, some loops have a blue waveform icon, while others have a green note icon. Blue loops are audio loops only: they can be used only as audio regions on audio tracks. Green loops are audio loops that also contain the MIDI region and the channel strip settings used to produce them. They can be used as audio regions on audio tracks (like blue loops), or as MIDI regions on instrument tracks. For more information, see Lesson 7, "Manipulating Tempo and Time Stretching."

Now you have a drums groove that will be the foundation of your song. Later, you will select more loops that match the feel and style of those drums, so you can keep building the arrangement. Now, let's learn how to find your way around your project.

Navigating the Project

One of the big advantages to producing music with a computer is that the whole song is laid out right before your eyes. This makes it extremely easy to jump to a certain part of the song, start playback, go back to the beginning, or continuously repeat a section.

Logic offers many ways to navigate a song. In the next two exercises, you will learn the Transport buttons and their keyboard commands; and you will learn to continuously repeat a section of the project, which will allow you to keep the drum loop playing as you preview more loops.

Using Transport Buttons and Key Commands

When producing music, time is of the essence. Many tasks are repetitive, and you will find yourself playing, stopping, and positioning the playhead every few seconds. Minimizing the time it takes you to perform those basic operations will greatly improve your work-flow and save valuable time.

While it may seem easier at first to click buttons with the mouse, using key command shortcuts can really speed up your workflow. Try to memorize at least the basic set of key commands corresponding to the transport buttons in the Transport bar.

> **NOTE** ▶ Key command shortcuts for Logic buttons can differ on desktops and lap-tops. Throughout the book, when key command shortcuts are available for buttons they appear in parentheses following the first use of the button in the text. For more information on specific key commands, consult the manual for your particular setup.

Let's tour the Transport buttons on the left of the Transport bar, and their corresponding default U.S. key commands.

> **TIP** ▶ In Logic, if you position your mouse pointer over a button and wait a couple of seconds, a yellow help tag appears displaying the name of the button. When a help tag appears, drag your mouse pointer over other buttons and their help tags will immediately appear.

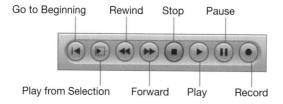

Transport Buttons and Key Commands

Transport Button	Standard Key Command	Laptop Key Command
Go to Beginning	Return	unassigned
Play from Selection	Shift-Enter	Function-Shift-Return
Rewind	<	<
Forward	>	>
Fast Rewind	Shift-<	Shift-<
Fast Forward	Shift->	Shift->
Stop	0	Return
Play	Enter	Function-Return
Pause	. *(on numeric keypad only)*	Command-Enter
Record	*	R

If you click the Stop button (or press 0, or Return on a laptop) when Logic is stopped, the playhead returns to the beginning of the project.

You can also press the Spacebar to toggle between play and stop.

1   Click the Play button.

The project starts playing, and you can hear the drum loop.

2   Click the Stop button.

The project stops.

3   Click the Stop button again.

The playhead returns to the beginning of the project.

4   Press the Spacebar.

The project starts playing.

5   Press the Spacebar again.

The project stops playing.

6   Click the background of the Arrange area.

The Trip Hop Jungle Beat region is deselected. Clicking in the background of the Arrange area deselects all regions.

Deselected region

7   Click the Trip Hop Jungle Beat region.

Selected region

The name of the region is highlighted, displayed in white letters over a black background, indicating that the region is selected. Notice the difference between the way Logic displays the region name when it is deselected and when it is selected.

8   Click the "Play from Selection" button (or press Shift-Enter).

The playhead jumps to the beginning of the selection (the Trip Hop Jungle Beat region) and playback starts.

9   Click the Forward button a few times (or press > (right angle bracket)).

As the project continues to play, the playhead jumps to the next bar each time you click the Forward button or each time you press >.

10   Press the Spacebar.

The project stops playing.

11   Click the Rewind button a few times, or press < (left angle bracket).

The playhead jumps to the previous bar each time you click the Rewind button or each time you press <.

12 Press the Spacebar.

The project stops playing.

Continuously Repeating a Section

You may often need to focus on a section of the arrangement and work on the section while it repeats over and over. In this exercise, you will turn on Cycle mode, adjust the cycle area to match the drums region, and continuously repeat that section as you preview and add more loops.

In the Bar ruler at the top of the Arrange area, you can see a rectangle in a lighter shade of gray, spanning bars 1 through 4. That rectangle indicates the positions of the left and right locators, which are the boundaries of the cycle area when the Cycle mode is on. The cycle area allows you to select a part of the song you want to continuously repeat.

1 In the upper part of the Bar ruler, click the gray locators stripe.

The cycle area turns green, indicating that Cycle mode is on.

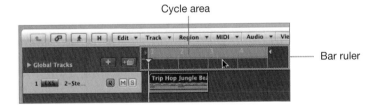

2 Select the Trip Hop Jungle Beat region if it is not already selected.

3 In the Toolbar, click the Set Locators button (or press Control-= (equal sign), or Control-' (apostrophe) on a laptop).

The cycle area matches the position and length of the selected region.

4 Press the Spacebar to start playback

Logic starts cycling over the first two bars, allowing you to hear your drums loop as you preview other loops.

5 While Logic is cycling through the drumbeat, at the upper left of the Loop Browser, click the Reset button.

The music-category buttons and search field are reset, and the Search Results list at the bottom is emptied.

6 Click the Bass button, enter *Bright Tone Bass* in the search field, and press Enter.

7 Click the first loop in the Search Results list.

You can hear the bass loop while the drums loop is playing. The bass loop plays in time with the drums, at the project's tempo.

8 If necessary, adjust the volume of the loop you are previewing by dragging the volume slider at the bottom of the Loop Browser.

9 Drag **Bright Tone Bass 03** below the drums track, in bar 1.

Logic automatically creates a new audio track, and the blue loop appears as an audio region.

10 Press Command-S to save your project.

Continue adding loops by dragging them below the last track in the Arrange area, in bar 1. Remember to click the Reset button before each new search and, if necessary, click the X at the right of the search field to clear the previous search.

Use the Loop Browser buttons and search field to find and add the following loops:

▶ **Deep Electric Piano 05** (click the Elec Piano button).

▶ **Orchestra Strings 03** (click both the Orchestral and the Strings buttons).

▶ **Wild Slide Distortion** (enter *Wild* in the search field).

11 Press the Spacebar to stop playback.

12 Press Return to go the beginning.

13 Click the Cycle area to turn the Cycle mode off.

Your Arrange area now has five tracks: drums, bass, piano, strings, and guitar.

NOTE ▶ Depending on your system, the tracks may be in a different order. To reorder the tracks, drag the track headers vertically.

Audio tracks   MIDI regions

Audio regions

Software instrument tracks

The green regions (drums and piano) are MIDI regions on software instrument tracks, while the blue regions (bass, strings, and guitar) are audio regions on audio tracks.

Now that you have chosen the Apple Loops you will use, you are ready to start building the song.

Building an Arrangement

In Logic, you build projects by arranging regions on tracks, positioned below the Bar ruler. You need to determine where a region starts, how many times it is looped, and where it stops. When editing regions in the Arrange area, the same techniques apply to both MIDI and audio regions.

Before you start building the arrangement, let's make sure you understand two fundamental concepts: Saving the project at regular intervals, and being able to undo the most recent actions.

Saving Your Work and Undoing Actions

Accidents do happen. While some of these will turn out to be happy events and improve your composition, at other times they turn out to be outright mistakes. It is therefore a good idea to save your song after every couple of steps. Remember that the key command to save your file is Command-S. Press it often!

On the other hand, don't be afraid to experiment and to make mistakes. It is easy to undo your last action by choosing Edit > Undo Action (or pressing Command-Z). You can press that key command several times to retrace the steps you most recently performed. By default, Logic can undo the previous 30 steps.

Command-S (Save) and Command-Z (Undo) will quickly become your two new best friends, so commit them to memory now!

Looping and Positioning Regions

The first step in building your arrangement is to decide where each instrument should enter. By introducing instruments one after the other, you constantly give something new to the listeners, which keeps them excited and eager to discover what's next.

1   From the Arrange area local menu bar, choose Edit > Select All (or press Command-A).

All five regions are selected and their names appear in white over black.

2   In the Inspector's Region Parameter box, click to select the Loop checkbox (or press L).

All selected regions are looped until the end of the song (the default length for a song is 16 bars). The dimmed sections to the right of each region represent the region looping over and over.

3   Click in the background of the Arrange area (or press Shift-Command-A).

All regions are deselected.

4   Drag the **Bright Tone Bass 03** loop toward the right and drop it on bar 2.

As you perform an operation on a region, a yellow help tag displays the following information:

▶   The operation you are about to perform (in the current step, it is Move Regions/Events)

▶   The number of the track where you are (2 in the current step)

▶   The name of the region you are working with (Bright Tone Bass 03)

▶   The position of the operation (1 1 1 1 before you drag, 2 1 1 1 after you drag)

▶   The length of the region (1 0 0 0)

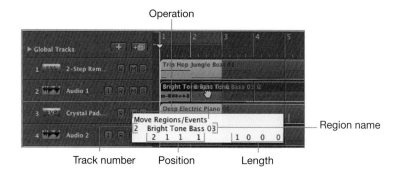

Operation

Track number   Position   Length

Region name

The help tag displays positions and lengths in bars (or measures), beats, divisions and ticks. You will often refer to a position or a length with those four numbers.

▶ The beat is the denominator in the time signature (1/4 note here).

▶ The division is set in the Transport bar, below the time signature (1/16 note here).

▶ A tick is the smallest possible time unit: there are 960 ticks in a quarter note, or 240 ticks in a 1/16 note.

So in this case, moving the Bright Tone Bass 03 region to 2 1 1 1 means moving it to bar 2, beat 1, division 1, tick 1: exactly on bar 2.

Playhead position   Time signature

Division

At the left of the Transport bar, the current playhead position is displayed in SMPTE units on the top line, and bars, beats, divisions, and ticks on the bottom line.

MORE INFO ▶ SMPTE time code is used to synchronize picture and sound in video. SMPTE units are hours, minutes, seconds, frames, and sub-frames. You will learn more about SMPTE time code in Lesson 12.

5   Drag the piano loop (**Deep Electric Piano 05**) to bar 5.

6   Drag the strings loop (**Orchestra Strings 03**) to bar 9.

7   Drag the guitar loop (**Wild Slide Distortion**) to bar 10.

8   Press Return to go to the beginning of the song.

9   Press the Spacebar to start playback.

You already have the foundation of a simple arrangement, starting with drum and bass patterns that groove together, and you've built on it by layering other elements like piano and strings as the song progresses.

Your next step is to decide where to eliminate some of the instruments and allow the arrangement to breathe a little.

Copying and Resizing Regions

Let's edit the bass track to make the intro lighter in texture, letting the full bass loop kick in at bar 5 with the electric piano.

1   Option-drag the Bright Tone Bass region to bar 5.

Dragging a region moves it, but Option-dragging makes a copy and lets you place the copy. Now you can manipulate the bass region in the intro; but, starting on bar 5, the full loop will play repeatedly. Notice that while you Option-drag a region the help tag now reads *Copy Regions/Events*.

TIP ▶ In Logic, when you use modifier keys such as Shift, Control, Command, or Option while dragging, it is most important which key is depressed at the time you release the mouse button. In fact, you can switch modifier keys while dragging, and the help tag will reflect the change, displaying the appropriate operation. To successfully copy a region by Option-dragging it, make sure you release the mouse button before you release the Option key.

2   In bar 2, select the Bright Tone Bass region.

3   In the Inspector's Region Parameter box, click to deselect the Loop checkbox (or press L).

The region's Loop parameter is turned off, and the region does not loop anymore.

You are about to shorten the bass region, but first you will zoom in on it so you can see individual bass notes in the waveform.

4   Press Control-Option-Z (the "Zoom to fit Selection" command).

The selected region fills the Arrange area and you can clearly identify individual notes in the waveform.

5   Click the "Play from Selection" button in the Transport bar (or press Shift-Enter).

Listen to your bass pattern while looking at the waveform. You are going to shorten the bass region to remove the last three notes.

6   Position your mouse pointer over the lower-right corner of the region.

The mouse pointer turns into a Resize tool.

You can use the Resize tool to adjust the start or end of a region.

7 While looking at the waveform, drag the corner of the region to the left, shortening the region to hide the last three notes.

The help tag length information should read . *2 2 0*: The edited region is two beats and two divisions (sixteenth notes) long. Let's zoom out. Depending on your zoom level, the Resize tool may snap to another value. Get it as close as possible, but don't worry if your help tag doesn't read exactly . 2 2 0.

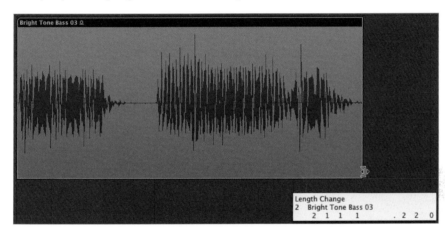

8 Press the Navigation: Back key command, Control-Z.

Logic returns you to the previous zoom level, displaying your whole arrangement. You now have a nice short bass pattern in measure 2 that is perfect for the introduction.

9 Choose File > Save (or press Command-S).

The project is saved.

You need to repeat the same bass pattern twice in bars 3 and 4, before the full bass loop kicks in at bar 5.

10 In the Arrange area's local menu bar, choose Region > Repeat Regions (or press Command-R).

The Repeat Regions/Events dialog opens, allowing you to create copies of the region and snap them to the desired grid unit.

11 In the Number of Copies text field, enter *2*. In the Adjustment menu, choose Bar, and click OK.

The shortened bass region is copied twice on the downbeats of bars 3 and 4.

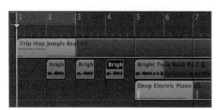

12 Press Command-S.

The song file is saved.

13 Go the beginning of the song and listen to your new introduction.

You now have a nice little introduction. The song starts with the drums groove, then a shortened version of the bass riff is introduced and repeated three times. On bar 5, the whole bass line starts just as the electric piano joins in.

Adjusting Loop Repetitions

Before you move on to arrange the strings and slide guitar parts, you will adjust the number of repetitions of the electric piano so it stops on bar 9, leaving some space in the mix for the next section.

1 Position your mouse pointer over the upper part of the piano loops (the dimmed parts to the right of the region).

The mouse pointer switches to a loop tool. You can use the tool to precisely adjust the point where a region stops looping.

2 Hold down the Loop-length tool at bar 9.

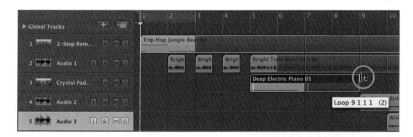

The help tag reads *Loop 9 1 1 1 (2)*, meaning that the region is looped until the first downbeat of bar 9, and the loop plays twice.

3 Press Command-S.

The song file is saved.

TIP ▶ Once you become more proficient with Logic, you can use the Loop tool by clicking where you want to cut off the loop without holding down the mouse button. For now, holding down the mouse button displays the help tag, which allows you to make sure the loop will stop exactly where you want. If the help tag doesn't read *9 1 1 1*, you can drag the mouse left or right until it does, then release the mouse button to perform the cut.

The song is starting to take shape! It has a nice sparse intro, then a fuller grooving section with the electric piano. Let's work on the strings and slide guitar section.

Arranging a Middle Section

One modern production trick is to recreate a music phrase composed of pieces of phrases from different instruments. It is the modern equivalent of the classic call-and-response dialogue that blues singers and guitarists perform when jamming: the singer sings a short phrase, and then the guitarist answers it with a short lick.

In this song, you are going to perform that trick using the strings for the call, and the slide guitar for the response.

1   Select the Orchestra Strings region.

2   Press L.

That region's Loop parameter is turned off, and the region does not loop anymore.

3   Position the mouse pointer on the lower-right corner of the strings region until the Resize tool appears. Drag to the left to halve the size of the region.

The help tag indicates that the resized region is one bar long.

4   Select the Wild Slide Distortion region.

5   Press L.

That region's Loop parameter is turned off, and the region does not loop anymore.

6   Drag the region's lower-right corner to bar 11.

The resized region is one bar long.

You have recreated a two-bar phrase composed of one bar of strings followed by one bar of slide guitar. The strings play a simple quarter-note motif. The slide guitar repeats and sustains the last note played by the strings, and then slides back into the first note of the strings motif. If you repeat that new phrase a few times, the slide guitar will take you right back into the strings motif.

You can use the same Repeat Regions command you used earlier to repeat a group of regions.

7   Click in the background and drag the mouse pointer, making sure that the rectangular green highlight touches both the strings and the slide regions.

Both regions are selected.

TIP ▶ When selecting regions, make sure you always start dragging in the background. If the mouse pointer is over a region when you start dragging, you will move the region.

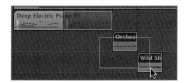

8   In the Arrange area's local menu bar, choose Region > Repeat Regions (or press Command-R). The Number of Copies field should still be set to 2, and the Adjustment menu to Bar, so click OK.

This time the whole selection, which contains two regions, is repeated twice.

9   Select the first Orchestra Strings region on bar 9.

10   Click the "Play from Selection" button (or press Shift-Enter).

Playback starts at the beginning of the selection, on bar 9, and you can listen to your new dialogue between the strings and the guitar.

Ending the Song

Now would be a good time to wrap up the song. You will bring back the electric piano, let it groove for a while, and create an ending for the song on bar 21. First, you will need to zoom out of the Arrange area to make space for the ending.

1   At the lower right of the Arrange area, drag the horizontal zoom slider to the left (or press Control–Left Arrow).

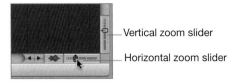
Vertical zoom slider
Horizontal zoom slider

The whole arrangement zooms out horizontally. Look at the Bar ruler, and try to display at least 23 bars in the Arrange area. Depending on your screen size, you might also want to zoom in vertically.

2   Drag the vertical zoom slider down (or press Control–Down Arrow).

The whole arrangement zooms in vertically.

The zoom sliders are an easy means of zooming the whole arrangement. Once again, commit the Control–Left Arrow/Right Arrow commands to memory, and save your right arm a trip to the sliders every time you need to zoom. The commands are listed at the end of this lesson.

3   Option-drag the Deep Electric Piano region to bar 15, right after the end of the last Wild Slide Guitar region.

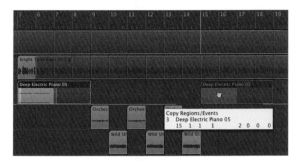

The region is copied along with its single loop. To create an ending for the song, you will stop all the still-looping regions at the same place. The last piano loop is still selected, so you will add the drum loop and bass loop to the selection by Shift-clicking them.

4   Shift-click the drums loop and the last bass loop (on bar 5).

Shift-clicking allows you to select several regions at once when there is no easy way to drag a rectangle across them as you did earlier for the strings and guitar regions.

5   Position the mouse pointer over the top part of one of the looping sections.

The mouse pointer switches to the Loop tool.

6   Option-drag the Loop tool to bar 21.

All three regions stop looping on bar 21. When using the Loop tool on multiple regions, holding down Option makes all the looping sections stop at the same place.

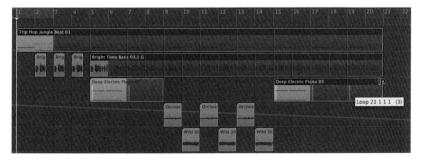

7   In the lower half of the Bar ruler, double-click about a bar before the end.

The playback starts where you double-clicked. It sounds a little abrupt: Usually musicians end a song by playing the last note on the downbeat of the last bar. Since the loops are cut off right on the downbeat, that last note is missing.

You can adjust the end of the bass and the piano loops so they play one more note on the next downbeat.

8   Press the Spacebar to stop playback.

9   Click in the background of the Arrange area.

All the regions are deselected.

This time, you need to zoom in on the ending of the bass and the electric piano tracks to precisely adjust where both instruments will end.

10   Control-Option-drag around the last bar (bar 20) on both the bass and the piano tracks.

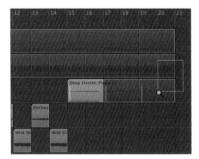

The mouse pointer switches to the Zoom tool, and the highlighted area is zoomed in.

11   On the bass track, drag the Loop tool to the right to uncover one more note, until the help tag reads *21 2 1 1*.

You can see the final note in the waveform.

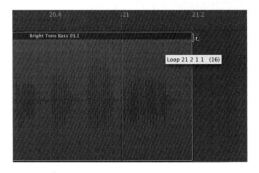

12 On the piano track, drag the Loop tool to the right to uncover the beginning of the first note in bar 21, until the help tag reads *21 1 3 1*.

On MIDI regions, notes are displayed as horizontal lines. Here, the low note is in the lower part of the looped region. As long as the attack of a note is visible, Logic will sustain the note for its whole length.

Now you can zoom out to see your entire arrangement.

13 Control-Option-click anywhere in the Arrange area.

The arrange area returns to the previous zoom level, showing you your complete arrangement.

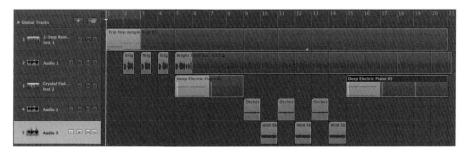

14 Listen to your arrangement.

You should now have a basic understanding of how to manipulate regions to create an arrangement in Logic. Your basic editing techniques are as follows:

▶ Drag a region to move it.

▶ Option-drag a region to copy it.

▶ Place the mouse pointer at the lower-corner of a region to resize it.

▶ Place the mouse pointer at the upper-right corner of a region to loop it.

You also learned basic zooming techniques:

▶ Control-Option-drag on an area to zoom in on that area, and Control-Option-click anywhere to return to the previous zoom level.

▶ Press Control–Right Arrow to zoom in horizontally, Control–Left Arrow to zoom out horizontally.

▶ Press Control–Down Arrow to zoom in vertically, Control–Up Arrow to zoom out vertically.

▶ Press Control-Option-Z to zoom in on the selection, and Control-Z to return to the previous zoom level.

Feel free to experiment on your own, and be creative! Try adding sections, or creating breaks in some parts. Use short breaks in the drums or bass tracks to trigger attention. They remove the foundation that listeners take for granted. You wake them up, then bring them back into the full groove.

As an additional exercise, try to stop the bass from looping just before the last section (on 14 2 1 1), and have it return for the end (on 15 1 1 1).

Mixing the Song

Once you have arranged the song, the next step is to mix the song before you can export it as a stereo file. Mixing is the art of blending the instruments, carefully balancing their volume and frequency spectrum, and giving them a place in the stereo sound field.

As you finish the project, you use the Mixer to adjust the level of each track and its stereo position, and add processing plug-ins to sculpt the sounds. In the following exercises, you will mix the middle section: the exchanges between the strings and guitar.

Preparing for Mixing

When mixing, you can use Cycle mode to repeat a section of the song, so you don't have to worry about navigating the song while you focus on making that section sound better as you work in the Mixer.

In this exercise, you will open the Mixer, rename the channel strips, and adjust the cycle area to match the middle section of the song.

1 At the bottom of the Arrange window, click the Mixer button (or press X).

The Mixer opens.

NOTE ▶ Depending on your screensize, you may need to resize the Mixer area so you can still see your tracks in the Arrange area. You may also have to scroll the Mixer area vertically to see the entire channel strips.

The Mixer shows you the channel strips that correspond to the tracks in the Arrange area. All those channel strips are mixed onto the Output 1-2 channel strip. The Arrange area stacks tracks vertically, while the Mixer stacks channel strips horizontally, so the channel strips are displayed left to right in the same order that they are displayed top to bottom in the Arrange area.

The names of the channel strips are not really descriptive. You can rename a channel strip by double-clicking the name in the corresponding track's header.

2   In track 1, double-click the drums track's name.

A text field appears.

3   Type *Drums,* and press Enter.

The first channel strip in the mixer displays the new name, *Drums.*

Set the remaining track names:

▶   Track 2 to *Bass*

▶   Track 3 to *Piano*

▶   Track 4 to *Strings*

▶   Track 5 to *Guitar*

In the Mixer, all the channel strips display the new names.

Now let's adjust the cycle area to the middle section of the song.

4   Select all six Orchestra Strings and Wild Slide Distortion regions.

5   In the Toolbar, click Set Locators.

The Cycle mode is turned on, and the cycle area adjusts to fit the selection.

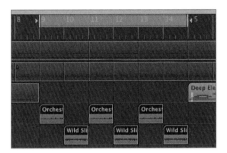

From now on, when you use the Spacebar to toggle between play and stop, playback will always start at the beginning of the first strings region at bar 9.

Adjusting Levels

Each channel strip has a level meter, a clip detector on top of the meter, a volume fader to adjust the level, and a Pan/Balance control to adjust the stereo position. Below the volume fader, a Mute button allows you to silence that channel strip, and a Solo button allows you to listen to that channel strip by itself.

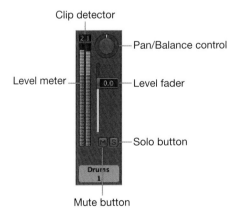

Notice that the Guitar channel strip is selected. The Guitar track was the last track selected in the Arrange area when you renamed it, which is why its channel strip is selected in the Mixer.

TIP ▶ In Logic, selecting something in one area or window usually results in the same element being selected in other Logic areas or windows. For example, selecting a track in the Arrange area results in the selection of that track's channel strip in the Mixer, and vice versa.

1   Play the song.

The clip detector at the top of the Output 1-2 channel strip is hitting the red. That's not good! Notice that it reads *3.0*. That means Logic's output is overloading by 3 dB.

2   In the Drums channel strip, drag the level fader down −8.2 (dB).

3   On the Output 1-2 channel strip, click the clip detector.

The clip detector is reset and starts tracking the new peak level. It no longer hits the red. Good.

4   On both the Drums and the Bass channel strips, click the Solo buttons.

The Solo buttons turn yellow, and you can hear only the Drums and the Bass tracks. This makes it easy to balance the level of the bass against the drums without the distraction of other instruments that are not yet mixed. Now that you've turned down the drums, you can hear that the bass needs a little taming.

5 In the Bass channel strip, lower the level fader to –2.7 (dB).

6 Option-click one of the yellow (engaged) Solo buttons.

Both Solo buttons turn off simultaneously.

In trip-hop, you want to keep the drums and bass "in your face." The only way to achieve that balance without overloading the mix is to turn down all the other instruments. If you feel your mix starts to sound weak, don't be fooled: simply turn up the volume on your audio interface or monitoring system.

7 In the Strings channel strip, lower the level fader to –9.1 (dB).

8 In the Guitar channel strip, lower the level fader to –20 (dB).

9 Press the Spacebar to stop playback.

Using Processing Plug-Ins

At the top of each channel strip, a Setting button gives you access to thousands of factory channel strip settings for both instrument and audio tracks. Again, a channel strip setting is a collection of all the plug-ins on a channel strip, along with their individual settings.

Below the Setting button are the EQ display and the Insert slots for processing plug-ins.

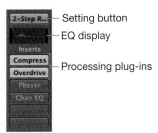

Another technique to keep the drums and bass sounding big is to make the other instruments sound thinner. First you will try a few channel strip settings to change the sound of the guitar.

1   At the top of the Guitar channel strip, click the Setting button to open the Channel Strip Settings menu, and choose 08 Warped Processors > 03 Lo-Fi Processors > Be Valved.

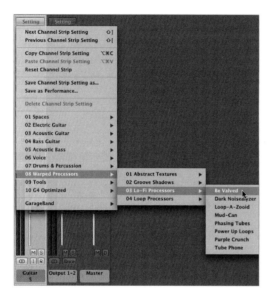

The channel strip setting loads, inserting a Limiter, a Bit Crusher, a Channel EQ, and another Limiter plug-ins and their settings to give that particular Lo-Fi sound. The Setting button now displays this channel strip setting's name, Be Valved.

2   Press the Spacebar.

Playback starts at the beginning of the cycle area, and you can hear the effect of the chosen channel strip setting on the guitar.

3   Hold down the mouse button on the Setting button for a moment to open the Channel Strip Settings menu again, but don't choose anything.

At the top of the menu you see the name of the current setting, and right below it, Next Channel Strip Setting and Previous Channel Strip Setting, with their corresponding key commands: Shift-] (right bracket) and Shift-[(left bracket).

TIP ▶ Once you find a function on a menu, it is a good habit to look at the corresponding key command. Then, close the menu and use the key command. By forcing yourself to use keyboard shortcuts the first time you execute commands, you are bound to memorize them faster, accelerating your workflow.

4   Keep the song playing and Press Shift-] .

The next channel strip setting loads, and the Setting button displays its abbreviated name, Dark Noi (for Noisealyzer).

5   Press Shift-] two more times, listening to the two following channel strip settings, and watch as the Setting button displays their names: Loop-A(-Zooid), and, the one you're going to use, Mud-Can.

The guitar is a little too loud, so let's lower its level.

6   In the Guitar channel strip, lower the fader to –27 (dB).

Panning Instruments and Copying Plug-Ins

Remember that your initial goal is to get the strings and the guitar to have a conversation. You will realize this concept by panning them to either side of the stereo field while making them sound a little more alike, placing them in the same range of frequencies. In the Mud-Can channel strip setting, the Guitar Amp Pro plug-in is mainly responsible for the resulting sound, so you will copy that plug-in and its settings on the Strings channel strip.

1   In the Strings channel strip, drag the Balance control down to –15.

Even though the Balance control is a rotary knob, you adjust it like any other setting in Logic: drag the Balance control vertically, starting dragging in the middle of the control knob.

The strings move to the left.

2   Drag the Guitar channel strip's Balance control up to +14.

The guitar moves to the right.

Now let's copy the Guitar Amp Pro plug-in from the Guitar channel strip to the Strings channel strip.

3   Option-Command-drag the GtrAmpPro plug-in to a Strings channel strip Insert slot on the left.

A copy of the plug-in, with identical settings, is inserted on the Strings channel strip. The Strings are now slightly too loud.

4   In the Strings channel strip, lower the fader to –11 (dB).

Now let's listen to a section with the electric piano to adjust its level.

5   In the Arrange area, select one of the Deep Electric Piano regions and click the "Play from Selection" button (or press Shift-Enter).

Logic starts playing the song from the selection, even though you have Cycle mode turned on.

6   In the Piano channel strip, lower the fader to –4.8 (dB).

7   Click the Mixer button again to close the Mixer, click the Cycle area to turn off Cycle mode, and listen to your song.

The song is finished! You started from nothing and used the Loop Browser to select five loops; created an arrangement by moving, looping, and editing regions; and mixed the five instruments. You can now export the mix and share it with your friends and family.

Exporting the Mix

When you are finally happy with the way your song sounds, it's time to export it. In this exercise, you will export an MP3 file. The process of rendering the mix into a single stereo file that you can burn onto a CD or use in other applications is called *bouncing*.

First, you must adjust the project length to define the bounce range. At the top of the Arrange area, look at the Bar ruler. The last region in your song is the bass, and it stops a little after bar 21. If you listen to the song's end, you'll notice that the last piano note sustains for a while, so you will end the song on bar 24 to avoid cutting off the last note.

1   In the Transport bar, below the Tempo display, drag the Project End display down to set the project length to 24 bars.

Let's make sure the song plays until the end.

2   Double-click the lower half of the Bar ruler around bar 20 to play the end of the song.

The last electric piano note is not cut off.

The bounce range can also be defined by the cycle area, or by selecting regions. To bounce the entire song, make sure Cycle mode is turned off and no regions are selected.

3   Click the background of the Arrange area.

All the regions are deselected.

4 Choose File > Bounce.

You are going to export the project as an audio file, so the Bounce window looks like a Save As window with name, location, and bounce options at the bottom.

Make sure the Start and End positions correspond to your entire song. Start should read *1 1 1 1* and End should read *24 1 1 1*. If they don't, you can adjust them now by dragging the digits vertically.

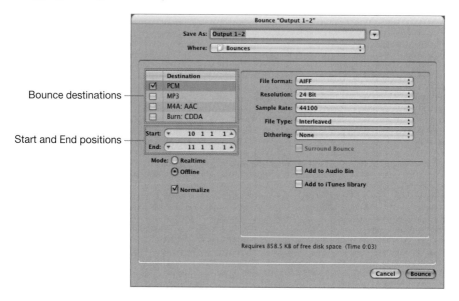

5 Name the bounce file *New Day*; and, in the Where pop-up menu, choose Desktop, or press Command-D.

You can choose from four different destinations for your bounce file:

▶ PCM: uncompressed audio file (AIFF, WAVE, CAF, and Sound Designer II)

▶ MP3: compressed audio file

▶ M4A: compressed audio file format used by iTunes and iPod

▶ Burn: a file burned directly from Logic onto a CD or DVD-A

6 Deselect PCM, and select MP3.

7 Click Bounce.

A progress indicator appears, tracking Logic bouncing the mix.

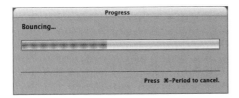

Once finished, a second progress bar tracks Logic as it converts the mix to an MP3 file.

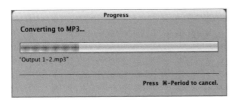

Once the Progress windows disappear, the file is ready.

8   On your desktop, double-click the file **New Day.mp3**.

> **TIP** ▶ You can use Mac OS X key commands to help complete this last step. Press Command-Tab to switch to the Finder, then press Option-Command-H to hide other applications so you can see your desktop. Type the first few letters of your song or use arrow keys to select it, and press Command–Down Arrow to open it.

The file opens in QuickTime (or in your default mp3 player) and you can listen to your very first Logic mix. Your MP3 file is ready to be shared in an e-mail or uploaded to a website!

Lesson Review

1. How many areas are in the Arrange window, and what are their names?
2. How do you know which area will respond to key commands?
3. How do you adjust a setting (such as the tempo) in Logic?
4. Which kinds of regions go on software instrument tracks and audio tracks?
5. What units displayed in the help tag indicate a length or a position in the project?
6. How do you move or copy a region in the Arrange area?
7. In what order are channel strips displayed in the Mixer?
8. What is a channel strip setting?
9. What are the steps to take to export your mix?

Answers

1. There are six areas in the Arrange window: Arrange area, editing area, Media or Lists area, Inspector, Toolbar, and Transport bar.
2. The area that has key focus responds to key commands and also has an illuminated title bar.
3. Drag a value up and down to increase or decrease it, or double-click to access a data field in which you can directly enter a new value.
4. MIDI regions go on software instrument tracks; audio regions go on audio tracks.
5. Bars, beats, divisions, and ticks.
6. Drag a region to move it; Option-drag a region to copy it.
7. Channel strips are displayed left to right in the same order that they are displayed top to bottom in the Arrange area.
8. The collection of all the plug-ins on a channel strip, including each plug-in's settings.
9. Adjust the project length, deselect all regions and turn off Cycle mode, choose File > Bounce, choose a destination, and click Bounce.

Building a Song

2

Lesson Files   Logic 8_Files > Lessons > 02 New Day_start

Logic 8_Files > Lessons > 02 We Shared Everything_start

Logic 8_Files > Lessons > 02 We Shared Everything_end

Time   This lesson takes approximately 60 minutes to complete.

Goals   Choose digital audio settings

Record single and multitrack audio

Record additional takes

Record in Cycle mode

Punch record both on the fly and automatically

Adjust count-in, metronome, and other settings

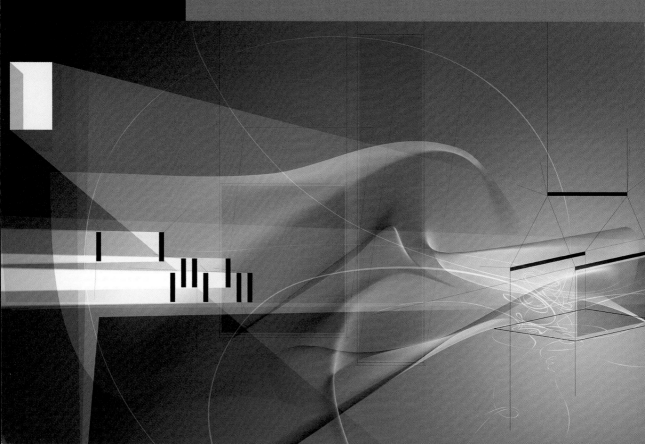

Recording Audio

To build a song, you need to come up with the raw material you will later arrange and mix. You may start with an idea you have in your head, a part you rehearsed on an instrument, a pre-recorded sample or loop, or you can start experimenting until inspiration strikes. To sustain and develop that initial inspiration, you need to master the various techniques Logic offers to record, create, or edit the audio and MIDI regions that constitute the building blocks for your project.

In addition to providing resources such as software instruments and Apple Loops, Logic Pro is a powerful digital audio workstation, offering you a complete set of tools to assist you in the most demanding recording sessions.

In this lesson, you will set up Logic for audio recording and study some situations that you will typically encounter when recording live musicians: recording a single instrument, recording additional takes of the same instrument, cycle recording, multitrack recording, punching on the fly, and automatic punching.

Setting Up Digital Audio Recording

When recording audio, Logic saves the digital data stream from the audio interface to an audio file on your hard disk. Assuming you have the correct settings, Logic does not exert any influence over the quality of your recordings. By choosing the right recording environment and using high-quality components in your signal chain, the quality of your audio recordings will be the same as the quality produced by a professional studio.

In the following exercises, you will set up Logic to prepare for a music recording intended for use on an audio CD.

▶ **Digital Recording, Sample Rate, and Bit Depth**

When audio is recorded in Logic Pro, sound pressure waves are turned into a digital audio file, as follows:

1. The microphone transforms sound pressure waves into an analog electrical signal.

2. The microphone preamp amplifies the analog electrical signal. A gain knob lets you adjust the signal level to avoid overloading the converter. The goal is to have a proper recording level but to avoid distortion.

3. The analog-to-digital (A/D) converter transforms the analog electrical signal into a digital data stream.

4. The audio interface sends the digital data stream from the converter to the computer.

5. Logic Pro saves the incoming data as an audio file displayed on the screen by a waveform representing the sound pressure waves.

To transform the analog signal to a digital data stream, the converters sample the analog signal at a very fast time interval, or *sample rate*. The sample rate identifies how many times per second the audio is digitally sampled. The *bit depth* identifies the number of data bits (0s and 1s) used to encode the value of each sample. The sample rate and bit depth settings both influence the quality of a digital audio recording.

NOTE ▶ Most audio interfaces include converters, and many include microphone preamps. Also, most modern Macintosh computers ship with a built-in audio interface. Many Mac notebooks and iMacs even have internal microphones. While they are not intended for professional-quality recording, internal microphones will allow you to perform the exercises in this lesson in the absence of an external microphone.

Setting the Sample Rate

The sample rate of a project should be set before starting your first recording. All the audio files used in a project should be recorded and played at the same sample rate. Playing an audio file at the wrong sample rate will result in the wrong pitch and tempo, much like playing back an audiotape or vinyl record at the wrong speed.

NOTE ▶ Make sure you read the section "Installing the Logic Lesson Files" in "Getting Started" before you continue.

You can set the project's sample rate in File > Project Settings > Audio, or you can customize the Transport bar to display the sample rate.

1   Go to Logic 8_Files > Lessons, and open **02 New Day_start**, or continue working in the project file you created in Lesson 1.

2   Control-click the Transport bar.

A shortcut menu appears (the menu may look different depending on where you click in the Transport bar).

3   In the shortcut menu, choose Customize Transport Bar.

A dialog opens from the Arrange area's title bar. The checkboxes allow you to select or deselect any of the buttons and displays you want the Transport bar to show.

4   In the Display column, select "Sample Rate or Punch Locators."

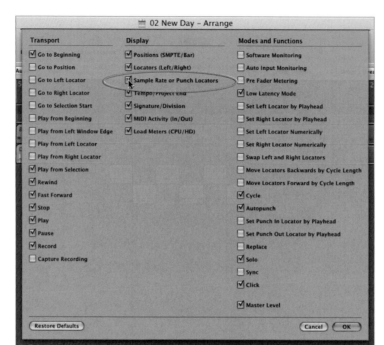

A new display is inserted into the Transport bar. It shows the current sample rate of the project: 44.100 kHz.

5   Click OK.

6   Click the Sample Rate display.

A menu appears allowing you to choose a new sample rate.

Data for an audio CD is encoded at a sample rate of 44.1 kHz (44,100 samples per second), and audio data for a standard video DVD is encoded at 48 kHz. While you can choose to work at other sample rates, using 44.1 kHz for music projects and 48 kHz for video projects avoids the need to convert the sample rate.

Since you are working with a music file for a CD, you'll work at 44.100 kHz, the current setting.

7   Click anywhere outside the Sample Rate menu.

The menu disappears and the sample rate still displays 44.100 kHz.

Setting the Bit Depth

While it is problematic to mix audio sample rates, Logic handles audio files of various bit depths in the same project without causing problems at playback.

Let's set the bit depth, and choose an audio interface.

1   In the main menu, choose Logic Pro > Preferences > Audio, or, in the Toolbar, click the Preferences button and choose Audio.

The Audio Preferences window opens.

2   From the Devices menu, choose the desired audio interface (and make sure "Enabled" is selected).

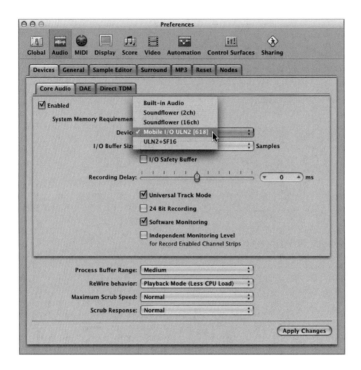

If you do not have an audio interface installed on your Mac, choose Built-in Audio or Built-in Microphone.

When 24 Bit Recording is not selected, Logic records at its default 16-bit depth. A 24-bit recording has a significantly greater dynamic range than a 16-bit recording. The extended dynamic range lets you record at lower levels, thereby decreasing the chances of clipping your recording.

3   Select 24 Bit Recording.

4   Close the Audio Preferences window (or press Command-W).

For some changes in the Audio Preferences window, Logic will automatically reinitialize the Core Audio engine. If you choose a new audio interface in the Devices menu and close Audio Preferences, a Progress window appears, indicating that the Core Audio engine is being initialized, and the Audio Preferences window closes when the initialization is completed.

MORE INFO ▶ Some additional options are available that seldom need to be changed from the default settings. For more information on these, see "Changing Recording and Metronome Settings" later in this lesson.

Recording a Single Track

In this example, you will record a single instrument. While the exercise describes recording an acoustic guitar, feel free to record any instrument you have, or your own voice if you do not have an instrument.

NOTE ▶ If you are using a laptop and want to use its built-in microphone, be sure that the microphone input is selected in the Sound pane of System Preferences.

Preparing a Track for Recording

To record audio, you first have to create a new audio track, select the correct input on your audio interface (the input connected to your microphone), and enable that new track for recording.

TIP ▶ To avoid feedback, turn off your speakers and monitor your recording using headphones. If you are working with a notebook computer's microphone, plug in the headphones or turn off the speakers before you enable a track for recording.

Since this project was originally saved on another computer, you will first consolidate the Project. This will update the record path for your computer, making sure any new audio recording goes in the audio folder inside the project folder.

1   Choose File > Project > Consolidate.

The Consolidate Project Options dialog opens.

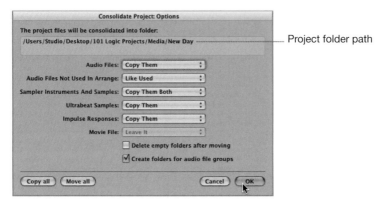

Project folder path

2   Don't change any options, and click OK.

A confirmation window opens.

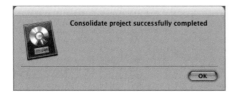

3   Click OK.

From now on, any new audio file recorded in that Project goes in the audio folder inside the project folder.

4   In the Arrange area, click the New Tracks button (+) at the top of the track list (or press Option-Command-N).

The New Tracks dialog appears.

5 In the Number field, enter *1*; in the Type menu, click to select Audio; and in the Format menu, choose Mono.

6 In the Input menu, choose the desired input of your audio interface. If you are using your Macintosh's built-in audio interface or your notebook's microphone, leave the option at Input 1.

7 Select Record Enable.

8 Select Open Library.

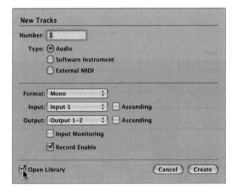

This selection will open the Library tab in the Media area so that you can select a channel strip setting for your new audio track.

9 Click Create (or press Enter).

A new record-enabled mono audio track is created, and, in the Media area, the Library opens showing all available audio channel strip settings. Logic automatically assigns the new track to the next available channel. Since three audio tracks were created when you dragged blue Apple Loops in Lesson 1 (remember that the green Apple Loops are on software instrument tracks), the new track is assigned to the Audio 4 channel and is automatically named Audio 4. Let's rename it.

You will record in an existing Logic project, and the audio files will automatically be placed in the audio folder inside that project folder.

NOTE ▶ If the Logic project was not already saved, a Save As dialog appears when you record-enable an audio track or create a new record-enabled audio track. Always save the project before you record audio and make sure that Include Assets is selected at the bottom of the Save As dialog. This ensures that all audio files recorded in that project will be placed in the audio folder inside the Logic project folder.

10 In the Audio 4 track header, double-click the name.

A text field appears with the current name selected.

11 Enter *Acoustic*, and press Enter or click outside the text field.

TIP ▶ Since Logic automatically assigns the name of a track to the audio files recorded on that track, it is a good idea to always name a track before recording on it. You will avoid populating your hard disk with files with nondescript names such as Audio 04#06, and more descriptive names will help you identify files later.

Note that the new track was created below the selected track. Let's move it to the bottom.

12 Drag the new track by its name or icon (the Pointer tool turns into a hand) below the Guitar track.

Before you start recording, you will expand the new track vertically to better see the waveform.

13 Position the Pointer tool near the lower-left corner of the track header.

The Pointer tool turns into the Finger tool.

14 Using the Finger tool, drag down to resize the new track.

> **TIP** ▶ When the Pointer tool turns into a hand, it indicates that you can drag an element to move it. When it turns into an index finger, it indicates that you can drag an element to resize it.

Because your new audio track is record-enabled (the R button on the track header is red), the next recording will create an audio region on that track. You can monitor the audio routed to record-enabled tracks while Logic is stopped, playing, or recording.

> **NOTE** ▶ If you are already using a hardware mixer or your audio interface's software to monitor the audio being routed to record-enabled tracks, turn off Software Monitoring in Logic's Audio Preferences. Otherwise you will be monitoring the signal twice, resulting in a flangy or robotic sound.

Adjusting the Recording Level

Before recording, make sure you can monitor the sound through Logic, and adjust the source audio level to avoid overloading the converters. On the channel strip, look at the clip detector, and make sure it never hits 0 dBFS (decibels full scale), which would indicate that you are *clipping* the input of your converter. Keep in mind that you need to adjust the audio level *before the converter input*, so use your microphone preamp gain knob. Allow for some headroom, especially if you know the artist might play or sing louder during the actual recording. It's better to work with a low-level recording than clipping the input.

> **MORE INFO** ▶ If you are using the Macintosh built-in line input or microphone, you can adjust the input level in the Sound pane's Input tab in System Preferences.

Let's adjust the recording and monitoring levels, tune the guitar, and find a cool acoustic guitar sound.

1   Ask the musician to play the loudest part of the performance you are about to record, and adjust the level on the microphone preamp as you watch the clip detector on the channel strip. If the clip detector turns red, lower the gain on the preamp, and click the clip detector to reset it. Make sure the maximum peak sits comfortably below 0 dBFS: the wider the dynamic range of the source, the more headroom it needs to avoid clipping.

   NOTE ▶ You may hear a small delay between when you play a note and when you hear it. This delay is called latency. You will learn how to reduce latency at the end of this lesson, in the section "Setting I/O Buffer Size."

—— Clip detector

2   Press the Spacebar to start playback, and play along the song. If the acoustic guitar is now too loud or too soft in comparison to the other tracks, adjust the monitoring level using the channel strip's fader.

   During recording, the channel strip's volume fader adjusts the monitoring level, but it does not alter the recording level. After the recording, the fader stays at the same position to play back the track at the same level.

3   In the Library tab, choose 03 Acoustic Guitar > Bright Acoustic.

The Bright Acoustic channel strip setting opens. The channel strip displays the name of the setting, and Channel EQ and Compressor plug-ins are inserted. The guitar sounds a little brighter, fitting better into the mix. The settings even include a Tuner plug-in, so you can verify that your instrument is in tune before you start recording.

4   Press the Spacebar to stop playback.

5   Double-click the Tuner plug-in in the first insert slot.

The Tuner plug-in opens. The Bypass button is orange, indicating that the plug-in is bypassed.

6   Click the Bypass button to turn off the bypass function.

The Bypass button turns black, indicating that the Tuner is now on.

7   Play the guitar's individual strings one after another, making sure that the Tuner displays the correct note and the meter stays as close as possible to the center position (red bar).

8   Bypass the Tuner.

9   Close the Tuner window.

You have set the desired sample rate and bit depth, adjusted the recording and monitoring levels, found a good-sounding channel strip setting, and tuned the instrument. You are now ready to start recording.

Recording Audio

Let's record a guitar part from bar 5 to bar 9.

1   In the Transport bar, click the Forward or Rewind button as needed—or press > (right angle bracket) or < (left angle bracket)—to position the playhead on bar 5.

2   Click the Record button (or press * (asterisk on the numeric keypad), or R on a laptop).

> **TIP** ▶ If no track is record-enabled, Logic automatically record-enables the selected track.

The playhead jumps one bar earlier and gives you a four-beat count-in with an audible metronome click before the recording starts. The Bar ruler turns red to indicate that Logic is recording. A progress window appears that shows the remaining recording time and the elapsed time. A new region with a red halo is created behind the playhead on the record-enabled track, and you can see the recording's waveform drawn in as you play or sing.

MORE INFO ▶ By default, the metronome automatically turns on when recording, and you get a four-beat count-in. You will learn to adjust both the metronome and the count-in settings later in this lesson.

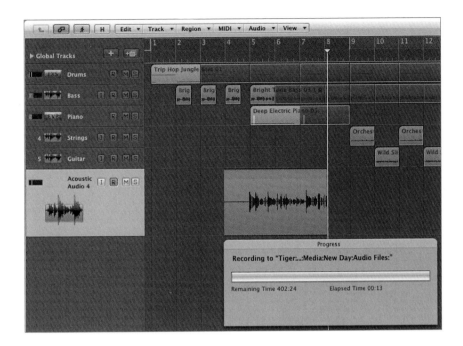

3 After you've recorded a few bars, in the Transport bar, click the Stop button (or press the Spacebar).

Your new recording appears as an audio region on the Acoustic track. Note that this new region is selected, making it easy to play, or to delete if you're not happy with it.

4 In the Transport bar, click the Play from Selection button (or press Shift-Enter).

The playhead jumps to the beginning of the recording and starts playing.

5 Stop playback.

6 Make sure the Arrange area is active, and press Delete on the main keyboard.

A Delete dialog appears. You can still click Cancel if you change your mind; but if you select Delete and click OK, the audio file will be permanently deleted from your hard disk. If you select Keep and click OK, the region is removed from the Arrange area, but the file is saved to your hard disk.

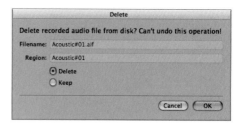

7   Click Cancel (or press Esc).

The new recording remains on the track.

Using the Audio Bin

When recording or importing audio files into a project, Logic uses the Audio Bin, located in the Media area, to track all the audio files and audio regions imported or recorded in the project. You can open the Audio Bin to make sure that files are recorded at the correct sample rates and bit depth settings and are properly named.

1   At the top of the Media area, click the Bin tab.

The Audio Bin opens, showing you the new **Acoustic#01.aif** file, as well as the three blue Apple Loops that you dragged into the Arrange area in Lesson 1.

For each audio file, the Info column displays:

▶   Sample rate

▶   Bit depth

▶   Status icon

▶   File size

You can click the disclosure triangle to the left of an audio file to display the regions associated with that audio file.

2   Click the disclosure triangle next to **Bright Tone Bass 03.aif.**

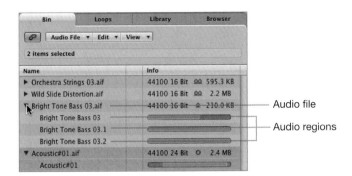

The regions associated with that audio file are displayed, including the one you short-ened in Lesson 1 for the intro of the song. The blue segment indicates which portion of the audio file the region contains.

Notice that the new **Acoustic#01.aif** audio file is selected, since the audio region you just recorded is still selected in the Arrange area. If you select a new region in the Arrange area, that region will be selected in the Audio Bin, and vice versa.

3   Click the **Acoustic#01.aif** audio file.

The audio file is selected and the Acoustic#01 region is deselected. The audio file's path is displayed at the top of the Audio Bin (or the beginning of the path if the path is too long to fit).

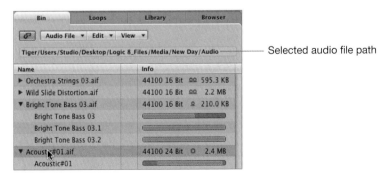

This is a quick way to ensure that the audio file was recorded in the correct location: in the audio folder inside the project folder.

In this case, the path is too long to be displayed in its entirety.

4   In the Audio Bin's local menu, choose Audio File > Show file(s) in Finder.

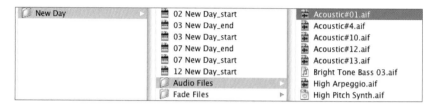

A Finder window opens, showing the selected audio file.

MORE INFO ▶ In Logic, you can also choose Window > Audio Bin to open the Audio Bin window, which displays the full path for each audio file.

5   Click the Arrange window (or press Command-Tab) to go back to Logic.

6   Click the first Bright Tone Bass 03 region in the Audio Bin.

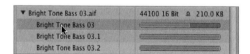

Bright Tone Bass 03 is selected in both the Audio Bin and the Arrange area. In the Arrange area you can see it's the shortened region used three times in the intro. Experiment by clicking regions in the Audio Bin or the Arrange area, and observe the same region being selected in the other location.

7   Click the disclosure triangle for the Bright Tone Bass audio file.

The regions associated with Bright Tone Bass are hidden.

Keep the Audio Bin open for the rest of this lesson to look at the new audio files created when recording.

Recording Additional Takes

When recording a live performance, musicians can make mistakes. Rather than delete the previous recording and repeatedly recording until you get a flawless performance, you can record several *takes* (performances of the same musical part), and later choose the best take, or even the best parts of each take, to create a *comp track* (composite track).

To record new takes in Logic, you can record the new performance over the previous one. All of the takes (including the original recording) will be placed into a *take folder*.

1   Make sure the track used to record your first performance (the Acoustic track) is still selected and record-enabled, and the Arrange area has key focus.

2   Position the playhead on bar 5.

3   In the Transport bar, click the Record button (or press * (asterisk), or R on a laptop).

Record a second take of about the same length as the first take.

The new recording seems to be recorded over the previous audio region.

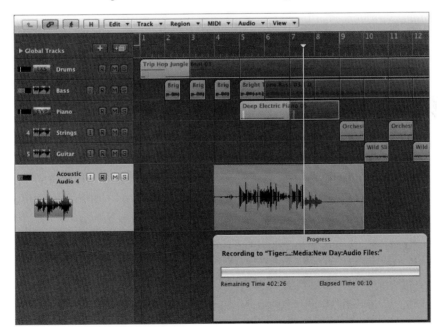

4   Stop the recording.

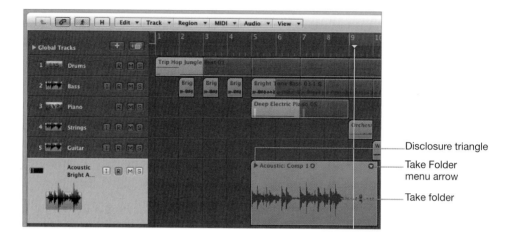

Disclosure triangle

Take Folder menu arrow

Take folder

Both the original take and the new take have been packed into a take folder. You can tell the region is a take folder by the presence of a disclosure triangle in front of the region name, and by the Take Folder menu arrow at the upper right of the region. Clicking the disclosure triangle displays all takes on individual sub-tracks. Clicking the Take Folder menu arrow allows you to access take-editing features.

5   Record a third take.

6   In the Acoustic track header, click the Record Enable (R) button.

The Record Enable button is disabled: the track is disarmed, and you can no longer hear the incoming sound.

If you listen to the song now, only the last recorded take will play back. The previous takes are muted. If the last take is shorter than another take you recorded previously, then playback automatically switches to that previous take at the end of the last take.

7   Click the disclosure triangle next to the take folder's name.

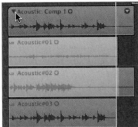

The take folder opens, showing you all the takes on lanes.

When the take folder is open, select the take you want to listen to.

MORE INFO ▶ The take turns blue and the others are dimmed (muted). Take folders and comping (creating a comp track) will be discussed in Lesson 3.

8   Click the disclosure triangle on the take folder.

The take folder closes.

TIP ▶ You can also double-click a take folder to open and close it.

Recording Takes in Cycle Mode

If you are both the engineer and the musician, it's not always practical to switch from playing your instrument to operating Logic between each take (and it can really destroy the vibe). Recording in Cycle mode allows you to repeatedly record a single section, creating a new take for each pass of the cycle. When you stop the recording, all the takes are packed inside a take folder.

1   Click the Go to Beginning button (or press Return).

2   Drag the horizontal zoom slider to the right (or press Control–Right Arrow a few times) to zoom in on the intro, so you can see at least the first five bars.

3   Drag a cycle from left to right between bars 3 and 5.

4   Start recording.

The playhead jumps a bar ahead of the cycle for a one-bar count-in and starts recording the first take. When it reaches bar 5, the end of the cycle area, it jumps back to bar 3 and starts recording a new take.

TIP ► You don't have to position the playhead when recording in Cycle mode: recording automatically starts at the beginning of the cycle, after the count-in.

Logic keeps looping the cycle area, recording new takes until you stop recording. Record 5 or 6 takes.

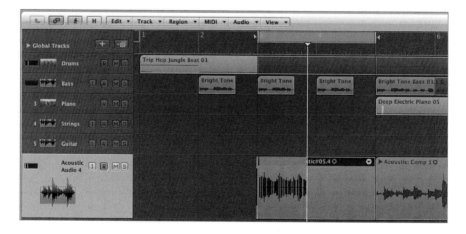

5   Click Stop (or press the Spacebar).

All the takes recorded in Cycle mode are placed in a take folder.

6   Look at the new audio file in the Audio Bin.

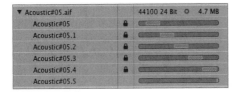

All the takes recorded in Cycle mode are displayed as successive regions of a single audio file.

Let's turn off the Cycle mode and return the Acoustic track to its original size.

7   Click the cycle area in the Bar ruler (or press / on the numeric keypad, or press C on a laptop).

Cycle mode is turned off.

8   Position your Pointer tool over the lower-left corner of the Acoustic track header.

The Pointer tool turns into the Finger tool, ready to resize.

9   Shift-click the track header.

The track zooms out and returns to the same height as the other tracks.

> **TIP** ▶ When tracks have different heights, Shift-clicking the lower-left corner of any track header using the Finger tool resets all the tracks to the same height.

Recording Multiple Tracks

You can use the same single-track techniques to record multiple tracks simultaneously. This allows you to record several instruments at once, placing each instrument on a separate track.

You first create as many tracks as needed, making sure each track is set to a different input and is record-enabled. (You can't record-enable channel strips that are set to the same input on your audio interface because they would all record the same input.)

In the following exercise, you will record two mono tracks at the same time, which you can do using the built-in Macintosh audio interface. To record more than two tracks simultaneously, you need an audio interface with more than two inputs.

1   At the bottom of the Arrange area, click the last track header.

This ensures the tracks you create now will be added below the last track.

2   At the top of the track list in the Arrange area, click the New Tracks… button (+) (or press Option-Command-N).

The New Tracks dialog appears.

3   Use the following settings:

▶   Number: 2

▶   Type: Audio

▶   Format: Mono

▶   Input: Input 1

4   To the right of the Input pop-up menu, select Ascending.

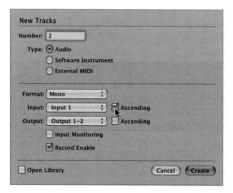

When creating multiple tracks, selecting the Ascending checkbox automatically sets the inputs (or outputs) to ascending settings. In this case, it will create two tracks and assign the first to Input 1 and the second to Input 2.

5   Select Record Enable.

6   Deselect Open Library.

The Library won't open. The Audio Bin will stay open, and you can see the audio files created as you record.

7 Click Create (or press Enter).

Two audio tracks are created, automatically assigned to the next available audio channels (Audio 5 and Audio 6). Their inputs are set to Input 1 and Input 2, and both are record-enabled.

TIP ▶ If you need to reassign a track's input, hold down the Input slot in the I/O section on the track's channel strip. A menu opens, allowing you to choose any input on your audio interface.

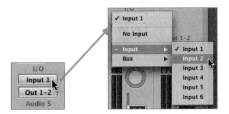

8 Rename the tracks *Piano* and *Voice*, or whatever you wish.

9 In the Transport bar, click the Go to Beginning button, or press Return.

10 Start recording.

The multitrack recording starts and, after a one-bar count-in, you see the playhead appear on the left of the Arrange area, creating two regions, one on each record-enabled track.

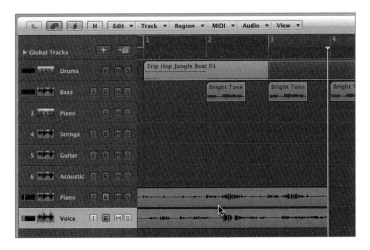

11 After a few bars, stop the recording.

You have a new audio region on each track.

You can use the same procedure to simultaneously record as many tracks as needed. If the tracks already exist in the Arrange area, make sure you assign them the correct inputs, record-enable them, and start recording.

Recording Additional Takes on Multiple Tracks

You can record additional takes on multiple tracks as you would record a single track: by recording over the existing multitrack recording.

1 Return the playhead to the beginning of the song.

2 Make sure both the Piano and Voice tracks are still record-enabled.

3 Start recording.

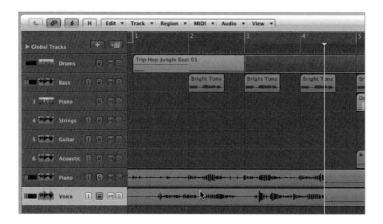

A new take is recorded on each record-enabled track.

4 Stop recording.

You have a new take folder for each track.

You can also use cycle recording to record multiple takes on multiple tracks.

First, let's clean up the project by deleting all the Piano and Voice recordings.

5   Make sure both the Piano and Voice take folders are selected.

6   Choose Edit > Delete (or press Delete).

A Delete dialog appears.

If you select Keep and click OK, the operation is nondestructive. The selected regions or take folders disappear from the Arrange area but remain in the Audio Bin, and the audio files remain on the hard disk.

If you choose Delete and click OK, the operation is destructive. The audio files are deleted from the hard disk. In that case, you cannot undo the operation and the audio files are removed permanently.

TIP ▶ Be very careful when deleting audio files. When in doubt, click Cancel to abort. Then, you can open the Audio Bin to preview all of the selected audio files before deciding what to do with them.

If you do not wish to keep the piano and voice recordings, delete them.

7   Make sure Delete is selected.

8   Select "For all."

When "For all" is selected, the choice of deleting or keeping the first audio file will be applied to all selected audio files.

9   Click OK (or press Enter).

The take folders disappear and the corresponding audio files are removed from the Audio Bin and permanently deleted from the hard disk.

10 In the upper half of the Bar ruler, click the gray locators stripe to turn on Cycle mode.

11 Make sure both the Piano and Voice tracks are still record-enabled.

12 Start recording.

Logic counts in four beats, then records one take on each track for every pass through the cycle area.

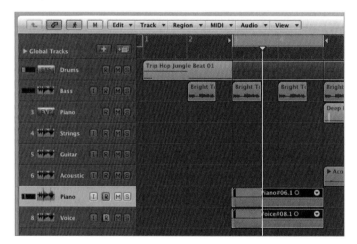

13 Stop recording.

You have two take folders containing each track's multiple takes.

Punching In and Out

When you want to correct a specific section of a recording—usually to fix a performance mistake—you can start playback before the mistake, punch in to engage recording just before the section you wish to fix, and punch out to stop recording immediately after the section. A take folder is created, automatically edited to play the only the new recording between the places where you punched in and out. Punching is nondestructive. At any time you can open the take folder and select the original recording.

There are two punching methods: on the fly and automatic. Punching on the fly allows you to use a key command to punch in and out while Logic plays, whereas automatic punching requires you to set the Autopunch area in the Bar ruler before recording. Punching on the fly is fast but usually requires an engineer to perform the punch in and punch out while the musician is performing. Automatic punching is ideal for the musician-producer who is working alone.

Punching on the Fly

To punch on the fly, you need to turn on the Punch on the Fly mode and use the Record Toggle key command to punch in and out. In the next exercise you will get familiar with the song and then experiment with punching on the last acoustic guitar track, Acoustic Right.

1   Close the current project and open 02 We Shared Everything_start.

When a project was originally saved on another computer, remember to consolidate the project before recording audio in it.

2   Choose File > Project > Consolidate, click OK, and when you get the confirmation pop up click OK again.

3   Play the song.

NOTE ▶ The first time you play a project, you may get System Overload alerts. If you do, click Continue and start playback again. The alerts will stop appearing after a while.

The last track, Acoustic Right, is missing an entire section. The guitar player made a mistake and stopped playing between bars 14 and 18. To make it easier to focus on that track, you can mute all the tracks except for the drum tracks.

4   Starting on the High Cello tracks, hold down the Mute button and drag down to the Acoustic Left track.

Tracks 7 through 14 (High Cello to Acoustic Left) are muted. Holding down a button in a track header and dragging down or up emulates the way engineers quickly mute or solo a whole section of the arrangement by sliding a finger across the buttons on a real mixing board.

5   Choose Options > Audio > Punch on the Fly; or, in the Transport bar, hold down the mouse button over the Record button and choose Punch on the Fly from the pop-up menu.

If you look at the menu again, a checkmark appears next to Punch on the Fly, indicating that the mode is active.

6   Click the lower half of the Bar ruler at bar 12 to position the playhead.

7 On the left Arrange channel strip, make sure the desired input is selected in the input slot, and click the Record Enable button.

The track is record-enabled.

8 Check your recording and monitoring levels.

Now that the project is ready to record, save it. You will revert to this record-ready state in the next exercise.

9 Choose File > Save (or press Command-S).

10 Start playback.

11 When the playhead reaches bar 14, press Shift-* (asterisk on the numeric keypad) or press Shift-R on a laptop and play your instrument.

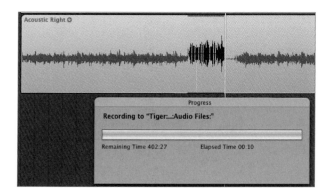

You just punched in. Logic starts recording over the current Acoustic Right audio region.

12 When the playhead reaches bar 18, press Shift-* (asterisk on the numeric keypad) or press Shift-R on a laptop again.

This time you punched out. Logic stops recording and reverts to playing back the current Acoustic Right audio region on the track.

13 Stop playback.

The Acoustic Right track now displays a take folder.

14 Open the take folder.

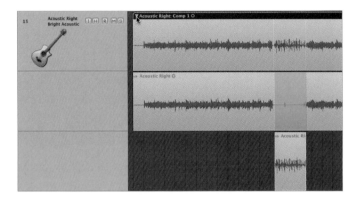

You can see that the comp take contains the original recording and the new recording between bars 14 and 18 where you punched in and out.

Using Automatic Punching

To prepare for automatic punching, you turn on the Autopunch mode and adjust the Autopunch area. You will also temporarily hide all tracks except for the one you record on, to clearly see what occurs.

1   Choose File > Revert to Saved.

An alert message appears, indicating that you are about to discard the changes you've made since the last time the song was saved.

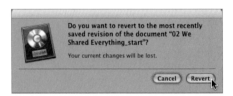

2   Click Revert.

The current project is closed without being saved, and the last saved version of **02 We Shared Everything_start** opens. It should be ready for recording, as you saved it before punching on the fly in the previous exercise.

Let's hide all the tracks but the one you're going to record on.

3   At the top of the Arrange area, click the Hide View button (or press H).

The Hide View button turns green, and a Hide button (with the letter H) appears in each track header.

4   Hold down the first track's Hide button and drag down to the Acoustic Left track to engage the Hide Track function for those tracks.

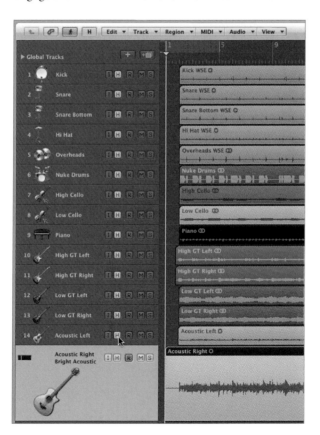

5 Click the Hide View button again (or press H).

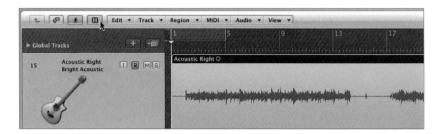

The Hide View button turns orange, and all the tracks with Hide buttons engaged are now hidden.

6 In the Transport bar, click the Autopunch button.

In the Bar ruler, a red autopunch strip appears from bar 1 to bar 5. The Autopunch area defines the section to be re-recorded.

TIP ▶ You can also toggle the Autopunch mode by Option-clicking the upper half of the Bar ruler.

7 Drag the Autopunch area so it extends from bar 14 to bar 18.

Notice the two red vertical lines on either side of the Autopunch area. These help you adjust the Autopunch area while you're looking at the waveform.

8   Position the playhead before the Autopunch area.

9   Make sure Acoustic Right is still record-enabled.

10 Click the Record button (or press * (asterisk on the numeric keypad), or press R on a laptop).

Playback starts. When the playhead reaches the beginning of the Autopunch area, Logic starts recording over the current Acoustic Right audio region. When the playhead reaches the end of the Autopunch area, Logic stops recording and reverts to playing the current Acoustic Right audio region.

11 Click Stop (or press Return).

The Acoustic Right track now displays a take folder.

12 Open the take folder.

You can see that the comp take contains the original recording and the new recording between bars 14 and 18 (corresponding to the Autopunch area).

You can hear the results of a successful punch recording in **02 We Shared Everything_end**, where the guitar player used Autopunch mode to replace bars 14 through 18 with a new take.

13 Close the current project and open **02 We Shared Everything_end**.

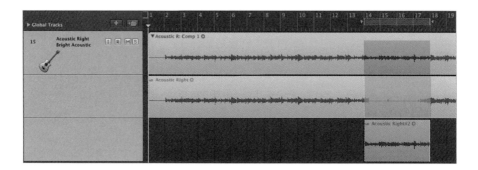

The Acoustic Right track is soloed and its take folder is expanded. The second take, Acoustic Right#2, is colored light red, so you can clearly see it in the comp at the top, under the Autopunch area.

TIP▶ To change the color of a region, click the Colors button in the Toolbar (or press Option-C) to open the Color palette. Then select the region(s) and click the desired color in the palette.

14 Choose File > Project > Consolidate and click OK.

15 Position the playhead just before the Autopunch area and start playback.

Listen to the transitions between the takes. Not bad!

16 Click the Solo button in the track header.

17 Click the Hide View button at the top of the Arrange area (or press H).

All tracks are now visible.

18 Listen to the Autopunch area again.

Notice the nice chorus effect produced by the two acoustic guitars panned left and right.

TIP▶ You can speed up the Autopunch recording process by using the Marquee tool described in Lesson 3. When a marquee selection is present, starting a recording automatically turns on the Autopunch mode, and the Autopunch area matches the marquee selection.

19 In the Bar ruler, Option-click the Autopunch area to turn Autopunch mode off.

Changing Recording and Metronome Settings

Some settings do not affect the quality of the audio recording but can change the behavior of your project when recording or the audio file format used for recordings. Although you can record audio using the default settings, sometimes you'll want to change them. The next few exercises will show you how those settings affect the audio recording process, and how to adjust them.

Setting the I/O Buffer Size

When communicating with the audio interface, Logic does not receive or transmit just one sample at a time. It places a number of samples in a buffer. When the buffer is full, Logic processes or transmits the entire buffer. The larger the buffer, the less work is required from the CPU. The advantage of using a larger buffer is that the CPU has more time to calculate other processes and you can use more plug-ins. The drawback to a larger buffer is that you have to wait a bit longer for the buffer to fill before you can monitor your signal. That means a longer delay between the original sound and the one you hear through Logic. That delay is called *latency*.

Usually, you want to have the smallest possible latency when recording, and the most CPU processing power possible when mixing, so you can use more plug-ins. You can adjust the I/O buffer size depending on the situation.

1   In the main menu, choose Logic Pro > Preferences > Audio, or click the Preferences button in the Toolbar and choose Audio.

2   Click the I/O Buffer Size pop-up menu.

The menu allows you to set the buffer size anywhere between 32 and 1024 samples.

3   Choose 32, and click Apply Changes.

Wait for the Core Audio engine to reinitialize.

4   Play the song.

Look at the CPU meter in the Toolbar. Depending on the CPU your computer has, you might see pretty big spikes. You might even hear pops and cracks while the song plays back, or get a Core Audio overload alert.

5   Set the I/O Buffer Size to 1024, and click Apply Changes.

6   Play the song.

The CPU meter should hit much lower. It doesn't have to work as hard with the larger buffer size. However, if you try to record audio with that setting, you will hear a delay between the notes you play and the notes you hear. That's latency. If you intend to do more audio recordings, find the lowest I/O buffer size setting that allows a clean monitoring.

Setting the Recording File Type

Logic can record in four digital audio file formats: Sound Designer II (an older audio file format developed by Digidesign), AIFF (the most commonly used audio file format on Macintosh computers), Broadcast Wave File (BWF, or WAVE), and Core Audio Format (CAF). The Audio Engineering Society recommends using BWF for most applications. CAF is practically unlimited in file size and can contain more than two channels, so it can be used for large audio files and multi-channel surround audio files.

1   At the top of the Audio Preferences window, click the General tab.

2   Set the Recording File Type to WAVE (BWF).

3 Close the Preferences window.

From now on, any new audio recorded in Logic will create BWF files.

Setting the Count-In

The count-in is the time you have to prepare yourself and get in the groove before the actual recording begins.

1 Choose File > Project Settings > Recording, or, in the Transport bar, hold down the Record button and choose Recording Settings.

The Recording Project Settings window opens.

2 Select "When Beginning: Count-in" and set it to 2 Bars.

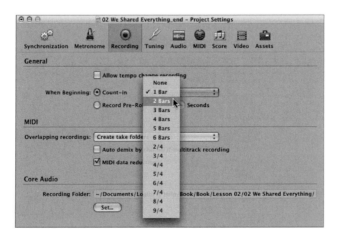

3 Record-enable any track.

4 Go back to the beginning of the song.

5 Start recording.

This time you can hear eight beats (two bars in 4/4) before the playhead appears and starts recording on the first downbeat of bar 1.

6 Stop the recording.

7 Choose Edit > Undo Recording (or press Command-Z).

Setting the Metronome

You can adjust the sound of the metronome in the Metronome project settings.

1 Choose File > Project Settings > Metronome, or click the Metronome button at the top of the Project Settings window.

TIP ▶ You can also access the Metronome project settings by holding down the Metronome button in the Transport bar and choosing Metronome Settings.

The Metronome Project Settings window opens. The Software Click Instrument settings are on the right of the window.

MORE INFO ▶ Preferences (such as the I/O buffer size and the Recording File Type set in previous exercises) are global settings that affect Logic's behavior in any project you work on. Project settings (such as count-in or metronome settings) are local settings that only affect the current project, and are saved with the project.

2 Start playing the song.

3 Click the Metronome button in the Transport bar.

4 In the Metronome Project Settings window, drag the Volume slider to the right.

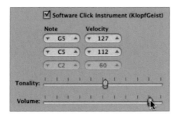

The metronome click increases in volume.

5 Drag the Tonality slider to the right.

The metronome sound changes and you can distinctly hear a pitch. Adjusting the tonality of the metronome is important: a pitched sound (slider to the right) will cut better through a busy mix but will also bleed through the musician's headphones into the microphone. A more muted sound (slider to the left) is more suitable for quiet mixes when you can't tolerate any metronome bleed.

Adjust the metronome so it is loud and clear.

When a project already contains a drum track, you may only need the metronome during the count-in to get into the groove before the song starts.

6 Under Options, select "Only during count-in."

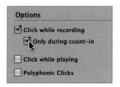

7 Position the playhead on bar 2, the beginning of the song.

8 Start recording.

You hear the metronome for two bars; then it stops playing as the song starts on bar 2.

9 Stop and undo the recording.

NOTE ▶ If you want your metronome to play a specific sound on an external hardware MIDI synthesizer or sampler, use the MIDI Metronome. In the MIDI Port menu, choose a port and connect a MIDI cable from that MIDI Out port on the MIDI Interface to the MIDI In port on your hardware sampler/synthesizer.

Lesson Review

1. Which settings affect the quality of a digital audio recording?
2. Where can you adjust those settings?
3. How do you record on one or several tracks?
4. How do you record additional takes?
5. What happens when you record in Cycle mode?
6. How do you punch on the fly?
7. How do you use the Autopunch function?
8. Where do you adjust the I/O buffer size?
9. How do you choose the best I/O buffer size?
10. Where do you set the recording file type?
11. Where do you adjust the count-in?
12. Where do you adjust the metronome settings?
13. How can you quickly access recording and metronome settings?
14. How can you hide tracks?

Answers

1. Sample rate and bit depth.
2. You adjust the sample rate in File > Project Settings > Audio, or you can customize the Transport bar to display it. Adjust the bit depth in the Devices tab of the Audio Preferences.
3. Record-enable the desired track(s) and click the Record button in the Transport bar.
4. Record over an existing audio region.
5. A new take is recorded for each pass of the cycle, and all the takes are packed into a take folder.

6. Make sure Punch On the Fly is enabled (choose Options > Audio > Punch On the Fly to toggle it on and off), start playback, and press the Record Toggle key command (Shift-*) to punch in and out.

7. In the Transport bar, click the Autopunch Mode button. Adjust the Autopunch range in the Bar ruler, and click the Record button.

8. In the Devices tab of Audio Preferences.

9. Choose a lower I/O buffer size when recording (for less latency), and a higher I/O buffer size when mixing (for more CPU processing power).

10. In the General tab of Audio Preferences.

11. In File > Song Settings > Recording.

12. In File > Song Settings > Metronome.

13. Hold down (or Control-click) the Record or Metronome buttons in the Transport bar.

14. At the top left of the Arrange area, click the Hide button. Click individual Hide buttons on track headers, and click the main Hide button again.

3

Lesson Files Logic 8_Files > Lessons > 03 New Day_start

Media Logic 8_Files > Media > New Day > Audio Files

Logic 8_Files > Media > Additional Media

Time This lesson takes approximately 60 minutes to complete.

Goals Create a composite take from multiple takes

Assign left-click and Command-click tools

Edit regions in the Arrange area

Apply fades and crossfades

Import audio files

Edit audio destructively in the Sample Editor

Position audio regions in the Arrange area

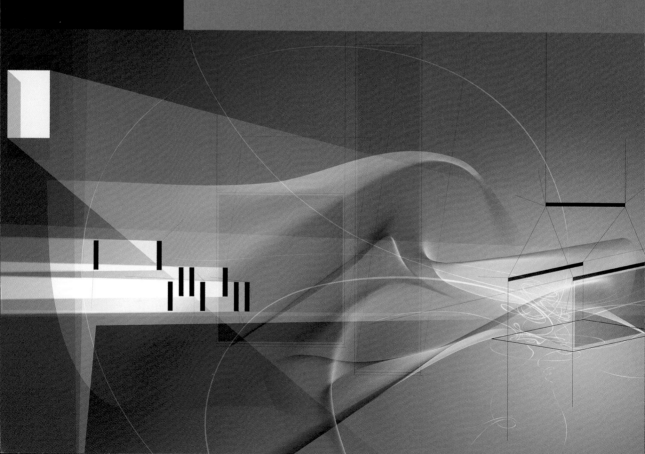

Editing Audio

Audio engineers have always looked for ways to edit recordings. In the days of magnetic tape, they used razor blades to cut pieces of a recording, then connected the pieces with special tape. They could create a smooth transition (or crossfade) between two pieces of magnetic tape by cutting them at an angle.

Digital audio workstations revolutionized audio editing the same way word processors revolutionized text editing. A waveform on the screen gives you a visual representation of the digital audio recordings stored on the hard disk. The ability to read the waveform and master the editing tools is the key to precise and flexible audio editing.

In this lesson, you will develop waveform reading skills, identify musical notes in the waveform, and perform edits just before the attack of a note. You will also create a single composite take using the multiple takes you recorded in the previous lesson, and create a drum loop from a drum recording you will import into the project.

As your ability to read waveforms and use Logic's editing tools develops, never forget to use your ears and trust them as the final judge of your work.

Comping Takes

In the previous lesson, you recorded several takes of acoustic guitar and packed them into a take folder. Now you will learn how to preview the individual takes and assemble a composite take by choosing sections from different takes, a process called *comping*.

Comping techniques are really useful when you have recorded several takes of the same musical phrase and each take has its good and bad qualities. Maybe in the first take the musician messed up the beginning but got the ending perfectly, while in the following take he nailed the beginning and made a mistake at the end. You can create a comp using the beginning of the second take and the ending of the first take.

The same technique can also be used to create a composite musical phrase by comping performances of different musical ideas. In the following exercises, you will create a new melody by comping takes of two different acoustic guitar melodies.

Previewing the Takes

Before you start comping, you need to get familiar with the takes you are going to comp.

1   Go to Logic 8_Files > Lessons and open **03 New Day_start**.

    A take folder is present on the Acoustic Guitar track.

2   Double-click the take folder.

    The take folder opens. The take folder is still displayed on the Acoustic track (track 6), with a disclosure triangle before its name, and a take folder menu at the top right. The individual takes are displayed on lanes below the acoustic track, with a take symbol before their name.

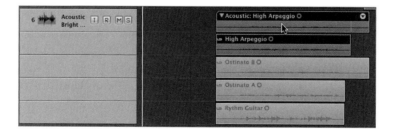

You can see that the High Arpeggio take at the top is selected (it is blue and has a black title bar). That's the one currently playing (the other takes are dimmed to indicate that they are muted).

Notice the name of the take folder: Acoustic: High Arpeggio. It's the name of the track and the name of the selected take.

3   In the Bar ruler, drag a cycle area from bar 5 to bar 9.

4   Press the Spacebar.

Playback starts on bar 5, and you can hear the first take, High Arpeggio. Note the names of the takes. They describe the musical ideas that they contain.

5   Stop playback.

6   Click the Ostinato B take.

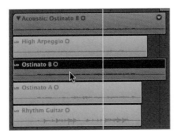

The Ostinato B take is selected, and the name of the take folder is now Acoustic: Ostinato B.

7   Press the Spacebar.

You are now listening to the second take, Ostinato B.

8   Stop playback.

> **MORE INFO** ▶ Logic can continue playing in Cycle mode as you select different takes. In that case, a brief delay will occur as Logic switches playback between takes.

Repeat these steps to listen to each of the other takes. High Arpeggio is a nice musical phrase and you will use it for this section. Ostinato A and Ostinato B are the same phrase, but Ostinato A is the weaker performance. Rhythm Guitar is interesting, but you will not use it for this section of the song.

While listening to High Arpeggio, notice that it's repeating the same two-bar phrase twice. The end of that two-bar phrase, going up in pitch, works well the first time, as it leads back into the arpeggio. However, it doesn't work so well the second time, just before the strings, because it doesn't sound as though it concludes the phrase.

Comping the Takes

In the following exercise, you will comp High Arpeggio with the end of Ostinato B, to provide a nice conclusion for the musical phrase.

1   Select the High Arpeggio take.

2   Click Ostinato B around bar 8 and drag to the right to select the ending of that take.

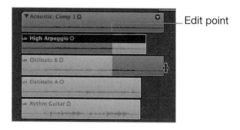

The comp is created. High Arpeggio will play until bar 8, and then Ostinato B will play. The name of the take folder is now Acoustic: Comp 1.

3   Listen to the comp.

The edit point is represented on the take folder as a white vertical line at bar 8. It shows the position where the comp stops playing High Arpeggio and starts playing Ostinato B. Unless you were very lucky, the edit probably sounds awkward. You will fine-tune the edit later in this lesson, but right now, let's get it in the ballpark.

4   On the takes lanes, zoom in on the edit point.

In this case, the fastest way to zoom in on the area is to press Control-Option to choose the Zoom tool, and drag over the area you want to zoom in on.

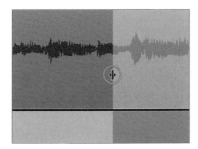

5   In one of the takes, place the mouse cursor over the edge of the blue selection.

The mouse cursor changes into a length-change tool pictured here:

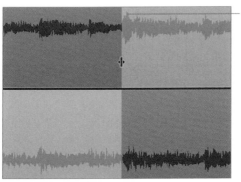

This tool allows you adjust the edit point between the two takes.

6   Drag the edit point to just before the attack of the note on bar 8.

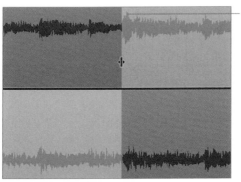

Note attack

Don't spend too much time finding the perfect edit point position. At this stage, you are making musical choices. You will fine-tune the edit point later.

7   In the Arrange area, Control-Option-click anywhere.

The area zooms out and you can once more see the whole song.

8   Listen to your new edit point.

It should sound better.

Once you have determined where to transition between takes, you can click sections of the other takes and experiment further to find the best takes for the sections on each side of the edit point.

Experimenting with the Comp

Before you begin experimenting, you need to make sure you can easily return to the comp you just created.

1   At the upper-right corner of the take folder, click the arrow.

The Take Folder menu opens, and you can see your four takes, the comp you just created (Comp 1: Comp 1), and a few commands you can apply to the take folder.

2   Choose New Comp.

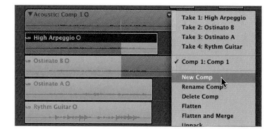

The take folder is now named Acoustic: Comp 2. From now on, you are editing Comp 2. If you are not happy with the results, you can revert to Comp 1 by choosing it from the Take Folder menu.

3   To the left of the edit point, click the Rhythm Guitar take.

Comp 2 is now composed of the Rhythm Guitar section before the edit point, and the Ostinato B section after. The edit point maintains the same position.

4   In Ostinato B, drag to select a one-bar section from approximately bar 6 to bar 7.

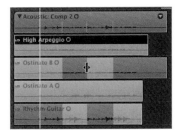

The section you dragged is selected (highlighted in blue), and Comp 2 is updated to play the blue sections of each take. Let's move that new section to the previous bar When you position the mouse cursor in the middle of a blue area, it turns into a two-headed arrow, and you can drag the blue area horizontally.

5   Drag the first blue area in the Ostinato B take to bar 5.

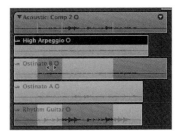

The selections in the Rhythm Guitar take are updated so that all the blue sections remain connected.

Take a moment to experiment further, creating a comp out of the four takes. Drag as many new sections as you want, slide them around, move the edit points, and click different sections of takes to select them, listening to your results.

Now let's go back to our original Comp 1.

6   From the Take Folder menu, choose Comp 1: Comp 1.

The take folder reverts to the comp created in the previous exercise. Now close the take folder.

7   Double-click the take folder.

The take folder closes.

You will flatten the take folder, replacing it with the audio regions that compose the current comp, Comp 1. Once you have audio regions instead of a take folder, you can refine the edit point and apply fades to the regions.

8   From the Take Folder menu, choose Flatten.

The take folder is replaced by the current comp: the selected sections of the takes in the take folder are now replaced by audio regions, and a crossfade is displayed at the edit point.

9   In the Bar ruler, click the cycle area to turn off Cycle mode.

Assigning Mouse Tools

Until now you have worked exclusively with the default tools. You also used keyboard modifiers such as Control-Option to choose the Zoom tool, and you used features that change the mouse cursor to tools such as the Resize tool or Loop tool, depending on its position.

When editing audio in the Arrange area, you will need to access more tools.

Two Tool menus are located at the upper right of the Arrange area. The left menu assigns the left-click tool and the right menu assigns the Command-click tool, which you access by pressing the Command key while clicking.

Command-click tool
Left-click tool

1   Position the mouse cursor over the Arrange area, and press Command.

The mouse cursor changes to the Command-click tool: the Marquee tool in this case. Let's assign the Text tool to the Command-click tool

2   From the Command-click Tool menu, choose the Text tool.

The Command-click Tool menu now displays the Text tool. The two Comp 1 regions are still selected, and you need to deselect them to rename them individually.

3   Click the background of the Arrange area with the Pointer tool.

Both Comp 1 regions are deselected.

4   On the Acoustic track, Command-click the first Comp 1 audio region.

A text field appears in which you can rename the region.

5 Type *High Arpeggio* and press Enter.

The region is renamed "High Arpeggio."

6 Rename the second region *Ostinato* and press Enter.

You can also press the Esc (Escape) key to open a Tool menu at the current mouse cursor position.

7 Make sure the mouse cursor is positioned over the Arrange area, and press Esc.

A Tool menu appears at the mouse cursor position. This key command will save you a lot of trips to the Tool menus.

TIP ▶ Each editor that can be displayed in the Editing area also has its own set of tools. You can change an editor's tools by using the tool menus in its title bar, or by positioning the mouse cursor over the editing area before pressing Esc.

8 Choose the Solo tool.

The left-click tool switches to the Solo tool. You can quickly reset the left-click tool to the Pointer tool by pressing Esc twice.

TIP ▶ Instead of choosing a tool from the menu using the mouse, you can use the keyboard shortcuts listed in the menu. For example, when the Tool menu is open, pressing 7 chooses the Solo tool as the left-click tool.

9 Hold down the mouse button over the beginning of the High Arpeggio region.

The region is outlined in yellow, and Solo mode is temporarily turned on. Playback starts and you can hear only the High Arpeggio region until you release the mouse button.

Let's switch the left-click tool back to the Pointer tool. You can quickly reset the left-click tool to the Pointer tool by pressing Esc twice.

10 Press Esc twice.

The left-click tool switches to the Pointer tool.

Now let's assign the Solo tool to the Command-click tool.

11 Press Esc.

The Tool menu appears. You can Command-click a tool to assign it to the Command-click tool.

12 Press Command as you choose the Solo tool.

The Solo tool is the Command-click tool. Now you can perform edits with the Pointer tool, and you can Command-click any region to hear it in Solo mode.

TIP ▶ If you have a two-button mouse, you can also assign a third tool to the right mouse button by choosing Logic Pro > Preferences > Global and clicking the Editing tab. Choose "Is Assignable to a Tool" from the Right Mouse Button pop-up menu. The Right-click Tool menu will appear to the right of the two existing Tool menus.

Editing Audio Regions in the Arrange Area

Editing audio regions in the Arrange area is nondestructive. Regions are merely pointers to an audio file that identify parts of the audio file. When cutting and resizing regions, or adding fades and crossfades in the Arrange area, no processing is applied to the original audio files, which remain unaltered on your hard disk. You can always adjust your edits later. As a result, editing in the Arrange area provides a lot of flexibility and room for experimentation.

Adding Fades

When editing audio, you want to avoid abrupt transitions on edit points—the region boundaries and the junctions between regions. You can use nondestructive fades in the Arrange area to create smooth transitions.

1   Select the Ostinato region.

2   Click Play from Selection (or press Shift-Enter).

Listen to the transition from the guitar part to the orchestra strings part in measure 9. The last acoustic guitar note is sustained too long and clashes with the melody of the strings.

3   Drag the lower-right corner of the Ostinato region toward the left to shorten it so it stops approximately on bar 9, just when the strings come in.

4   Click Play from Selection (or press Shift-Enter).

The transition works better, but the guitar dies abruptly on bar 9. Let's add a fade-out at the end of the Ostinato region. You might need to zoom in to apply the fade.

5   Press Esc and choose the Crossfade tool (or press Esc-0).

The left-click tool switches to the Crossfade tool.

6   Drag the Crossfade tool over the boundary of the region. Start dragging in the background to the right of the region, and drag toward the left, covering the end of the region with the blue shaded rectangle.

Make sure that you drag over the boundary of the region, or nothing will happen. You can create fades only over region boundaries.

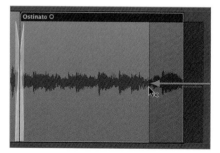

A fade-out is created. The length of the drag area determines the length of the fade.

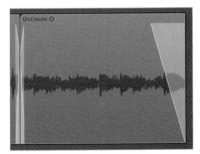

7   Listen to the fade-out.

It probably sounds unnatural. Let's lengthen the region so the note sustains a little longer. You will need the Crossfade tool to adjust the fade later, so make the Pointer tool the Command-click tool.

8   Press Esc and Command-click the Pointer tool.

9   Press Command as you drag the lower-right corner of the region a little further to the right to sustain the last note a little longer.

Now let's curve the fade.

10   Press Control-Shift as you drag up the Crossfade tool on the fade.

Control-Shift-dragging the Crossfade tool vertically on a fade changes the mouse cursor to a broken arrow, which allows you to change the fade's curve.

The fade sounds more natural, but with the new curve a longer fade would sound even better.

11   Drag the Crossfade tool over the boundary of the region again, this time drawing a longer fade. As long as the blue shaded rectangle covers the boundary of the region it doesn't matter whether you drag the Crossfade tool from left to right or from right to left.

The fade lengthens while retaining its curve shape.

Feel free to continue adjusting the curve and length of the fade until it sounds just right. There are no rules as to what the perfect curve and shape of a fade should be, so experiment and trust your ears.

Adding Crossfades

It is usually a good idea to crossfade audio regions that are back to back. The first region will fade out as the next fades in, ensuring a smooth transition without audible clicks.

When you previously comped the acoustic guitar in the take folder, a crossfade was automatically added. The crossfade was displayed when the comp was flattened. In the next exercise, you will delete that crossfade, fine-tune the position of the edit and add a new crossfade.

1   On the Acoustic track header, click the Solo button.

From now on, you will hear only that track. You may need to zoom in horizontally around bar 8 so that the Bar ruler displays the third beat of each bar (7.3, 8.3, and so on).

2   Drag a one-bar cycle area over the crossfade that overlaps bar 8 (from 7.3 to 8.3).

You can now play that section and listen to your edit without repositioning the play-head every time you start playback.

3   Control-Option-drag to zoom in on the crossfade between High Arpeggio and Ostinato.

Zoom just enough so you can still see the whole cycle in the Bar ruler.

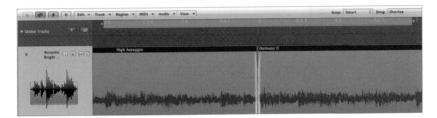

4   With the Crossfade tool chosen, Option-click the crossfade.

Option-clicking a fade with the Crossfade tool deletes the fade. You may need to zoom in closer to be able to delete the fade.

Let's assign the Pointer tool to the left-click tool so you don't have to press Command to edit the regions.

5   Press Esc twice.

The left-click tool is reset to the Pointer tool.

6   Position the mouse cursor over the edit point in the upper half of the waveform.

Junction pointer

The cursor changes into the Junction pointer. Dragging the Junction pointer horizontally changes the position of the junction between the regions while keeping both regions connected and not overlapping.

Make sure the mouse cursor is positioned on the upper half of the waveform. When the mouse cursor is on the lower half, it switches to the Resize tool, and you will resize one of the regions, creating gaps or overlaps between the regions.

7   Drag the Junction pointer slightly to the right.

The Junction pointer jumps in rough increments. Logic snaps to a virtual grid that has a resolution dependent on the current zoom level. You can hold down Control to gain a little more precision, and hold down Control-Shift to get tick precision (there are 240 ticks in a sixteenth note).

TIP ▶ For really fine resolution editing, zoom in close to the edit point. You can then perform edits with sample precision (down to the individual digital audio sample resolution).

8   While dragging the Junction pointer, press Control-Shift to disable snapping, and position the edit point close to bar 8.

Holding Control-Shift allows you to smoothly adjust the position of the edit point.

Press the Spacebar to listen to the junction, and adjust its position if necessary. You may hear a click at the junction of the regions. You will fix that with a crossfade. For now, you are only trying to find the best position to transition from High Arpeggio to Ostinato B.

9   Zoom in on the junction.

10 Press Esc and choose the Crossfade tool (or press Esc-0).

11 Drag the Crossfade tool over the junction of the regions.

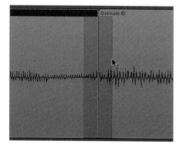

A crossfade is created. Again, use your ears to adjust the crossfade. A short crossfade works best here. You can redraw the crossfade to adjust its length and position.

12 Control-Shift-drag the Crossfade tool up or down on the crossfade.

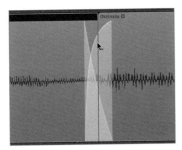

The shape of the crossfade changes.

13 Unsolo the Acoustic track, turn off the Cycle mode, and listen to the whole acoustic guitar section.

Reset the left-click tool for the next exercises.

14 Press Esc twice.

The left-click tool is the Pointer tool.

Don't spend too much time perfecting the crossfade. Crossfades between two performances sometimes sound a little odd when the track is soloed. If you can get the crossfade close, the result will usually be satisfying in the whole mix.

Previewing and Adding Audio Files

The Audio Bin lists all the audio files that were imported or recorded in the project, even if they are no longer used in the Arrange area. In the Lesson 2, you used the Audio Bin to keep track of the audio files recorded in the project. You will now use it to preview and add an audio file to the project.

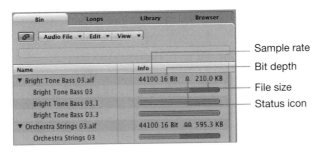

The Info column displays the audio file's information: sample rate, bit depth, status, and file size. The status icon indicates whether the file is mono or stereo, and whether it's an Apple Loops, a regular or compressed audio file. In front of each region, the dark gray bar represents the length of the audio file, and the colored section represents the region.

Let's import and add the Rhythm Guitar take that you chose not to use earlier when comping takes.

> **MORE INFO** ▶ You can also open the full-featured Audio Bin window from the main Window menu. The Audio Bin window displays the region's waveforms and also allows you to edit the regions.

1   In the Audio Bin, choose Audio File > Add Audio File.

The Audio Bin file selector box opens. When you comped the acoustic guitar takes earlier in this lesson, the unused takes' audio files were deleted from the Audio Bin, but they are still in the Audio Files folder inside the project folder.

2   Navigate to Logic 8_Files > Media > New Day > Audio Files and select **Rhythm Guitar.aif**.

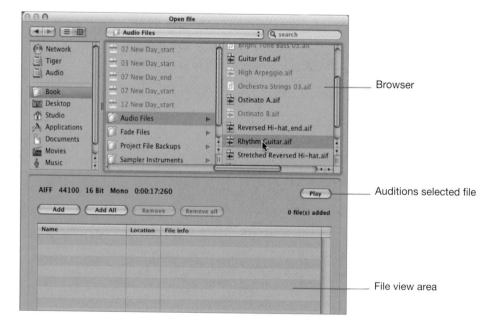

Think of the Audio Bin file selector box as a shopping experience. At the top, the Browser represents the shelves of a store where you look for audio files that you can preview by clicking the Play button. At the bottom, the file view area is your shopping cart.

You can double-click files in the Browser to add them to your file view area. When you click Done, all the files in the file view area are added to the Audio Bin.

3   Click the Play button.

You are previewing **Rhythm Guitar.aif**.

4   Click the Stop button.

5   Click the Add button (or double-click **Rhythm Guitar.aif**).

Rhythm Guitar.aif is added to the file view area.

6   At the bottom of the Audio Bin file selector box, click Done.

Rhythm Guitar.aif is added to the Audio Bin.

7   At the lower left of the Audio Bin, click the speaker button.

The selected region starts playing.

8   In the Arrange area, zoom out so you can see the whole arrangement.

9   From the Audio bin, drag the Rhythm Guitar region onto bar 14 of the Acoustic track.

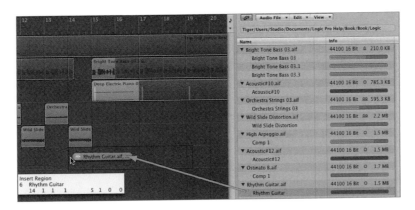

The Rhythm Guitar region is inserted in the Arrange area where you dragged it.

10 Listen to the section where you just dragged the Rhythm Guitar region.

Since the region was recorded with a one bar count-in, the musical phrase starts on bar 15, right at the beginning of the last section. The region fits rather well, except that it's too short for the section. You will resolve that in the next exercise.

Cutting and Copying Regions

Since the Rhythm Guitar region is too short for the last section, you can cut a portion of the region and repeat it so that it covers the whole section.

In the next exercise, you will use the Marquee tool to select a portion of a region and drag it to the end of the song. You will use No Overlap mode to make sure that the regions don't overlap.

1 At the upper right of the Arrange area, click the Drag menu and choose No Overlap.

When No Overlap is chosen, dragging one region over another automatically trims the region underneath to make space for the new one, avoiding region overlaps.

2 Press Esc to open the Tool menu, then Command-click the Marquee tool.

The Command-click tool is now the Marquee tool, and the left-click tool is the Pointer tool. This is a very powerful tool combination when editing audio in the Arrange area. You can select a portion of an audio region with the Marquee tool, and move or copy that selection with the Pointer tool.

3 Zoom in on the Acoustic track for the whole last section (bars 15 to 21).

4 Command-drag in the Rhythm Guitar region from bar 15 to bar 17.

The Marquee tool selects that portion of the Rhythm Guitar region, which is now highlighted.

5   Press the Spacebar.

The playhead jumps to bar 15 and plays the marquee selection. It corresponds exactly to a two-bar pattern of the guitar, what you need to add at the end to complete the rhythm guitar part.

TIP ▶ When a marquee selection is present, playback starts at the beginning and stops at the end of the marquee selection, even if Cycle mode is turned on.

6   Option-drag the marquee selection to bar 19.

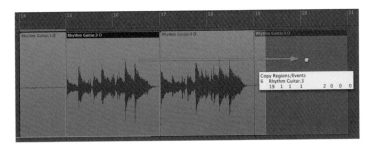

Option-dragging a marquee selection will automatically divide, copy, and paste the selection to a new location regardless of region boundaries. When the mouse button is released, the original region is automatically restored.

Here the two-bar guitar pattern is copied and pasted at bar 19. The end of the original region is trimmed at bar 19 so that it does not overlap with the region you just pasted.

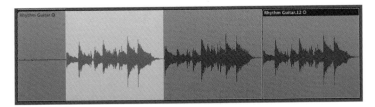

Now that the rhythm guitar part is complete, you can fine-tune the junction between the two regions, and add a crossfade to avoid any clicks at that junction.

7   Zoom in on the junction between the two Rhythm Guitar regions.

It looks as though the edit point is in the middle of the note attack. It would be better if placed a little further to the left, in the silence.

8 Position the mouse cursor over the junction on the upper half of the waveform.

The mouse cursor switches to the Junction pointer.

9 Drag the Junction pointer to the left.

> **TIP** ▶ When using the Junction pointer, the help tag can sometimes get in the way, hiding part of the waveforms in the audio regions. To get the help tag out of the way, position the mouse cursor in the upper part of the junction to get the Junction pointer, hold down the mouse button and drag the Junction pointer down in the lower part of the regions, then drag horizontally to adjust the position of the edit.

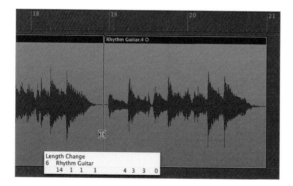

Now the junction of the two regions occurs in the silence.

10 Press Esc and choose the Crossfade tool.

11 Drag the Crossfade tool over the junction.

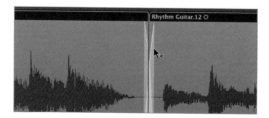

Make sure the crossfade is placed on the silence, not over any of the guitar notes.

Now that you know how to apply fades, take a minute to create a fade-in at the beginning of the first Rhythm Guitar region, and a fade-out at the end of the last Rhythm Guitar region. If you decide to resize the beginning of the first region to eliminate the noise in the guitar recording during the first bar of count-in, make sure that you first deselect the second region or you will be resizing both regions at the same time.

Deleting Unused Audio Files

When recording audio in Logic, storage space appears unlimited at first. When you are not totally happy with a recording, you usually keep it "just in case" and record another take. And another. . . You focus on recording the best performance, delaying the process of sorting out the good takes from the bad for the editing stage.

Once in the editing stage, you choose the best takes and comp them, or you edit the regions you need in the Arrange area. The leftover regions sit unused in the Audio Bin and can quickly pile up, crowding your hard disk space.

In the next exercise, you will delete unused audio files from your hard disk to reduce the size of the project folder.

1   In the Audio's Bin local menu bar, choose Edit > Select Unused (or press Shift-U).

All the audio files and regions that are not in use in the Arrange area are selected.

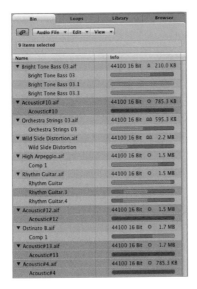

If you need to make sure you won't need the unused files again, you can select them one by one and listen to them by clicking the speaker button at the lower left of the Audio Bin. If you are sure you want to delete them all, press Shift-U again to select all the unused audio files and regions.

You have two choices: You can delete the unused audio files from the Audio Bin but keep them on your hard disk (if you think you might still need them later), or you can permanently delete them from the hard disk.

First, try deleting them from the Audio Bin, but keep them on your hard disk.

2   From the Audio Bin local menu bar, choose Edit > Delete (or press Delete).

The selected audio files and regions are deleted from the Audio Bin but not from your hard disk. This will not reduce the size of your project folder, but it will clean up your Audio Bin.

Since the operation is nondestructive, you can undo it and see the files again.

3   Press Command-Z.

All the audio files are once again displayed in the Audio Bin.

This time, you will delete the files from your hard disk. Be very careful whenever you permanently delete audio files: the operation is destructive, and you will not be able to recover those deleted files.

4   Choose Edit > Select Unused (or press Shift-U).

The unused audio files and regions are selected.

5   Choose Audio File > Delete File(s).

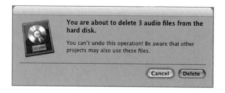

After a few seconds, an alert appears. Read it carefully! If you are sure you want to delete the audio files forever, click Delete.

6   Click Delete.

The files are permanently deleted from the Audio Bin and from the hard disk.

Editing an Audio Drum Loop

You will now perform destructive editing on an audio file. Starting with a rock drum recording, you will select a two-bar pattern from the recording and edit it so that it loops perfectly.

> **NOTE** ▸ In Lesson 7, "Manipulating Tempo and Time Stretching," you will adjust the tempo of that loop to match the song.

Previewing and Importing Audio Files

Earlier in this lesson, you added audio files to the Audio Bin. You can also drag audio files from the Audio Bin directly to the Arrange area. But, instead of opening the Audio Bin, you can browse your hard disk within the Logic interface.

In the Media area, the Browser tab allows you to look for files without leaving your project.

> **NOTE** ▸ The Browser displays only media files supported by Logic.

First, create a new audio track, and then use the Browser to find the rock drum recording and import it into the project. Remember that the new track will be created below the selected track, so in the track list, select the last track header if you want the new track to appear below the last track in the Arrange area.

1   At the top of the track list in the Arrange area, click the New Tracks button (+) (or press Option-Command-N).

Create one stereo audio track and deselect Record Enable.

2   In the Media area, click the Browser tab.

The Browser opens.

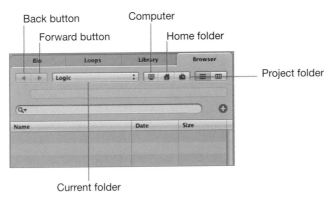

The Browser is like a mini Finder window inside Logic. At the top, you can see Back and Forward navigation buttons to step through your navigation history. The Path menu displays the current folder and allows you to move up in the Finder hierarchy. Three bookmark buttons provide quick access to the volumes on your computer, your home folder, or the project folder.

3   Click the Home button.

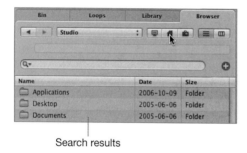

Search results

The contents of your Home folder are displayed in the search results.

You can choose the way the search results are displayed using the List View and Browser View buttons. The Browser view displays columns, allowing you to see the folder hierarchy.

4   Click the Browser View button.

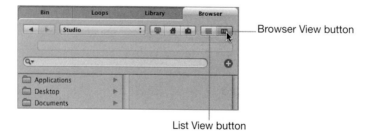

Browser View button

List View button

The search results are now displayed in two columns.

5   Click the Desktop folder.

The contents of your Desktop folder are displayed in the right column.

6   Navigate to Logic 8_Files > Media > Additional Media and select **Rock Drums.aif.**

Selected file information

The file's information is displayed at the top of the Browser.

TIP ▶ If you know the name of your file, use the search field at the top of the Browser. You can also click the plus button (+) to the right of the search field to set conditions that will limit your search by date, comments, length, and so on.

7   At the lower left of the Browser, click the speaker button.

The selected file starts playing. That's the rock drum recording you are going to use to create a drum loop. You will add the rock drum recording to the playhead position on the selected track, so make sure the new Audio 5 track is selected and the playhead is at the beginning of the song, on 1 1 1 1.

8   Double-click **Rock Drums.aif**.

A new Rock Drums audio region is inserted in the Arrange area at the playhead position on the selected Audio 5 track.

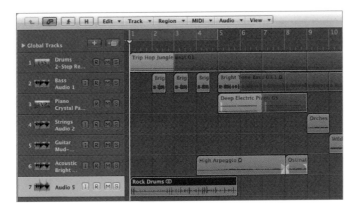

9   In the Media area, click the Bin tab.

You can see the **Rock Drums.aif** audio file in the Audio Bin.

Editing a Loop

In this exercise, you will cut a two-bar portion of the drum recording that will later be used as a drum loop.

1   In the Arrange area, click the Rock Drums region with the Pointer tool to select it.

2   Press Control-Option-Z.

     The region fills the Arrange area.

3   In the Audio 5 track header, click the Solo button.

4   Start playback.

     Keep in mind that the audio region's tempo does not match the tempo of the project. The bars in the Bar ruler don't correspond to the bars of the audio region. You will have to use your waveform-reading skills to resolve this.

     Listen to the drum pattern while paying close attention to the waveform. The groove is six bars long, composed of three two-bar patterns. Each two-bar pattern starts with two hits of the tom-toms. You want to cut the second two-bar pattern that starts on the third bar, where the drums really kick in. Listen to the tom-toms, and locate them on the waveform.

     You will first select that section with the Marquee tool. You don't need to be very precise, as you will fine-tune the loop later. It is better to include a little more rather than a little less of the desired section.

5   Make sure the Marquee tool is the Command-click tool.

6   Command-drag the Marquee tool from the first tom-tom hit of the second two-bar pattern to the first tom-tom hit of the third two-bar pattern.

     While selecting, look at your help tag. The marquee selection should start on 2 3 3 1 and end on 4 2 1 121.

     If you get the marquee selection wrong the first time, you can adjust it by Shift-dragging outside the selection with the Marquee tool. But remember that the Marquee tool is your Command-click tool, so in this case, you'll have to Shift-Command-drag. You may need to zoom in further to adjust the marquee selection with more precision.

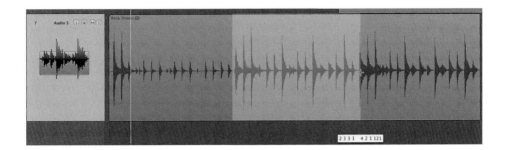

7   Shift-Command-drag the Marquee tool to adjust one of the boundaries of the marquee selection.

Make sure you first click outside the marquee selection, then drag left or right. If you click inside the marquee selection, the selection is lost.

Continue to adjust the selection until the help tag reads 2 3 3 1 on the left and 4 2 1 121 on the right.

8   Press the Spacebar.

The playhead plays the marquee selection once. You should hear the two-bar loop you're going to work on, with just the attack of the crash cymbal.

9   Click the marquee selection.

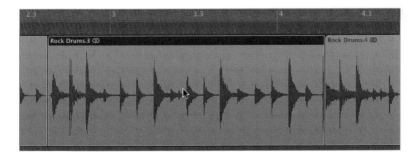

The Rock Drums region is divided at the borders of the marquee selection. You will now open that region in the Sample Editor to adjust its length and clean it up.

Using the Sample Editor

The Sample Editor allows you to perform destructive audio editing. Although performing nondestructive editing on audio regions in the Arrange area keeps the parent audio file intact, processing an audio region in the Sample Editor actually modifies the audio file associated with that region.

Instead of performing destructive audio editing on the original audio file, you can save the selection (which still corresponds to your marquee selection from the previous exercise) as a new audio file, and work on that new audio file while leaving the original audio file intact.

1   In the Arrange area, double-click the region you divided in the previous exercise.

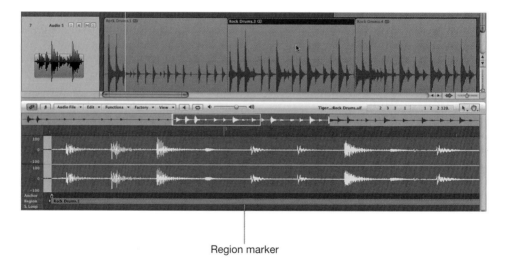

Region marker

The region opens in the Sample Editor and appears in the editing area. You may need to resize your screen or scroll down to see the editing area. Notice that the Sample Editor displays the whole audio file. The region you double-clicked is selected (white waveform over dark gray background), and displayed as a region marker in the region area below the waveforms. The region marker has the same color and name as the region in the Arrange area or the Audio Bin.

Let's save a copy of the selection, which corresponds to the region you double-clicked.

2   From the Sample Editor's local menu bar, choose Audio File > Save Selection As (or press Option-Command-S).

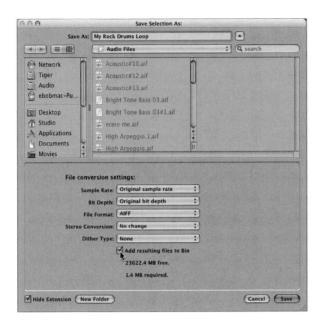

The Save Selection As dialog appears. The location is automatically set to the Audio Files folder inside the project folder.

3   Name the new audio file *My Rock Drums Loop*.

Leave the "File conversion settings" menu options unchanged, but make sure "Add resulting files to Bin" is selected.

4   Click Save (or press Enter).

A new audio file is created and added to the Audio Bin.

Since you are going to work in the Sample Editor, open the new audio file in a Sample Editor window.

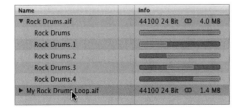

5   In the Audio Bin, select **My Rock Drums Loop.aif**.

6 From the main menu bar, choose Window > Sample Editor.

A Sample Editor window opens, displaying My Rock Drums Loop.

7 At the upper left of the Sample Editor, click the zoom button (the rightmost button of the three window controls).

The Sample Editor fills the screen, and the waveforms are displayed nice and big. You are ready to do some serious destructive audio editing!

Trimming an Audio File

First, you need to adjust the start and end points of the audio file to create a file that will loop perfectly in time later in the Arrange area. The file should start exactly on a downbeat and end exactly on a downbeat.

Use the Sample Editor to trim the drum loop.

1 Click the speaker button (or press the Spacebar).

The audio file plays once.

2 Drag over the waveform to select a portion of the audio file.

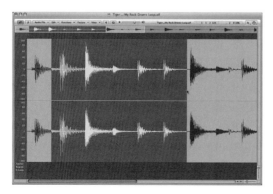

The selection is displayed as a white waveform over a dark gray background.

3   Press the Spacebar.

The selected portion plays.

4   Click the Cycle button, and press the Spacebar.

The selected portion plays and loops repeatedly. You can choose to keep the selection looping as you adjust it.

5   Choose Edit > Select All (or press Command-A).

Now the whole two-bar pattern is looping, and you can fine-tune the boundaries of the selection, listening to make sure the timing is good. You need to adjust the selection to start just before the first transient, and end just before the first transient of the first note in the next pattern, the crash cymbal.

6   Zoom in on the beginning of the waveform to see the attack of the first downbeat.

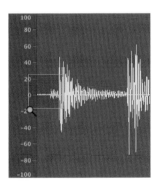

You can adjust the start of the selection by Shift-clicking (or Shift-dragging) on the waveform. There is a little bit of noise before the first hit, and you want to start the selection after the noise, just before the first transient (attack).

7   Shift-drag the selection start to the right, stopping just before the first transient.

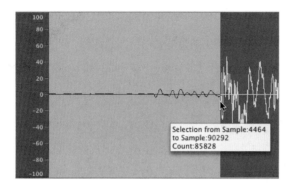

When you release the mouse button, the selection start automatically snaps to the nearest point where the waveform crosses the zero line. Since abrupt transitions in a waveform result in audible clicks, working with a selection that starts and ends on zero crossings avoids clicks.

However, in this case you want to trim the loop precisely on the attack of the first drum hit, so let's turn off this feature. In the next exercise, you will apply fades to the audio file's beginning and end borders to make sure the loop doesn't click.

8 Control-click (or right-click) the waveform.

A shortcut menu appears.

9 Choose Search Zero Crossings to deselect it.

Search Zero Crossings is turned off.

10 Shift-drag the selection start to the first transient.

This time the selection start does not snap to the nearest zero crossing, and you can adjust it precisely where you want it.

Now you need to adjust the end of the selection. You will use the waveform overview at the top of the Sample Editor to navigate your audio file.

11 At the top of the Sample Editor, click the end of the waveform overview.

The waveform overview shows the whole audio file, and the white frame represents the section visible in the main waveform display.

Waveform overview   White frame

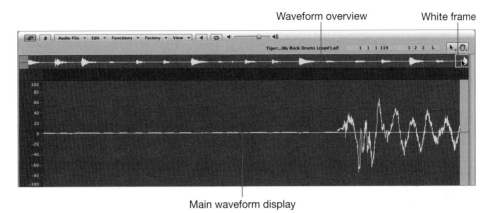

Main waveform display

The white frame moves where you clicked, and in the main waveform display, you can see the end of the audio file. At the very end, you can see the beginning of the crash cymbal.

12 Shift-click just before the transient of the crash cymbal.

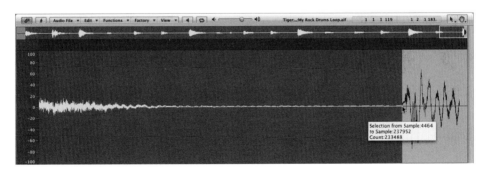

Look at the selection in the waveform overview. It starts on the transient of the first note, and ends on the transient of the attack of the cymbal.

13 Listen to your loop.

It now loops perfectly in time.

14 Choose Functions > Trim.

An alert message appears asking if you are sure that you want to trim the selection. When you are about to perform a destructive edit such as trimming, Logic requires a confirmation.

15 Click Process.

The audio file is trimmed so that only the selection remains.

Adding Destructive Fades

Now that the audio file is trimmed, you can apply destructive fades at its beginning and end. The waveform will then start and end on zero crossings, and you won't hear any clicks when looping the file.

1 At the end of the waveform, drag a small selection toward the right, dragging all the way to the end of the audio file.

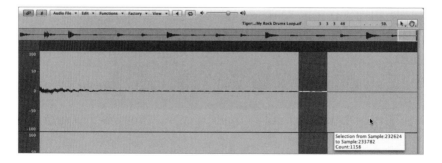

2 Choose Functions > Fade Out.

A confirmation dialog appears.

3 Click Process.

A destructive fade-out is applied to the selection. Since this selection is almost silence, you barely see any difference.

4   Click at the very beginning of the waveform overview.

The beginning of the audio file is displayed in the main waveform display.

5   Zoom in closely on the beginning of the waveform.

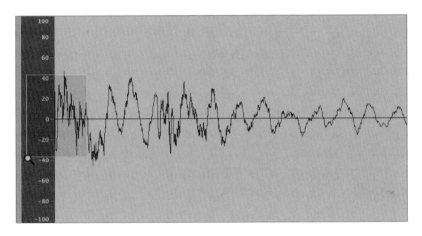

Don't hesitate to zoom in twice if you have to.

6   Drag a small selection around the beginning of the waveform.

This time, drag from right to left to make sure you select the beginning.

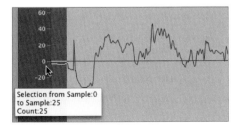

You don't want to fade the attack of the first drum hit, so make sure your selection is really short (the help tag counts only about 25 samples). You can clearly see the waveform does not start on a zero crossing.

7   Choose Functions > Fade In, and click Process.

8   A destructive fade-in is applied to the selection.

The waveform now starts on a zero crossing.

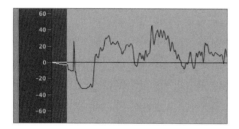

Reversing a Sample

The loop is trimmed, it starts and ends on a zero crossing, and it is ready to be used. But let's have a little fun with this drum loop. In this exercise, you will reverse one of the hi-hat hits.

1   At the top of the Sample Editor, press and hold down the mouse button in the middle of the waveform overview.

The mouse cursor turns into a speaker icon and you can preview the audio file from the point where you clicked the waveform.

2   Using the waveform display to navigate, along with your favorite zoom techniques (the Zoom tool, zoom control and sliders, or key commands) make sure you can see at least the last six drum notes in the main waveform display.

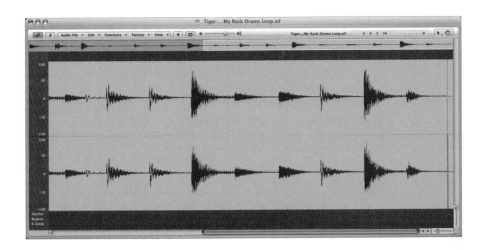

3   In the ruler, drag the mouse cursor left or right.

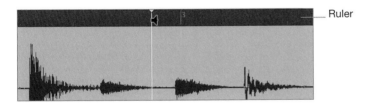

The mouse cursor turns into a speaker icon, and you can use it to drag the playhead left and right, scrubbing the audio file.

TIP ▶ Once you hold down the mouse button, drag the mouse down onto the waveform to scrub over the waveform rather than scrubbing in the ruler.

4   From the last six notes, select the first hi-hat after the first snare.

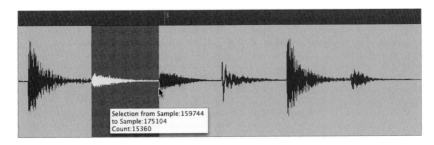

Start the selection just before the attack, and end the selection just before the attack of the next note.

5   Choose Functions > Reverse, and click Process.

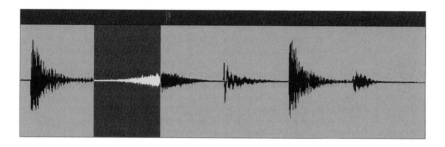

The selection is reversed.

6   Choose Edit > Select All (or press Command-A).

7   Press the Spacebar.

The whole loop plays and you can hear the reversed hi-hat.

The effect is interesting, but it would sound even better if you reversed the next hi-hat note instead of that one.

8   Choose Edit > Undo Change Selection (or press Command-Z).

The same hi-hat note is selected again.

9   Choose Edit > Undo Reverse (or press Command-Z).

The hi-hat is returned to normal.

Although editing in the Sample Editor is destructive, note that you can undo the five most recent destructive edits.

TIP▶ You can set the number of Sample Editor undo steps in the Sample Editor tab of the Audio Preferences.

10 Drag over the next hi-hat note to select it.

11 From the Sample Editor's local menu bar, choose Functions > Reverse, and click Process.

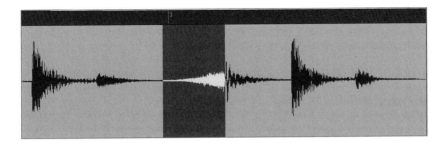

Save the reverse hi-hat so you can use it in the next exercise.

12 Choose Audio File > Save Selection As (or press Option-Command-S), name the file *Reversed Hi-hat*, and save it.

The file is saved in the default location—the Audio Files folder in your project folder—and it is added to the Audio Bin.

13 Press Command-A and listen to the whole loop.

Now the reverse hi-hat sounds great. It gives a little bounce to the groove.

14 Close the Sample Editor window.

Positioning an Audio Region in the Arrange Area

Audio regions have an anchor, which is used to position the region in the Arrange area. When you drag a region in the Arrange area, the anchor position is the position displayed in the help tag, and the anchor is used to snap the region to the grid.

By default, the anchor is located at the start point of an audio region. While this makes sense for most audio regions, sometimes the attack of a sound is not at the beginning of a region. If you want to line up the attack with the grid, you need to position the anchor right on the attack. That is the case with reversed sound, where the attack is near the end of the region.

In the following exercise, you will move the anchor to the amplitude peak of the reversed hi-hat that you saved in the previous exercise. Then, you will line up the amplitude peak of the reversed hi-hat with the first downbeat of the ending section of the song.

1 In the Arrange area, zoom out so you can see the whole song.

2 Zoom in on the beginning of the last section, at bar 15.

Make sure that you can see the bottom track, Audio 5.

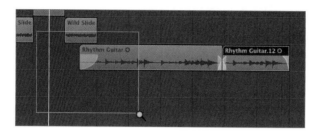

3 From the Audio Bin, drag **Reversed Hi-hat.aif** to bar 15 of the Audio 5 track.

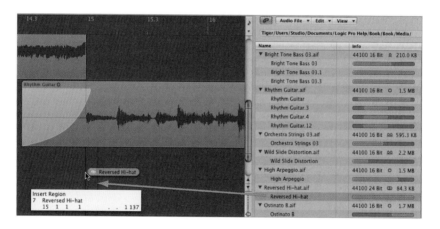

4 Position the playhead before the Reversed Hi-hat region and start playback.

By default, the audio region's anchor is at its start point, so the reversed hi-hat swell starts on bar 15. For the reversed effect to work, the region needs to start earlier and reach its maximum amplitude peak exactly on bar 15.

To do that, you will need to move the anchor in the Reversed Hi-hat region. At the lower left of the Sample Editor, you can see the anchor, represented by an orange indicator below the waveform.

5 Drag the anchor to the maximum amplitude on the waveform, almost at the end of the Reversed Hi-hat region.

Anchor

Notice that the Reversed Hi-hat region moves in the Arrange area and the anchor stays on bar 15.

6 In the Arrange area, zoom in on the Reversed Hi-hat region.

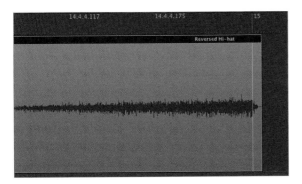

The position of the anchor is represented by a white vertical line, and you can see it lined up with bar 15. You can try adjusting the position of the anchor in the Sample Editor and see the region's position change in the Arrange area.

7 In the Audio 5 track header, click the Solo button to turn it off.

8 Zoom out and start playback around bar 14.

Listen to the effect of the reversed hi-hat: it sounds great! Now the reversed hi-hat really sucks you into that final section of the song.

You now know how to read a waveform, as well as identify notes and their attacks to perform precise and clean edits. You acquired skills with a number of editing tools—such as the Marquee tool, Crossfade tool, Junction pointer, and take folders—that you will continue using as you edit recordings and arrange projects. You can now increase your workflow by choosing the appropriate left-click and Command-click tools for the job. As you produce more music in Logic, you will continue sharpening those skills, making you a proficient audio engineer.

Lesson Review

1. How do you open a take folder?
2. How do you preview the takes?
3. How do you comp takes?
4. How can you see the result of your comp as regions?
5. How can you assign the left-click tool?
6. How can you assign the Command-click tool?
7. How do you add a fade-in or fade-out to a region?
8. How do you crossfade between two regions?
9. Identify three ways you can import an audio file into your project.
10. How can you select a portion of an audio region?
11. When you choose Edit > Select Unused in the Audio Bin, which files are selected?
12. What kind of audio editing can you do in the Sample Editor?
13. What is a zero crossing?
14. Why should regions start and end on zero crossings?
15. What is the anchor?

Answers

1. Double-click a take folder to open it.
2. Click the takes you want to preview. The blue-shaded take is the take playing; the others are muted.
3. Open the take folder, and drag over the desired sections of each take to highlight them. The take folder assembles a comp made of all the blue sections.
4. In the take folder menu, choose Flatten.

5. In the Left-click Tool menu, choose the desired tool, or press Esc and choose the desired tool.

6. In the Command-click Tool menu, choose the desired tool, or press Esc and Command-click the desired tool.

7. Drag the Crossfade tool over the boundaries of a region.

8. Drag the Crossfade tool over the junction of the regions.

9. You can drag the audio file from the Finder to the Arrange area, drag it from the Audio Bin file selector box, or double-click it in the Media area's Browser tab.

10. Use the Marquee tool to select a portion of an audio region.

11. Choosing Edit > Select Unused selects all the audio files and regions that are not currently used in the Arrange area.

12. Destructive audio editing.

13. A point where the waveform crosses the center line.

14. To avoid audible clicks.

15. The anchor is a point in an audio region used to position the region to the grid in the Arrange area.

4

Lesson Files   Logic 8_Files > Lessons > 04 Funky Groove_start

Time   This lesson takes approximately 60 minutes to complete.

Goals   Record MIDI performances

Quantize MIDI recordings

Merge a MIDI recording with an existing MIDI region

Record MIDI in take folders

Punch record a MIDI recording

Capture a performance as a recording

Record MIDI using Step Input mode

Filter incoming MIDI events

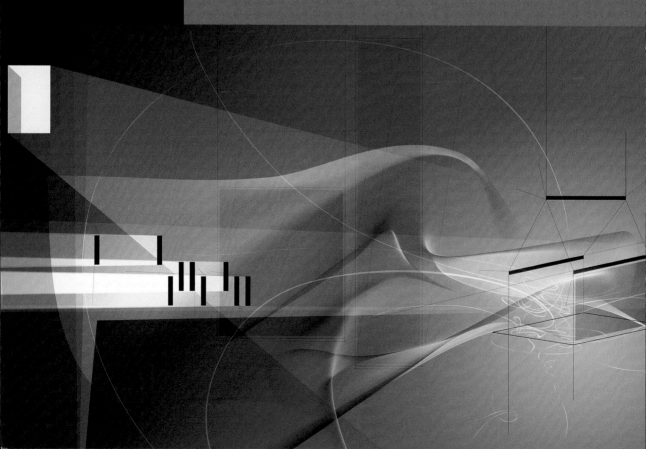

Recording MIDI

MIDI (the Musical Instrument Digital Interface) was created in 1981 to standardize the way electronic musical instruments communicate. Today, MIDI is extensively used in the music industry, from cell phone ringtones to major-label albums. Most TV and film orchestra composers use MIDI to sequence large software sound libraries, getting ever closer to productions that sound like a real orchestra.

MIDI sequences can be compared to piano rolls, the perforated paper rolls once used by mechanical player pianos. Like the punched holes in piano rolls, MIDI events do not contain audio. They contain note information such as pitch and velocity. To produce sound, MIDI events need to be routed to a software instrument or to an external MIDI instrument.

There are two basic types of MIDI events: MIDI note events that trigger musical notes, and MIDI continuous controller (MIDI CC) events that control parameters such as volume, pan, or pitch bend.

For example, when you hit C3 on a MIDI controller keyboard, the keyboard sends a Note On MIDI event. The Note On event contains the pitch of the note (C3) and the velocity of the note (which indicates how fast the key was struck, measuring how hard the musician played the note).

By connecting the MIDI controller keyboard to Logic, you can use Logic to route the MIDI events to a virtual software instrument or to an external MIDI instrument. The instrument reacts to the Note On event by producing a C3 note, and the velocity determines how loud the note sounds.

> **MORE INFO** ▶ To learn more about the MIDI standard specification, visit the MIDI Manufacturers Association website at http://www.midi.org/.

Recording MIDI

In Logic, the techniques used to record MIDI are very similar to the techniques you used to record audio in Lesson 2. When a MIDI controller keyboard is connected to your computer, and its driver is properly installed (some devices are class-compliant and don't require a driver installation), you can use that keyboard to record MIDI in Logic. Logic automatically routes all incoming MIDI events to the record-enabled software instrument or external MIDI track.

> **TIP** ▶ If you don't have a MIDI controller keyboard, press the Caps Lock key on your computer keyboard to turn your Mac keyboard into a polyphonic MIDI controller keyboard. A representation of your computer keyboard is displayed, showing the letter keys assigned to musical notes. The number keys allow you to choose the octave range, and the lower row of keys lets you choose the note velocities. Keep in mind that you may need to disable the Caps Lock keyboard to access some of Logic's key commands.

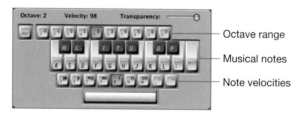

To record a MIDI performance triggering a software instrument, you need to create a software instrument track, insert an instrument plug-in or choose a channel strip setting from the Library, and click Record.

1 Go to Logic 8_Files > Lessons and open the **04 Funky Groove_start** project.

That project has a single audio track with a drum loop, which will provide a timing reference to record your new instrument.

2 At the top of the track list, click the New Tracks button (+) (or press Option-Command-N).

The New Tracks dialog appears.

3 In the Number field, enter *1*. Select Software Instrument as the Type. Select the Open Library checkbox, and click Create.

A software instrument track is created, and it is automatically record-enabled. The Library opens, displaying software instrument channel strip settings.

By default, audio tracks have a blue icon and audio regions are blue. Software instruments have a green icon and MIDI regions are green.

4 Choose a channel strip setting from the Library.

For this exercise, choose 04 Keyboards > 01 Electric Piano > Suitcase V2.

LOGIC EXPRESS ▶ For this exercise, choose 04 Keyboards > 01 Electric Pianos > Tines Electric Piano, and in the following exercises, substitute Tines Electric Piano when you see Suitcase V2.

In the Inspector, the software instrument channel strip loads the necessary plug-ins. In the Arrange area, the name Suitcase V2 is displayed on the Inst 1 track header.

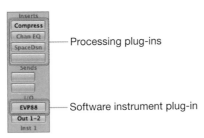

—— Processing plug-ins

—— Software instrument plug-in

While audio channel strip settings contain only processing plug-ins, software instrument channel strip settings also contain the software instrument plug-in. On the channel strip, the software instrument plug-in is loaded in the Instrument slot of the I/O section.

5   Play some notes on your MIDI controller keyboard.

You should hear the electric piano. In the Transport bar's MIDI In display, the incoming MIDI note events are displayed as notes are played. If you play a chord, the display shows the chord name.

You are now ready to record, but first open the Piano Roll Editor so that you can see the MIDI notes appear as you record them.

6   At the bottom of the Arrange area, click the Piano Roll button.

The Piano Roll Editor opens in the editing area.

7   Go to the beginning of the project.

8   In the Transport bar, click the Record button (or press * (asterisk) on the numeric keypad, or press R on a laptop).

The playhead jumps back one bar, giving you a four-beat count-in with an audible metronome click before recording starts. The Bar ruler turns red to indicate that Logic is recording.

9   When you can see the playhead, play some notes.

Play a simple bass line in an eight-note pattern (try a melody in the key of A minor). You will record more notes in that region later in this lesson.

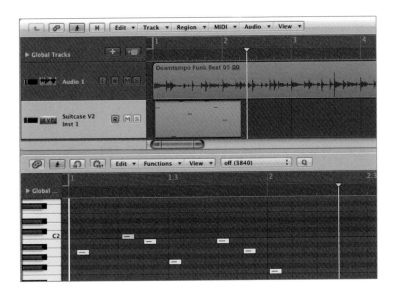

When you play the first MIDI note, a new MIDI region with a red halo is created on the record-enabled Suitcase V2 track. The region's length constantly updates to include the most recent MIDI event played.

The MIDI notes appear in the Piano Roll Editor as you record them.

10 Stop recording.

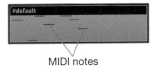

MIDI notes

In the MIDI region, the notes are displayed as small beams. As in the Piano Roll Editor, the vertical positions of the notes indicate their pitches (with the high pitches at the top).

11 Go back to the beginning and listen to your MIDI recording.

If you are not happy with your performance, you can undo it (Command-Z) and try again.

TIP▶ If you record-enable several software instrument tracks, incoming MIDI events will be routed to all record-enabled tracks, allowing you to layer the sounds of several instruments.

Quantizing MIDI Recordings

If you are not happy with the timing of your MIDI performance, you can correct the timing of the notes. The time-correction process is called *quantization*. To quantize a MIDI region, you choose a grid resolution from the Quantize menu in the Region Parameter box. Each note inside the region will snap to the nearest position on the chosen grid.

Quantizing MIDI Regions

In the following exercise, you will quantize the recording you made in the previous exercise to correct its timing, so that the piano notes are in sync with the drums.

1 Select the new #default MIDI region.

First, rename the region so you can easily identify it later.

2 In the Inspector's Region Parameter box, click the name of the region and enter *Piano*.

The region is renamed Piano.

Now choose the Quantize value, which determines the resolution of the grid used to quantize the notes.

3 Set the Quantize parameter to 1/8-Note while looking at the notes in the Piano Roll Editor.

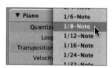

All the MIDI notes snap to the nearest eighth note.

4 Go to the beginning and start playback.

You can hear your performance, perfectly in time with the drums. Unless of course the performance timing was really poor, in which case some of the notes may not snap to the desired 1/8 note.

In Logic, quantizing is a nondestructive operation. You can always go back to the way the performance was originally recorded.

5   With the Piano region selected, open the Quantize parameter menu and choose "off (3840). "

The MIDI notes return to their original recording positions.

MORE INFO ▶ The (3840) indicator identifies the shortest resolution of Logic's MIDI sequencer, the tick. When the time signature is 4/4, there are 3840 ticks in a bar (or 240 ticks in a sixteenth note). When Quantize is set to "off (3840)," the notes snap to the closest tick.

6   Choose Edit > Undo Parameter Change (or press Command-Z).

The region's Quantize parameter is reset to 1/8-Note, and the notes snap to the grid.

MORE INFO ▶ The Quantize menu also offers Swing settings. The Swing settings delay the position of every other note in the grid to obtain a swing, or shuffle groove, common in many music genres such as blues, jazz, hip hop, or house music. The amount of delay goes from no delay (A = no swing) to a lot of delay (F = hard swing). For example, 8B Swing will subtly delay the second eighth note of each beat.

Setting a Default Quantization Grid

You can set a default quantization value so that any new recording will automatically be quantized to that grid resolution. This is very useful if you are not confident of your timing chops. Since the Quantize setting is nondestructive, you can always adjust it or turn it off for that region after the recording is done.

1   Click in the background of the Arrange area.

All regions are deselected, and the Region Parameter Box now displays the MIDI Thru settings. The MIDI Thru parameter settings are automatically applied to any new MIDI region that you record.

2   Set the Quantize parameter to 1/16-Note.

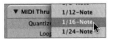

3   Select the Piano region.

The Region Parameter Box displays the region's name and settings. You can see the Quantize setting you applied to that region in the previous exercise: 1/8-Note.

4   Press Delete.

The region is deleted.

5   Go to the beginning of the track and click the Record button (or press * (asterisk) on the numeric keypad, or press R on a laptop).

Record a new simple bass line as you did previously.

6   Stop recording.

In the Piano Roll Editor, the notes immediately snap to the nearest sixteenth note. The new MIDI region is selected, and the Region Parameter box now displays its parameters: Quantize is automatically set to 1/16-Note, the MIDI Thru Quantize setting you set in step 2.

7   Set the Quantize parameter to "off (3840)."

The notes return to their original recorded positions.

8   Set the Quantize parameter back to 1/16-Note.

Merging Recordings into a MIDI Region

Sometimes you may want to record a MIDI performance in several passes. For example, when recording piano, you can record only the left hand and then record the right hand in a second pass. Or, when recording drums, you can record the kick drum in the first pass, the snare in a second pass, and the hi-hat in a third pass.

In Logic, when recording MIDI events on top of an existing MIDI region, you can merge the new events with the existing ones. You only have to select the existing MIDI region before recording, and the new notes will be recorded inside the selected region.

Recording into a Selected MIDI Region

In the previous exercise, you recorded a simple bass line onto a piano track. Now you will play chords as you listen to the bass line and record the new chords inside the same MIDI region.

1   Select the Piano region.

2   Go to the beginning and start recording.

Try to play some chords that complement the bass line you recorded previously.

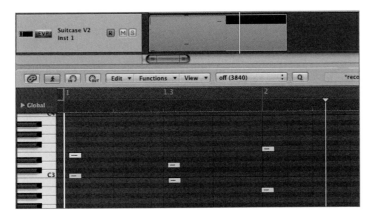

NOTE ▶ While you are recording, you are temporarily recording a new region on top of the existing one. The new region will be merged with the existing one as soon as you stop recording. The Piano Roll Editor displays the contents of the new region you are recording, and although the contents of the existing region are not displayed while you are recording, you can still hear the existing notes played back.

3   Stop recording.

The new recording is merged with the existing region and you can see all the notes in the Piano Roll Editor. (You might have to scroll or resize the Piano Roll Editor window to see all the notes.)

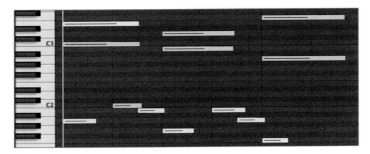

TIP ▶ You can also use this technique to add MIDI Controller events such as pitch bend or modulation to a region after you have recorded the MIDI notes.

Merging Recordings in Cycle Mode

Recording in Cycle mode allows you to continuously repeat the same section and only record new events when you are ready. This can be very useful to record a drum pattern, for example. While repeating a one-bar or two-bar section, you can add new elements to the pattern during each pass of the cycle, while listening to everything that you have recorded.

When you are recording in Cycle mode, notes recorded in all consecutive passes of the cycle are merged into a single MIDI region. In this exercise, you will use Cycle mode to record drums—first recording the kick, then the snare, then the hi-hat—switching in and out of record mode as the cycle repeats so you can practice each drum instrument before you record it.

1   In the Arrange area, mute both existing tracks.

Remember that you can click the Mute button on the first track header and drag down the mouse to mute both tracks.

2   At the top of the track list, click the New Tracks button (+) (or press Option-Command-N).

The New Tracks dialog appears.

3   In the Number field, enter *1*. Make sure that Type is set to Software Instrument and Open Library is selected, and click OK.

This time you will insert the software instrument in the Inspector, on the Arrange channel strip.

4   In the I/O section of the channel strip, click the Instrument slot.

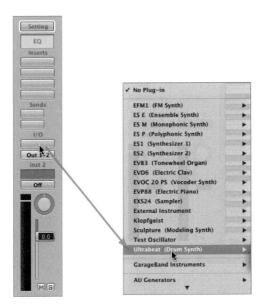

A menu appears, allowing you to choose one of Logic's software instruments.

5   Choose Ultrabeat (Drum Synth).

NOTE ▶ When you place your mouse cursor over Ultrabeat (Drum Synth), a menu opens on the right that allows you to choose between Stereo and Multi-Outputs. For now, do not use the lower-level menu, and simply choose Ultrabeat (Drum Synth). By default, a stereo Ultrabeat will be inserted.

The Ultrabeat plug-in is inserted in the Instrument slot of the channel strip, and the Ultrabeat plug-in window opens.

6   Close the Ultrabeat window.

MORE INFO ▶ For now you will use Ultrabeat to produce drum sounds as you record MIDI in Cycle mode. In Lesson 6, "Programming Drums." you will to use the Ultrabeat interface to program a drum pattern.

Notice the white frame around the Ultrabeat plug-in on the channel strip. A white frame indicates the selected section of the channel strip, whose settings are automatically displayed in the Library. The Library now displays Ultrabeat settings.

7   In the Library, choose 01 Drum Kits > Funk Boogie Kit.

Wait a few seconds while Ultrabeat loads the kit. When the kit is fully loaded, the drum kit name is displayed on the Inst 2 track header in the Arrange area.

Selecting a software instrument track automatically record-enables it, but the instrument is not always in live mode. When an instrument is not in live mode, the first note you play will take about 100 ms (milliseconds) to trigger the instrument, which is then placed in live mode.

You can put an instrument in live mode by sending any MIDI event to it (playing a dummy note, moving the modulation wheel, and so on), or by clicking the Record Enable button in its track header.

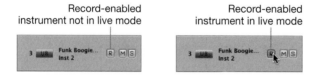

First, locate the notes on your controller keyboard that trigger the kick, the snare, and the hi-hat. In Ultrabeat, you will use:

▶   C1: kick

▶   E1: snare

▶   F♯1: hi-hat

8   Play the lowest C note on your MIDI controller, while watching the MIDI Activity display in the Transport bar.

If the MIDI In display doesn't show a C1, press your MIDI controller keyboard Octave Up and Down buttons until the lowest C plays a C1.

NOTE ▶ If your MIDI keyboard has a C lower than C1, locate the C1 on a higher octave.

MORE INFO ▶ If you are using the Caps Lock keyboard, press 4 to set the right octave, and press A to trigger a C1 MIDI note.

When you can trigger a kick with C1, locate E1 (two white notes to the right) to play the snare, and F♯1 (the next black note to the right) to play the hi-hat.

9   In the Bar ruler, click the cycle area.

Cycle mode turns on, and the cycle area is shown as green.

10   Resize the cycle area so that it spans one bar starting at the beginning of the song.

You will now record the drums, one at a time.

11   Click in the background of the Arrange area.

The Region Parameter box displays the MIDI Thru parameters.

12   Set the Quantize parameter to 1/8-Note.

13   Start recording.

You hear a four-beat count-in before the playhead reaches the beginning of the cycle area. Play two C1 notes: one on the first beat, one on the third beat. In the Piano Roll Editor's Bar ruler, the first beat is on 1, the third beat on 1.3 (bar 1, beat 3).

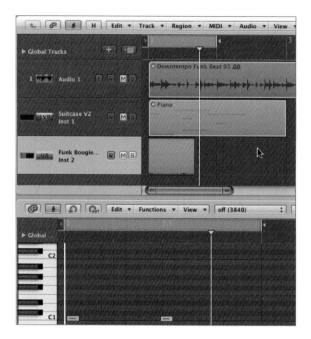

When a new cycle begins, you can hear the kick drum notes you just recorded. Notice that the notes snap to the nearest 1/8 note since you chose that grid resolution for your default MIDI Thru parameters.

You have all the time in the world before you continue to record. As long as you don't play anything, there are no MIDI events, and Logic keeps cycling over the existing region, playing back your kick drums. If you feel the need to practice the snare before recording, you can return to play mode while cycling continues.

14 Click the Play button (or press Enter).

Logic is no longer in record mode (and the metronome stops clicking), but playback continues as Logic repeats the cycle area without interruption. Notice that the two C1 notes are now quantized to the grid.

On your MIDI keyboard, locate the snare (E1) and practice a snare pattern. Try to hit the snare on beats 2 and 4.

15 Click the Record button.

Playback continues without interruption, but Logic reenters record mode. When you feel ready, record the snare.

When the playhead jumps to the beginning of the cycle, you can see the two kick notes and the two snare notes in the Piano Roll Editor.

TIP ▶ If you switched to play mode before recording the snare, the snare recording is considered a new operation. Staying in record mode, you can press Command-Z to undo the snare recording, keeping only the kick notes, and record the snare again.

Use the same techniques to record your hi-hat (F♯1) on every eighth note in the same MIDI region.

16 Stop recording.

The merge MIDI-recording techniques you used in the two previous exercises provide a lot of flexibility, and allow you to take your time, recording a single part of a performance. These techniques will work in many situations. For example, consider recording a violin or cello on a software instrument track; then, on a second pass, record the movements of the pitch bend wheel to add vibrato to some of the notes.

Recording MIDI Takes

When you want to nail a performance, or experiment with various musical ideas, you can record different takes and later choose the best one. The techniques to record MIDI takes are similar to the techniques you used to record audio takes in Lesson 2. You can record over an existing MIDI region, or you can use cycle recording to record one take for each pass of the cycle.

Cycle mode should still be turned on from the previous exercise. Let's record takes in Cycle mode and experiment using different melodies for a bass line.

1   In the Transport bar, hold down the Record button and choose Recording Settings from the pop-up menu (or press Option-* (the asterisk on the numeric keypad), or press Option-R on a laptop).

The Recording Project Settings dialog opens.

2   In the MIDI area, from the "Overlapping recordings" pop-up menu, choose "Create take folders."

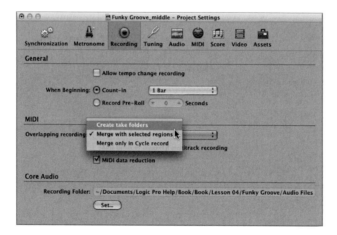

3   Close the Project Settings window.

4   In the Arrange area, unmute track 1 (Drums/Audio 1) and mute track 3 (Funk Boogie Kit/Inst 2).

5   Create a new software instrument track and open the Library.

6   In the Library, choose 02 Bass > 02 Electric Bass > Attitude Bass.

LOGIC EXPRESS ▶ Choose 02 Bass > 02 Electric Bass > Rock Fretless, and in the following steps substitute Rock Fretless when you see Attitude Bass.

7   Start recording and play a different melody for each pass of the cycle until you have 4 takes.

A MIDI take is recorded for each pass of the cycle where you play MIDI notes. If you don't play anything for a whole cycle, no take is recorded. The takes are packed into a take folder.

When a new cycle begins, the take you just recorded is automatically muted. You can listen to it by switching to play mode.

8   Click the Play button (or press Enter).

You are now in play mode, and you can hear the last take you recorded.

9   Open the take folder menu and choose the take you want to hear.

You can also double-click the take folder to open it, and click the take you want to hear. Double-click the take folder to close it.

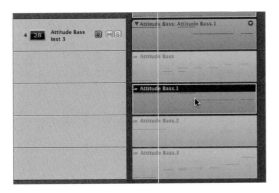

MORE INFO ▶ Unlike audio take folders, you cannot comp the takes in a MIDI take folder.

10 Stop playback and turn off Cycle mode.

Recording a Performance in Play Mode

When looking for musical ideas, you often simply play back the project and experiment on your MIDI keyboard. But how many times have you jammed along in play mode, only to later wish that you had recorded your performance?

In Logic, the good news is that every MIDI performance is recorded in memory, even in play mode. However, only the most recent performance is kept in memory. If you are happy with your previous performance, you can capture it as a recording right after you stop playback.

1   Mute the Attitude Bass track.

2   Select the Suitcase V2 track.

The MIDI region on the track is selected. If you have several MIDI regions on that track, all the regions are selected.

NOTE ▸ Make sure that Cycle mode is turned off. If Cycle mode is turned on, selecting a track selects only those regions within the cycle area (and the regions that overlap the cycle area).

3   Press Delete.

All the selected MIDI regions are deleted.

4   Start playback.

5   Play your MIDI controller keyboard for four or five bars.

6   Stop playback.

7 Press Control-* (the asterisk on the numeric keypad) (or press Control-Option-Command-R on a laptop), the Capture as Recording command.

The performance you just played is captured as a recording. The MIDI region is created on the track, and the notes are displayed in the Piano Roll Editor.

Capture as Recording only works immediately after you stop playback. If you press 0 to go back to the beginning of the project, or start playback again, the performance is lost.

This technique can also be useful to fool a musician into thinking you are not recording. Some musicians perform better without the pressure of the red light!

Using Punch Recording

You can use the punch-on-the-fly and autopunch techniques you learned for audio recording to punch on MIDI recordings. However, the default behavior when recording MIDI is to merge the punched-in MIDI recording with the existing region on the track. If you want to use punching techniques to correct a portion of a performance, you'll have to turn on the Replace mode.

Let's customize the Transport bar to display the Replace Mode button, and use the Autopunch function to punch in on the piano recording you captured in the previous exercise.

1 Control-click the Transport bar and choose Customize Transport bar from the shortcut menu.

The Customize dialog opens.

2 In the Modes and Functions column, select Replace and click OK.

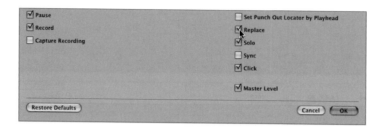

The Replace button is displayed in the Transport bar.

3   Click both the Autopunch and Replace buttons.

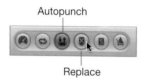

In order to merge the new events you are going to record over the Autopunch area with the existing region on the track, you need to change your recording settings back to the default settings.

4   In the Transport bar, hold down the mouse button on the Record button and choose Recording Settings from the pop-up menu.

The Recording Project Settings dialog opens.

5   In the MIDI area, from the "Overlapping recordings" pop-up menu, choose "Merge with selected regions."

6   In the Bar ruler, adjust the Autopunch area around a section of the Piano you want to record over.

Make sure the Autopunch area is placed over a section of the piano performance you captured in the previous exercise.

7   Go to the beginning of the project and make sure the Suitcase V2 track is still record enabled.

8   Click the Record button and start playing right away.

In the MIDI Piano region, the notes below the Autopunch area are deleted.

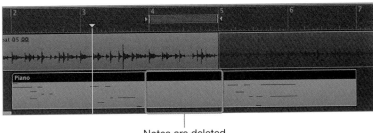

Notes are deleted

You can hear the notes you are playing, but only the notes played within the Autopunch area are recorded inside the MIDI region.

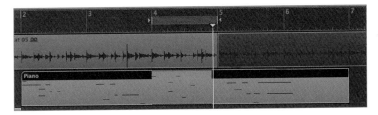

9   Turn off the Autopunch and Replace modes.

Using Step Input Recording

Instead of recording a real-time performance, you can record notes one at a time. In Step Input mode, you position the playhead and play a note or chord on your MIDI keyboard. The note(s) are recorded, and the playhead moves one step ahead, waiting for the next note(s).

This mode is very useful for recording complex musical phrases that you can't perform in real time, such as complicated chord patterns or really fast arpeggios (a great technique for dance music).

1   Select the Suitcase V2 track and press Delete.

All the regions on the track are deleted.

TIP ▶ If you don't want to select the regions on a track when selecting the track, open Global Preferences, click the Editing tab, and deselect "Select Regions on Track selection."

You start by creating an empty MIDI region using the Pencil tool (as the Command-click tool). You will step-record notes inside that new region.

2   Press Esc and Command-click the Pencil tool.

3   Command-click the Suitcase V2 track between bars 1 and 2.

The Pencil tool creates an empty one-bar MIDI region.

4   Resize the region so it is four bars long.

5   At the upper left of the Piano Roll Editor, click the In button.

The button turns red and MIDI Step Input Recording is turned on.

MORE INFO ▶ You can also enable Step Input Recording in the Score Editor or the Event List.

6 Go to the beginning of the project.

7 Play a single note on your MIDI keyboard.

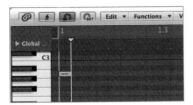

A sixteenth note is recorded at the playhead position, and the playhead moves forward one sixteenth note. The recorded note has the pitch and velocity of the note you played.

The length of a step is identified by the division setting in the Transport bar, below the time signature.

8 In the Transport bar, click the division setting and drag down until it reads /8.

In the Piano Roll Editor, the grid resolution is the same as the division setting. The vertical grid lines are now placed at eighth-note intervals.

9 Play a chord.

An eighth-note chord is recorded at the playhead position, and the playhead moves forward one eighth note.

You can also use the Step Input Keyboard to exercise more control over your step input recordings.

10 From the main menu bar, choose Options > Step Input Keyboard.

Note-length buttons

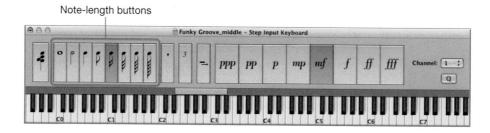

The floating Step Input Keyboard appears. The selected note-length button overrides the division setting in the Transport bar.

11 On the Step Input Keyboard, click the quarter-note button.

12 Play a note.

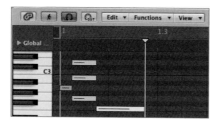

A quarter note is recorded at the playhead position, and the playhead moves forward one quarter note.

If you were recording a quarter-note pattern and wanted to record a single half note, you could click the half-note button, record your half note, and click the quarter-note button again to record the next quarter note.

An easier way is to use the Sustain Insert Note button.

13 Play a note and hold down the key on your MIDI keyboard.

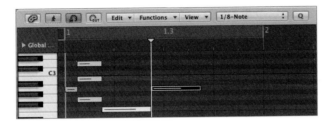

A quarter note is recorded. You need to hold down the MIDI key for the next step, so that the note you are recording remains selected in the Piano Roll Editor.

TIP ▶ You can also release the key on your MIDI keyboard and click the inserted note to select it.

14   On the Step Input Keyboard, click the Sustain Inserted Notes button.

The selected note is lengthened by a quarter note, so it is now a half note. You can click the Sustain Inserted Notes button several times to lengthen the selected notes by the current step length.

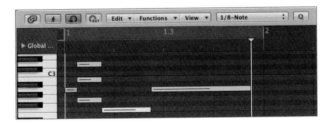

You can now release the key on your MIDI keyboard.

Now let's record quarter notes starting on bar 2.

15   With the pointer positioned over the lower half of the Bar ruler on bar 2, hold down the mouse button.

The playhead snaps to bar 2.

16 Play three notes, one at a time.

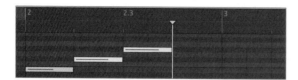

Now you want to insert a quarter-note rest.

17 On the Step Input Keyboard, click the Sustain Inserted Notes button.

The playhead jumps forward one quarter note. When no notes are selected, the Sustain Inserted Notes button makes the playhead move one step ahead, and you can resume step input recording.

Try using step input recording techniques to record fast sixteenth-note arpeggios or even crazy chord patterns. With a little experimentation, you will quickly end up with cool musical phrases that couldn't possibly be performed live.

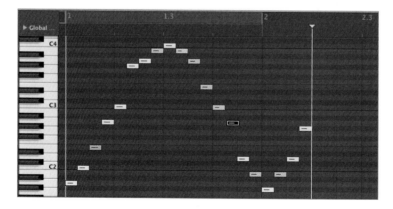

18 Click the In button to turn off Step Input recording.

Filtering Incoming MIDI Events

Sometimes your MIDI controller keyboard sends MIDI events that you may not want to record in Logic. Maybe you are using an older MIDI keyboard that generates random pitch bend events, or your keyboard is sending aftertouch MIDI events when you apply pressure to the keys, but the instrument you are recording does not react to aftertouch.

Logic allows you to filter out undesired incoming MIDI events so they are not recorded. Since input filter settings are project settings, you can adjust them to filter various types of events in different projects.

1   In the Toolbar, click the Settings button and choose MIDI from the pop-up menu.

2   Click the Input Filter tab.

In this tab, you can select the MIDI events you want to filter.

3   In the Arrange area, click the Suitcase V2 track header.

The track is selected and record-enabled.

4   Play some notes on your MIDI controller keyboard and move the pitch bend wheel.

You can hear the note pitches change as you move the pitch bend wheel.

5   In the MIDI Project Settings window's Input Filter tab, select Pitch Bend.

6   Play some notes on your MIDI controller keyboard and move the pitch bend wheel.

This time the pitch bend MIDI events are filtered at their input into Logic, and your pitch bend wheel movements have no effect on the pitch of the notes you play.

Separating the MIDI data from the audio signal produced by the instrument allows for very flexible recording. Throughout this lesson you quantized your notes to a grid and chose to merge new recordings into an existing MIDI region or to record separate takes in a MIDI take folder. You also used step input recording to enter notes one step at a time, without the pressure of recording a real-time performance.

After a MIDI performance is recorded, you can still change the sound of the instrument independently of the MIDI events, or edit the MIDI events independently of the instrument's sound. Those vast sound- and performance-editing possibilities take you to a new realm of experimentation. Enjoy it!

> **MORE INFO** ▸ To learn how to use external MIDI instruments with Logic, read the Appendix, "Using External MIDI Devices."

Lesson Review

1. How does Logic route incoming MIDI events?
2. How can you time-correct a MIDI region?
3. How do you choose the default quantize settings for new MIDI recordings?
4. How do you record notes into an existing MIDI region?
5. How do you record MIDI takes?
6. What do you need to do before you can punch in on a MIDI track to replace a portion of a MIDI region?
7. How do you turn on Step Input mode?
8. When recording in Step Input mode, identify two ways you can adjust the step length.

Answers

1. All incoming MIDI events are routed to the record-enabled track(s).
2. In the Inspector's Region Parameter box, choose a grid resolution value from the Quantize menu. The MIDI notes in the region will snap to the nearest position on the chosen grid.
3. Deselect all regions to choose the MIDI Thru parameters in the Region Parameter box.
4. Make sure the region is selected and record on the same track, on top of the selected region.

5. Open the Recording project settings and choose Overlapping recordings > Create take folders, then record on top of an existing record, or record in Cycle mode.

6. You need to turn on the Replace mode.

7. Click the In button in the Piano Roll Editor, Score Editor, or Event List.

8. In the Transport bar, adjust the division setting; or open the Step Input Keyboard and use the note-length buttons.

5

Lesson Files	Logic 8_Files > Lessons > 05 Funky Groove_start
Media	Logic 8_Files > Media > Additional Media
Time	This lesson takes approximately 60 minutes to complete.
Goals	Import MIDI files into a project
	Insert and edit MIDI notes in the Piano Roll and Score editors
	Quantize and mute individual notes
	Edit note velocity and pitch using a MIDI keyboard
	Draw and edit MIDI continuous controller automation using Hyper Draw and the Hyper Editor
	Clean up MIDI regions in the Event List

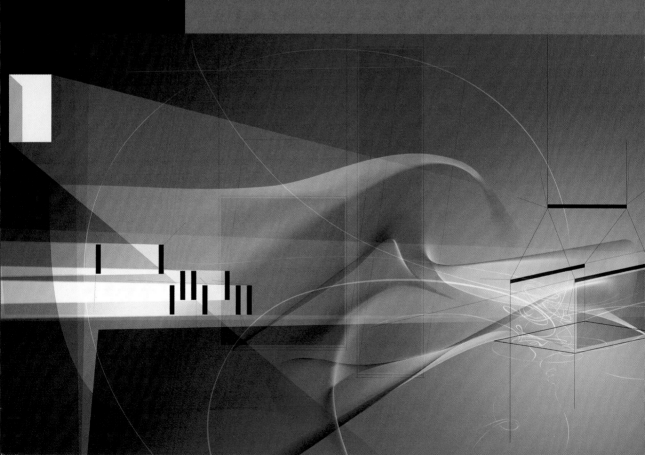

Programming and Editing MIDI

When you work with MIDI sequences, the flexibility of separating the performance data from the instrument playing it gives you total control over the performance data, even after it is recorded. You can open the MIDI region in a MIDI editor to precisely fine-tune each note's position, pitch, velocity, and length. You can edit or add MIDI controller events to automate the instrument's volume, panning, pitch, and many other parameters. You can also write music from scratch, creating notes in MIDI editors using only your mouse, similar to the way a composer writes music on staff paper.

Writing music in MIDI editors is also called *programming MIDI sequences*. Logic includes several MIDI editors for this purpose, and while they all display the same MIDI events, each does it in its own way. For example, the Score Editor shows you musical notes on a staff, while the Piano Roll Editor shows you notes as beams on a grid.

In this lesson, you will use Logic's MIDI editors to program and edit MIDI events. You will write a bass line and a simple horn riff, edit a real-time recording of a MIDI performance, and program MIDI control automation to breathe life into your MIDI sequences.

Programming in the Piano Roll Editor

The Piano Roll Editor is the most straightforward MIDI editor. It borrows its name from the perforated paper roll used by mechanical player pianos, in which the position and length of a punched hole determined the pitch and length of the note it triggered. In Logic, the Piano Roll Editor represents MIDI notes as beams on a grid, positioned below a Bar ruler, much as the Arrange area displays regions on a grid below a Bar ruler. In fact, most of the techniques for editing regions in the Arrange area also apply to notes in the Piano Roll Editor.

Creating Notes with the Pencil Tool

In the Piano Roll Editor, you create notes by clicking in the grid with the Pencil tool. As you write your musical part using the Pencil tool, you can also use it to resize, move, copy or delete notes.

You will use the Pencil tool to program a simple bass line in the key of A minor (using only the white keys on the musical keyboard).

1   Go to Logic 8_Files > Lessons > and open **05 Funky Groove_start.**

    Cycle mode is turned on, and the cycle area spans the first two bars. You are going to write a two-bar bass line, so leave Cycle mode on and listen to the drums.

2   In the Arrange area, select the Attitude Bass track.

    You will use the Pencil tool (currently the Command-click tool) to create an empty MIDI region on that track.

3   Command-click the Attitude Bass track in bar 1.

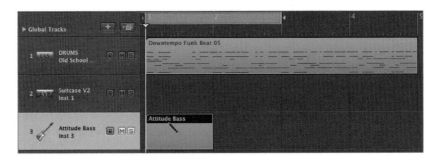

An empty one-bar MIDI region is created.

4 Resize the region so that it is two bars long.

In the editing area, the Piano Roll Editor displays the contents of the selected Attitude Bass region, which is currently empty. You can use the piano keyboard on the left to audibly preview the notes before you create them.

5 In the Piano Roll Editor, click the keys on the piano keyboard.

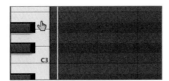

The keys trigger the bass software instrument and you can hear the bass notes. Scroll down to find A1, two white keys below C2.

6 In the Piano Roll editor, make the Pencil tool the left-click tool, and the Velocity tool the Command-click tool.

The Pencil tool and the Velocity tool are the two most important tools when you're creating notes in the Piano Roll Editor, and this tool combination will make you proficient at programming MIDI.

As you position the mouse pointer over the grid, look at the info display at the top of the Piano Roll Editor. It displays the pitch and position of the note you are about to create.

Info display

In the Piano Roll Editor's grid, light gray lanes correspond to the white keys on the piano keyboard, and dark gray lanes correspond to the black keys. This song is in the key of A minor, and you will use the natural A minor scale, which contains only white keys. Therefore you will insert notes only on the light gray lanes.

7 Using the Pencil tool, hold down the light gray lane at 1 1 1 1 in front of the A1 key.

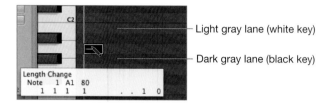

Light gray lane (white key)

Dark gray lane (black key)

TIP ▶ You can customize the colors of the Piano Roll Editor lanes in View > Piano Roll Colors.

A note is created, and since you are holding down the mouse button, a help tag appears that verifies the note is an A1.

MORE INFO ▶ The help tag reads *Length Change*. Later in this lesson, you will use the Pencil tool to change the length of a note as you insert it.

8 Position the Pencil tool over the lower-right corner of the A1 note.

The mouse pointer changes to a Resize pointer.

9 Drag the corner of the note toward the right to lengthen the note to make it a quarter note.

Note length

The help tag will show the note length as . 1 0 0 (period one zero zero), which indicates the length as 0 bars, 1 beat, 0 divisions, and 0 ticks. In other words, a single quarter note.

10 Insert a C2 on 1 2 1 1 (the second beat).

Remember to watch the info display as you position the Pencil tool. When the info display shows the desired note pitch and position, you can click to insert the note.

A quarter note C2 is inserted. The Pencil tool inserts notes of the same length and velocity as the last selected note.

11 Shorten the C2 so it is an eighth note.

While you resize to an eighth note, you may need to hold down Control-Shift to disable snapping. The help tag shows the note length as . . 2 0 (two divisions, or two sixteenth notes, make an eighth note).

Instead of creating the note and then resizing it, you can hold down the Pencil tool to insert the note, then drag the tool left or right to resize the note. This allows you to insert and resize a note in one action.

12 Hold down the Pencil tool to create an A1 on 1 2 3 1 (right after the last note), and drag the Pencil tool toward the left to shorten the note to a sixteenth note.

To make the note a sixteenth note, drag until the help tag displays the note length as . . 1 0. Depending on your zoom level, you may have to hold down Control-Shift as you drag the Pencil tool to disable snapping.

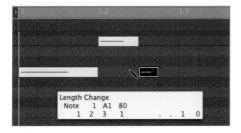

13 Hold down the Pencil tool to insert an E1 note right on 1 2 4 1 (right after the last note) and drag to lengthen it to a quarter note.

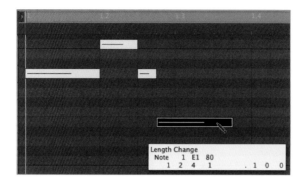

You just wrote a one-bar bass riff.

14 Press the Spacebar.

Listen to your bass riff. It works well with the drums. You will fill in the second bar in the next exercise.

Copying and Deleting Notes Using the Pencil Tool

Writing music is often about repeating musical phrases while introducing subtle differences. When programming MIDI, it is easy to select all the notes that form a musical phrase, copy them, and edit the copy to slightly change the repeated phrase.

In the following exercise you will use the Pencil tool to copy the one-bar bass riff to bar 2, and delete a note to change the second riff.

1 Make sure that the Piano Roll Editor has key focus, then choose Edit > Select All (or press Command-A).

All the notes are selected in the Piano Roll Editor.

Now you will copy the whole bass riff to bar 2. When you position the Pencil tool over the middle of a note, it turns into a Pointer tool. You can then use the Pointer tool to move the notes or Option-drag to copy the notes.

2 Position the mouse pointer over the middle of the first note.

The Pencil tool becomes a Pointer tool.

After you start dragging notes in the Piano Roll Editor, you can hold down Shift to limit the dragging to a single direction, either horizontal or vertical. Holding down

Shift while you Option-drag the selection will ensure that you don't accidentally copy the notes to another pitch.

TIP Limiting dragging to a single direction is a very useful feature. If you prefer it, you can make it the default behavior. Choose Logic Pro > Preferences > Global, click the Edit tab and select Limit Dragging to One Direction In (Piano Roll and Score) and (Arrange). When those options are selected, you can hold down Shift when you do *not* want to limit the dragging to one direction.

3   Option-drag the whole selection to 2 1 1 1, but press Shift immediately after you start dragging to limit dragging to horizontal.

To align the copy of the riff on 2 1 1 1, watch the help tag and also the vertical and horizontal white dashed guidelines that appear when you drag a note.

The riff now plays twice. To make the second riff slightly different, you can delete its first A1 note by double-clicking the note with the Pencil tool. But first you need to deselect all the notes.

4   Choose Edit > Deselect All (or press Shift-Command-A).

TIP Holding down Shift with a key command often gives you the result opposite to the command. In this case, Command-A selects all, Shift-Command-A deselects all.

5   Double-click the first A1 note of the second bass riff.

The note is deleted.

6   Start playback and listen to your bass line.

Editing Note Velocity

When you play a MIDI keyboard, you need to control how loud each note is played. To judge how hard you press the keys, MIDI keyboards measure the speed at which each key is depressed. That speed is called *velocity*. When you press a key, the MIDI keyboard sends a *note-on* MIDI event that contains the pitch and velocity values of the note.

Higher velocities usually result in louder notes. Depending on the patch or program you're using, higher velocities can also trigger different sounds or different samples, as they do in the sampler instrument you're using on the Attitude Bass track. The result will sound more real, as the higher-velocity notes trigger samples of a bass string that was actually plucked harder.

You assigned the Velocity tool to the Command-click tool in the first exercise. You will now use the Velocity tool to edit the velocities of the bass notes to extend the dynamic range of your bass line and make it sound more natural. Using the Velocity tool, you can drag a note up to increase its velocity or drag down to decrease it.

1 Command-drag the first bass note up and down.

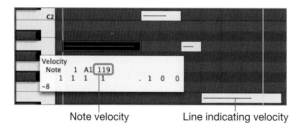

Note velocity   Line indicating velocity

In the help tag, you can see the value of the note velocity (to the right of the note pitch), ranging from 1 to 127.

The velocity value is indicated by the color of the note, ranging from violet (the lowest velocity) through blue, turquoise, green, yellow, orange and red (the highest velocity). It is also represented by the length of the line in the middle of the note beam.

While you drag the Velocity tool up and down, the MIDI note is triggered repeatedly so that you can hear the sound of the note at different velocities. Notice how high-velocity (red) notes trigger bass sounds that are plucked very hard, while very low-velocity (violet) notes trigger ghost bass sounds in which the string is barely touched.

2   Adjust the velocities of the other notes to make the bass line more dynamic.

You can experiment with placing accents on individual bass notes by raising their velocities to change the groove of the riff. Subtle random differences in velocities also help make the bass line sound more realistic.

3   Choose Edit > Select All (or press Command-A).

4   Using the Velocity tool, drag up and down on one of the notes.

When using the Velocity tool on multiple notes, all of the note velocities are offset by the same amount, and the differences in velocity between the notes are retained.

5   Choose Edit > Deselect All (or press Shift-Command-A).

6   Start playback.

7   Adjust the velocity of some notes while the project is playing.

As you drag the Velocity tool, MIDI notes are triggered over the playback, making it difficult to hear the result of your velocity changes on the bass line.

At the upper left of the Piano Roll Editor, you will see a MIDI Out button. By default, that button is turned on (green) and any note you create, select, or edit is automatically played. While playing the project in Cycle mode, it's a good idea to turn off MIDI Out.

8   Click the MIDI Out button.

The MIDI Out button is dimmed, and MIDI notes are no longer triggered when you're editing them. You can keep the project playing and adjust velocities while listening to the result.

9   Keep the project playing and adjust the velocities of some notes while listening to the result.

Editing a MIDI Recording

When you're recording a MIDI performance, MIDI events are created in real time at the playhead position and placed in a MIDI region on the record-enabled track. You can then use the MIDI editors to fine-tune the performance.

In the following exercises, you will import a MIDI file containing a piano recording. You will use editing tools to mute undesired notes, shorten notes to get a better musical feel, and quantize individual notes to correct their timing.

Importing a MIDI File

You can import any MIDI file into an existing project. You can choose File > Import and select your MIDI file, or just drag the MIDI file to a track.

1   Open a Finder window, then go to Logic 8_Files > Media > Additional Media, and locate **Piano.mid**.

2   Drag **Piano.mid** to the Suitcase V2 track, at 1 1 1 1.

A Piano MIDI region is created.

3   Double-click the Piano MIDI region.

The contents of the Piano MIDI region are displayed in the Piano Roll Editor. You may have to scroll or zoom to see all the notes in the Piano MIDI region.

4   Play the project.

Listen to the piano performance you just imported.

Editing a Recorded MIDI Sequence

When opening a MIDI performance in the Piano Roll Editor, you can see all the imperfections. Some notes shouldn't have been played, and some are sustained for too long. This is a good time to polish the performance.

In the current project, the Piano region includes several elements that could be improved. First, the two blue A notes on the fourth downbeat of measure 1 play at the same time as the snare. This is a funky groove, and one of the "rules" of groove is to leave space for the snare! You could delete the two notes, but you might want to change your mind later. For now, you can just mute the notes.

1   Press Esc twice to revert the left-click tool to the Pointer tool.

2   Drag to select the two blue notes at the end of measure 1.

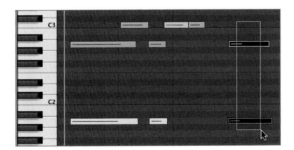

3   Press Esc.

The Tool menu appears.

4   Choose the Mute tool.

5   Click one of the two selected notes.

The notes are dimmed, indicating that they are muted. While the notes are still present in the region, they will not trigger any MIDI events. This is a great way to experiment with removing notes nondestructively. You can always unmute the notes later by clicking them again with the Mute tool.

To mute notes, you don't have to select them before clicking them with the Mute tool; but if you select multiple notes, one click of the Mute tool will mute them all.

TIP You can also mute and unmute selected notes by pressing M.

6   Press the Spacebar to start playback.

When the playhead reaches the fourth beat, the muted notes don't play, making room for the snare. That snare really "snaps" now! Much better.

Notice how the riff's high note in bar 2 is more staccato and sounds funkier? Look at the two final chords. They are very short. In measure 1, the second high chord (the two green notes) is sustained too long for that groove. Let's shorten it.

Sustained chords   Staccato chords

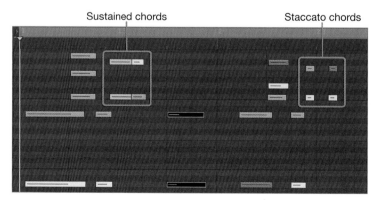

7   Press Esc twice.

The left-click tool switches back to the Pointer tool.

8 Position the mouse cursor over the lower-right edge of one of the green notes.

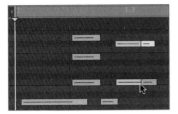

No matter where you position your mouse cursor, it will not display the Resize pointer allowing you to resize the green notes. Let's figure out why.

9 Hold down one of the green notes.

The note's shadow appears. The green note's right edge is below the orange note to the right. When notes overlap, you can use the Finger tool to resize them.

10 Press Esc and choose the Finger tool.

11 Drag to select both green notes.

12 Using the Finger tool, drag one of the green notes to the left.

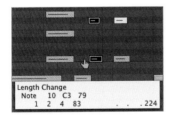

The Finger tool resizes the notes. Listen to the result.

The first two notes of the Piano region are slightly off the beat. You could quantize the MIDI region as you did in Lesson 4, but then you would correct all the timing nuances of the performance and lose its human feel. Instead, you will use the Quantize tool to quantize just those two notes.

13 Press Esc and choose the Quantize tool.

14 Drag to select the two first notes.

15 Hold down one of the selected notes with the Quantize tool.

The Quantize menu appears.

16 Choose 1/4-Note.

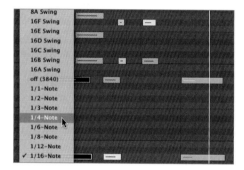

The selected notes snap to the nearest quarter-note grid line, on the first downbeat.

17 Press the Spacebar and listen to your edited piano.

Using the Score Editor

The Score Editor displays MIDI notes as standard musical notation. If you have a classical training, this could become your editor of choice. In these exercises, you will use the Link modes to change the relationship between the Score Editor and the Arrange area displays, and use the Score Editor to create a simple horn part.

Using the Link Modes

You can use Link modes to control what an editor displays when you work in another area. By default, MIDI editors open in Content Link mode (indicated by a yellow link button) and display the contents of the selected MIDI region in the key focus area.

1 At the bottom of the editing area, click the Score button.

Link button

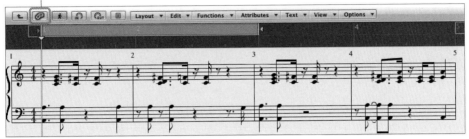

The Score Editor opens in Content Link mode and displays the contents of the Piano region. The notes you are seeing are the same notes you just edited in the Piano Roll Editor, but they're displayed as musical notation.

NOTE ▶ If the Score Editor shows you the contents of all the regions, in the Arrange area, click the background to deselect all the regions, then click the Piano region to select it. Click the background of the Score editor to give it key focus.

Notice that the Inspector updates to display the score parameters and a Part box full of score symbols. You will use these in the next exercise to create notes on a staff.

2   In the Arrange area, click the Attitude Bass region to select it.

The Score Editor displays the contents of the Attitude Bass region, and you can see your bass line as musical notation.

When you unlink an editor, it will keep displaying the same contents independently of your actions in other areas. This is useful when you need to manipulate regions in the Arrange area without changing what a MIDI editor displays.

3   In the Score Editor title bar, click the Link button.

The button is dimmed and the Score Editor is now in No Link mode.

4 In the Arrange area, select different regions.

The Score Editor does not update and still shows the contents of the Attitude Bass region.

In the Same Level Link mode, a MIDI editor displays all the contents of the key focus area. When the Arrange area has key focus, the Same Level Link mode allows a MIDI editor to display all the MIDI regions in the Arrange area.

5 In the Score Editor title bar, click the Link button.

TIP ▶ You can also hold down the mouse button on the Link Button and choose a link mode from the pop-up menu, allowing you to switch from the Content Link mode to the Same Level Link mode without clicking the Link button twice.

The button is purple, indicating that the Score Editor is in the Same Level Link mode. The Score Editor now displays the contents of all the MIDI regions in the Arrange area.

On the top staff, the high notes are hidden under the title bar. You can drag the first clef vertically to move the staves down.

6 Drag the first G clef down.

All the staves move down and you can now see the highest notes.

In the next exercise, you must see the contents of a new MIDI region to create a horn line, so you will need to reset the Content Link mode.

7   Double-click the Link button.

The Link button turns yellow and the Score Editor is in Content Link mode. It displays the contents of the selected region in the Arrange area.

Creating a Horn Line in the Score Editor

You will now use the Score Editor to program a simple horn riff. First you need to create a new software instrument track and load a horn channel strip setting.

1   Create a new software instrument track, making sure Open Library is selected.

2   In the Library, choose 07 Pop Horns > Studio Horns.

You may have to scroll to the left to see the all the instrument categories.

You can play a few notes on your MIDI keyboard to hear the sound of the studio horns.

3   Command-click in bar 1 of the Studio Horns track.

An empty one-bar region is created and displayed in the Score Editor.

4   Resize the region so that it is two bars long.

5   Zoom in the Score Editor by dragging its vertical zoom slider at the bottom right.

The Score Editor has key focus again, and the Inspector displays the Part box.

In the Score Editor, you can insert notes and symbols by dragging them to the staff from the Part box.

6   In the Part box, drag a quarter note to the upper staff as an A3 at 1 1 1 1.

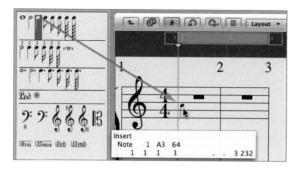

When creating notes in the Score Editor, look at the help tag to make sure you drop the note at the desired pitch and position. Notice the note length in the help tag. The inserted note is a few ticks shorter than a quarter note. This is done to avoid creating overlapping notes in the Score Editor.

The note is blinking to indicate that it is selected. If you click the background, the note is deselected and stops blinking.

You could continue to drag notes from the Part box, but in the Score Editor it is usually easier to copy existing notes.

7   Option-drag the A3 note to A2 (one octave below) at 2 1 1 1.

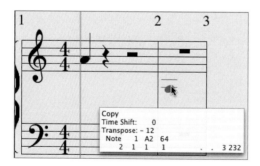

A new quarter note is inserted on the lower staff as an A2. Listen to your horns. Does it sound like the simplest horn line you have ever heard? Well, in funk music, sometimes simple works the best. Still, let's add a little lead-in note just before that last note, to make it groove.

8 From the Part box, drag a sixteenth note to G2 at 1 4 4 1.

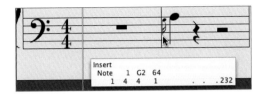

As you drag the note to 1 4 4 1, it looks as though it's going to be dropped inside the second bar, but don't trust the display; always trust the help tag, and make sure it reads 1 4 4 1 before you release the mouse button. When you do, the Score Editor will display the correct position and automatically fill in the blanks with the necessary rest symbols.

9 Click the Piano Roll button (or press P).

Your new horn notes are displayed as note beams in the Piano Roll Editor.

The Inspector now displays the Studio Horns channel strip.

10 Adjust the Studio Horns volume to suit yourself, and listen to your groove.

Editing Notes with a MIDI Keyboard

You can adjust the pitch and velocity of selected notes using your MIDI controller keyboard. The notes will retain their position and length, and they will update their pitch and velocity according to the note you played on the MIDI keyboard.

In this exercise, you will use your MIDI keyboard to experiment with the pitch and velocity of the horn notes you just entered in the Score Editor.

1   In the Arrange area, make sure that the Studio Horns track is record-enabled.

2   At the bottom of the editing area, click the Score button.

The Score Editor opens, showing you the three horn notes you inserted in the previous exercise.

3   Click the first note.

The note is blinking to indicate that it is selected.

4   At the top of the Score Editor, double-click the In button.

The In button is the button you clicked to activate step input recording in the previous lesson. When you double-click the In button, the MIDI connector icon inside the button turns black, and you can now edit the selected note's pitch and velocity using your MIDI keyboard.

5   Play a note on your MIDI keyboard.

The selected note is changed to the pitch and velocity of the MIDI note that you played.

You will actually keep the A3 pitch but experiment with different velocities using the keyboard. Try to find the original A3 pitch on your keyboard (you can use the MIDI In display in the Transport bar).

6   Start playback.

With that first note still selected in the Score Editor, on your MIDI keyboard, press the A3 really hard or really soft. You can hear the note you play, and you can watch the selected A3's velocity updated depending upon how hard you pressed the key. Each time the playhead jumps back to the beginning, you will hear the A3 played with the new velocity.

Continue experimenting in the same way with the other two horn notes. Try placing the accent on the second note or the third note, and listen to how it affects the groove.

Let's use the same technique in the Piano Roll Editor to alter the velocities of the notes in the bass riff.

7   At the top of the Score Editor, click the In button to turn it off.

8   In the Arrange area, click the Attitude Bass track header.

The Attitude Bass track is selected and record-enabled.

9   Double-click the Attitude Bass region.

In the editing area, the Piano Roll Editor opens and displays the contents of the Attitude Bass region.

10 At the top of the Piano Roll Editor, double-click the In button.

11 Select the first bass note, and play a note on your MIDI keyboard.

If the note you play has a very high pitch, the selected note will disappear from the visible area in the Piano Roll Editor. Play a few lower-pitched notes until the selected note reappears.

Find the original pitch (A1) on your MIDI keyboard, and experiment hitting the note at various velocities while playing the project.

12 Click the In button to turn it off.

Editing MIDI Continuous Controller Events

When playing a MIDI keyboard, you can add expression to your performance using knobs, sliders, or wheels, such as the pitch bend wheel or a volume pedal. Manipulating those controllers sends a stream of MIDI continuous controller (CC) events that represent the movement of the controller and trigger the intended action on the instrument.

When programming MIDI, you can draw the stream of MIDI CC events to automate an instrument's volume, pitch, and other parameters. In the following exercises, you will use Logic's MIDI editors to create pitch bend, volume, and pan automation in the bass and piano MIDI regions.

> **MORE INFO** ▶ Producers often refer to automated MIDI CC events as "region-based" automation, as opposed to "track-based" automation, which you'll explore in Lesson 10, "Automating the Mix and Using Control Surfaces."

Editing Note Velocity Using Hyper Draw

Note velocities are not MIDI CC events. Velocity is one of the parameters of a MIDI note-on event. However, Hyper Draw offers a different way to edit note velocities that is especially useful for creating velocity ramps, crescendos, and decrescendos.

Let's apply a decrescendo to the bass line.

1   In the Arrange area, make sure the Attitude Bass region is selected.

    The bass line is displayed in the Piano Roll Editor. If necessary, zoom to make sure all the bass notes are visible, and switch your left-click tool back to the Pointer tool.

2   Solo the Attitude Bass track.

3   At the bottom left of the Piano Roll Editor, click the Hyper Draw button.

    A gray Hyper Draw area appears at the bottom of the Piano Roll Editor.

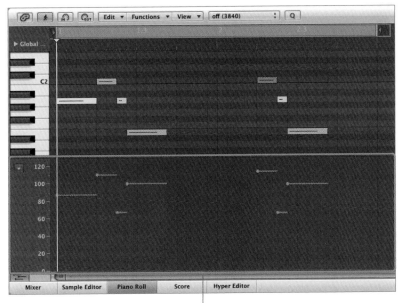

Hyper Draw area

Since no MIDI CC events are present in the region, the Hyper Draw area displays the velocity of each MIDI note as a node along with a line representing the length of the note. The height of each line represents the velocity of the note above it on the grid, according to the scale on the left. You can adjust the velocity of a note by dragging the node (not the line) vertically.

4   Drag a node up or down.

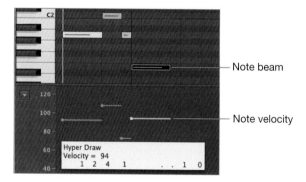

A help tag shows you the note's velocity as you adjust it. When you release the mouse button, the note's beam changes color to reflect the new velocity.

Let's use the Line tool to create a decrescendo.

5   Hold down the mouse button in the background of the Hyper Draw area.

A Start Line help tag appears, helping you to precisely adjust the position and value of the beginning of the decrescendo. Keep holding down the mouse button as you position the pointer where you want to start the decrescendo.

6   Drag to the upper left of the Hyper Draw area until the help tag reads 1 1 1 1, Velocity = 127.

7   Release the mouse button and locate the End Line position, where you want the decrescendo to stop.

The help tag moves to the top of the Piano Roll Editor so you can see the entire Hyper Draw area, and it now says *End Line*.

8 Position the mouse cursor and drag all the way down and to the right.

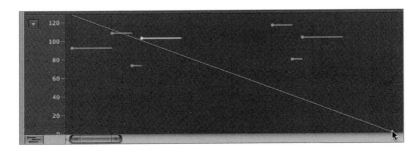

A green line appears between the Start Line position and the pointer position.

9 Click at the mouse cursor position.

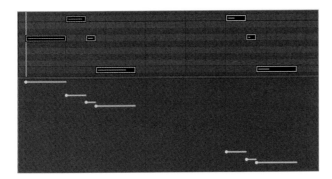

All the note velocities are aligned to the green line you just drew.

10 Listen to your bass line.

The Line tool can be very useful to create velocity crescendos and decrescendos, but in this case, having a decrescendo on a bass line doesn't really work for a funky groove, and the last few notes are now too quiet to be heard.

11 Press Command-Z.

The original velocities reappear. The original accents you programmed by adjusting the note velocities with the Velocity tool work better for the bass line, so you will keep the note velocities as they are now.

Automating Pitch Bend Using Hyper Draw

Pitch bend events are MIDI CC events. Adding subtle pitch glides at the beginning or end of notes can help make a MIDI sequence more musical. By creating pitch bend automation on the first bass note, you will emulate the sound of the bass player sliding into the note.

1   At the upper left of the Hyper Draw area, click the arrow button.

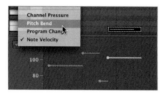

A menu appears allowing you to choose which MIDI controller automation you want to display in the Hyper Draw area.

2   Choose Pitch Bend.

The Hyper Draw area shows a blank slate where you can start creating and editing pitch bend events.

The black center line indicates the normal pitch of the note. You will create automation that starts at the minimum pitch bend value and goes back up to the normal pitch.

Although a single click is enough to create a node, dragging the mouse cursor allows you to create the node and use the help tag to position it.

3   In the Hyper Draw area, position the pointer at 1 1 1 1. Hold down the mouse button and drag until the help tag displays the lowest possible pitch bend value (–64). Release the mouse button.

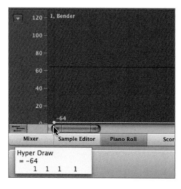

A node is created at the position where you released the mouse button.

Now you need to create a second node to return the pitch to the normal note pitch.

4   Click slightly to the right of the first node, as close to the black center line as possible.

A second node is created. Notice that the pitch bend value is displayed next to each node.

5   Drag the new node. While watching the help tag, position the node to a value of 0 (original note pitch) near the center of the first bass note.

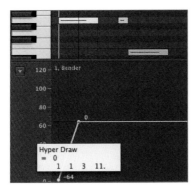

6   Press the Spacebar to hear the results.

You can hear the pitch glide. It's getting there, but it still doesn't sound quite right. You can curve the pitch glide to make it sound more natural.

7   Control-Option-drag the line between the two nodes.

Make sure that the tip of the Pointer tool is positioned exactly on top of the line when you're Control-Option-dragging to create a curve (zoom in if you need to). If the Pointer tool is slightly off position, you will be Control-Option-clicking in the background and, as a result, zooming. You may want to zoom in horizontally before you create the curve.

Drag up or down to create a convex or a concave curve, respectively. Drag left or right to create a horizontal or vertical S curve, respectively. You can also Control-Option-click the line to revert to a straight line. Note that you can create a curve only between nodes of different values. You can't curve a horizontal line.

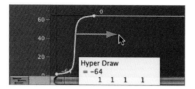

8 Try Control-Option-dragging to the right to create a vertical S curve.

9 Press the Spacebar to hear the result.

The result sounds much more natural, very close to what a real bass player sliding into a note would sound like. Still, the slide is a little slow.

10 Drag the second node to the left.

The S curve is shortened. Keep listening and adjusting the position of the second node and the shape of the curve until you find the perfect-sounding slide.

11 In the Arrange area, click the Solo button on the Attitude Bass track header to turn it off.

Automating Volume Using Hyper Draw

You can add expression to a MIDI sequence by creating volume automation.

Because using MIDI CC automation intrinsically ties the automation to the MIDI region you are editing, it is called *region-based* automation. It is useful when you want to add expression to a musical phrase (for example, a volume swell on the first two notes), and want the same volume changes to occur every time you repeat the musical phrase. Copying or repeating the MIDI region in the Arrange area will copy or repeat all the notes and MIDI CC automation contained in the region.

In Lesson 10, you will use track-based volume automation, which is useful when you want to create dynamic changes that spread over several regions, such as a slow decrescendo over several copies of the same region.

You will now add dynamic expression to the piano performance by creating MIDI CC volume automation.

1   In the Arrange area, click the Suitcase V2 track header.

The Suitcase V2 track is selected, and its channel strip appears in the Inspector.

The Piano region is also selected and its contents are displayed in the Piano Roll Editor. You may have to zoom and scroll to see the piano notes.

2   At the left of the Hyper Draw area, click the arrow to open the Hyper Draw menu, and choose Volume.

There are currently no MIDI volume events in this region, and a black horizontal line representing the current volume is displayed in the Hyper Draw area. It corresponds to the position of the volume fader on the channel strip in the Inspector.

To create the volume automation, you do not have to be precise when positioning the nodes. Click to create the nodes, and don't worry about the help tag. The goal is to accent the second beat.

3   Create a node on the second beat that is 5 to 7 dB higher than the current volume.

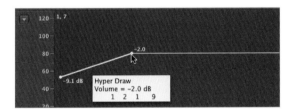

4   Create a node on the third beat to return to the original volume.

You may want to start dragging to insert the node and position it to the same value as the first node. If you can't get the same value, zoom in vertically, or hold Control as you drag the node.

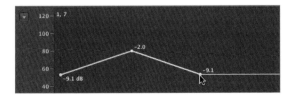

5   Control-Option-drag the second line to curve it.

Don't hesitate to listen to the results and experiment as you're drawing automation. Also, close your eyes and focus on hearing the actual result, uninfluenced by the visual representation of the Hyper Draw automation.

If you make a mistake and create a node you don't want, click the node to delete it.

TIP ▶ You can also draw freehand automation by dragging the Pencil tool in the Hyper Draw area.

When you are happy with the accent in bar 1, you can copy the same accent to measure 2. To select several automation nodes, hold Shift as you drag to select them.

6   Shift-drag to select all three nodes.

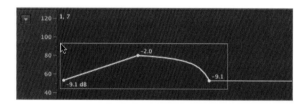

The whole automation is highlighted, indicating that it is selected.

7   Hold down one of the selected automation lines, and Option-drag the selection to bar 2, using the help tag to position the copy as close as possible to 2 1 1 1.

Depending on your zoom level, the automation may snap to different values. If you want more precision when positioning automation nodes, you need to zoom in horizontally. In this exercise, it doesn't matter if the volume automation is a few ticks off.

The selected automation is copied to bar 2. Now copy the automation in measures 1 and 2 to measures 3 and 4.

8   Shift-drag around all the nodes in bars 1 and 2.

This time you will use a new technique to copy automation: you will copy the selection to the Clipboard, position the playhead where you want the copy, and paste the Clipboard.

9   Choose Edit > Copy (or press Command-C).

The selected automation is copied to the Clipboard.

10   Press / (slash) on the main keyboard, the Go to Position command.

A dialog appears, prompting you to enter a new position for the playhead.

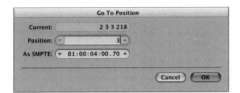

11   Type 3, then press Enter.

The playhead is positioned on 3 1 1 1.

12   Choose Edit > Paste (or press Command-V).

The automation in the Clipboard is pasted at the new playhead position. Zoom out to see the whole region.

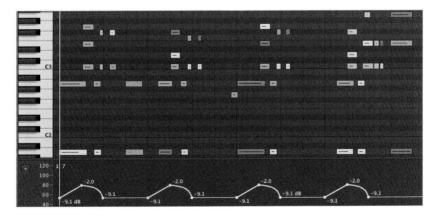

13 Turn off the Cycle mode, return to the beginning, and listen to the whole Piano region.

In the Inspector, the volume fader will move, following the volume automation you just created.

> **TIP** ▶ You can also display and edit MIDI CC automation in the Score Editor by clicking the Hyper Draw button, and in the Arrange area by choosing View > Hyper Draw and selecting the desired MIDI controller.

You have created volume MIDI CC automation in the Piano region. You could now arrange a song by copying, moving, or looping the Piano region. The volume automation you created would be present for each instance of the Piano region.

Automating Pan in the Hyper Editor

Although they share a similar name, Hyper Draw and the Hyper Editor are quite different. Hyper Draw is the name of the technique you previously used to draw MIDI CC automation by creating nodes and adding curves.

The Hyper Editor is a highly customizable MIDI editor, capable of displaying any type of MIDI event on its own lane. You can use the Pencil tool to draw events on a music grid, and each lane can have its own grid resolution. This makes it the editor of choice to draw drum rolls, as you will do in Lesson 6, "Programming Drums."

In the Hyper Editor, you can also display and edit multiple types of MIDI CC on their own individual lanes. Let's use the Hyper Editor to draw some pan automation in the Piano region.

1 At the bottom of the Piano Roll Editor, click the Hyper Editor button.

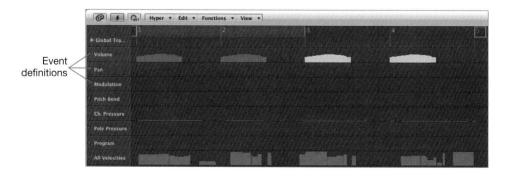

In the Hyper Editor, each lane allows you to display and edit one type of MIDI event, determined by its *event definition*. An event definition can be a MIDI note or a MIDI CC such as volume or pan. On each lane, events are represented by vertical beams on a grid. The height of a beam represents the value of the MIDI CC event, or the velocity of the MIDI note the beam represents. A collection of event definitions is called a *hyper set*.

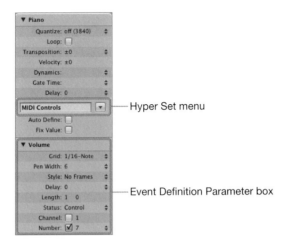

Hyper Set menu

Event Definition Parameter box

The Inspector now displays Hyper Editor parameters. The Hyper Set menu lets you choose which Hyper Set you want to display in the Hyper Editor. The Event Definition Parameter box allows you to adjust parameters for the selected event definition.

The default hyper set is called MIDI Controls. It includes the basic MIDI controller events: volume, pan, modulation, pitch bend, and a few others. If you are still looking at the Piano region, you can see the volume automation you created in the previous exercise.

2   Click the Pan event definition.

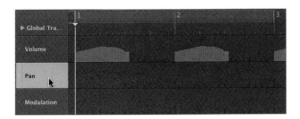

The Pan parameters are displayed in the Event Definition Parameter box.

3   Press Control–Down Arrow a few times.

The Hyper Editor zooms in vertically so you can better see the Pan event definition lane.

4   In the Inspector, set Grid to 1/32-Note.

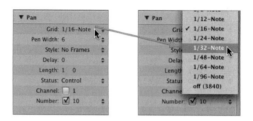

The Pan lane's grid now has a finer resolution. Notice that the grids on the other lanes did not change.

Now you will enter some pan automation. You will use the Pencil tool (Command-click tool) to draw the automation in the lane.

5   In the first two bars, Command-drag in the Pan lane to create pan events.

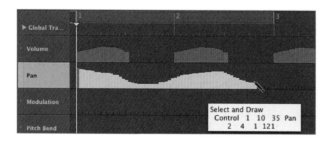

You can now use the Line tool to shape the events you just created.

6   Press Esc and choose the Line tool.

The Line tool in the Hyper Editor works the same way as the Line tool you previously used in Hyper Draw to edit bass note velocities: Hold down the mouse button to find the Start Line position, release the mouse button, find the End Line position, and click to end the line. You will now use the Line tool to create a smooth movement of the Piano from one speaker to the other over the first 2 bars.

7   Hold down the Line tool in the Pan lane and find your starting position, at the top of the lane on 1 1 1 1.

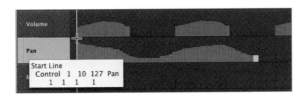

8   Release the mouse button and find your ending position, over the last pan event just before bar 3.

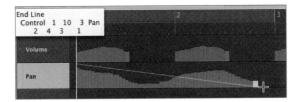

A green line appears.

9   Click the end of the line.

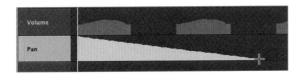

All pan events are aligned to the green line, producing a smooth panning of the piano from right to left.

You can also use the Line tool to create events.

10 Using the same technique to start and end the line, use the Line tool in bars 3 and 4, which have no events at present.

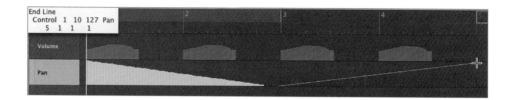

Pan events are created on each grid mark, along the green line.

11 In the Arrange area, click the Suitcase V2 track header.

The Inspector shows the Suitcase V2 channel strip.

12 Go to the beginning and listen to the project.

You can hear the pan automation you just created, and see the Pan knob move in the Inspector.

With each lane placed in its own grid, and having the ability to draw events while snapping them to the grid of your choice, you can create interesting step automation. You could use swing grid resolution on a lane that controls the filter cutoff of a synth to generate some trippy filter sweeps! The Hyper Editor is also a great tool to program drum beats, as you will learn in Lesson 6, "Programming Drums."

Editing in the Event List

The Event List displays all the MIDI events contained in a region as text and numerical values. It offers powerful ways to filter events and to select and edit the desired events with the most accuracy, displaying the exact numerical value of each event's parameter.

Cleaning Up a MIDI Region

Sometimes a MIDI recording can contain undesired MIDI events that were not filtered during input. When you don't know which MIDI events a region contains, you might not know where to look for them in the other editors. The Event List can show all the MIDI events in a region, so you can use it to get a comprehensive view of the MIDI data a region contains.

In this exercise you will examine the contents of the Piano region you imported at the beginning of this lesson, and delete the unwanted events.

1   In the Toolbar, click the Lists button.

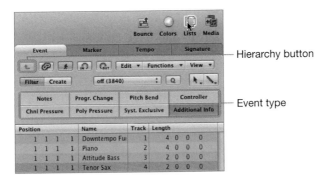

The Event List opens. It displays the contents of the Arrange area, listing all its regions and their positions and lengths.

NOTE ▸ If the Event List displays the contents of a region, click the Hierarchy button at the upper left of of the Event List to see a list of all the regions in the Arrange area.

You can display the contents of a region by double-clicking the region in the Event List, or by selecting the region in the Arrange area. When you are looking at the contents of a region, you can once again display all the regions in the Arrange area by clicking the Hierarchy button.

MORE INFO ▸ The Event List is the only MIDI editor that can display a list of regions and their positions. It is the only editor in which you can quantize the position of regions in the Arrange area, which is very useful for quantizing the positions of audio regions (for example to quantize drums).

2   In the Event List, double-click the Piano region.

A list of all the MIDI events contained in the Piano region is displayed.

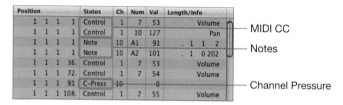

If you look at the Status column, you'll see that some events are note events, some are controller events, and some are channel pressure (C-Press) events. In the Length/Info column, some of the controller events are volume; others are pan. Those are the MIDI controller events created by the automation you drew in the previous exercises.

Some MIDI controller keyboards send channel pressure events (also known as *after-touch*) when pressure is applied to the keys. Channel pressure events can be config-ured to control instrument parameters such as vibrato or filter cutoff. But sometimes they are unused or may affect a modulation that you don't want.

Let's clean up the Piano region by deleting all channel pressure events. Since the Filter button is turned on (it is located under the Hierarchy button), you can click event type buttons to filter out the display of that event type.

3   Click the Notes button.

The Notes button is shaded, and all note events are hidden.

4   Click the Controller button.

The Controller button is shaded, and all controller events (volume and pan) are hidden.

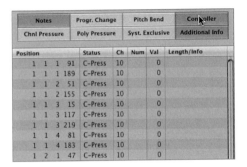

Now only the channel pressure events are displayed. In the Event List, only the currently displayed events will be affected by editing commands.

5   Choose Edit > Select All (or press Command-A).

All the displayed events (the channel pressure events, in this case) are selected. Notice that the channel pressure events are also highlighted in the Hyper Editor. (You might have to scroll down to see the Channel Pressure lane.)

6   Press Delete.

All channel pressure events are deleted. You can also see the channel pressure events deleted from the Hyper Editor.

7   Click both the Notes and Controller filter buttons.

The Notes and Controller events are displayed again.

Quantizing Note Lengths

When playing a real drum kit, you do not usually control the length of the drum sounds. For example, when you hit a snare, the snare rings until the sound dies.

Similarly, when playing a MIDI drum kit, you don't usually control the length of the drum sounds. By default, drum synthesizers and samplers trigger mostly *one-shot* sounds. A one-shot sound always sustains only for its duration, independent of the length of the MIDI note that triggers it.

Since the length of the MIDI note generally does not influence the playback of your drum sounds, you may want to clean up a recording of MIDI drums so that all drum notes have exactly the same length, making them visually easier to edit in the Piano Roll Editor.

1   In track 1 of the Arrange area, click the Downtempo Funk Beat 05 region.

The contents of the selected region are displayed in the Event List.

2   At the bottom of the editing area, click the Piano Roll button.

The Piano Roll Editor also displays the contents of the drum region. You can see the notes as they were recorded. They all have different lengths, which can look confusing when you're editing drums.

3   In the Event List, choose Edit > Select All (or press Command A).

Holding down Shift-Option as you adjust a single value assigns the same value to all the selected events.

4   Shift-Option-drag down the length of one of the selected notes.

Position				Status	Ch	Num	Val	Length/Info
1	1	1	1	Note	1	G-1	108	. . . 1
1	1	1	1	Note	1	A-1	108	. . . .
1	1	1	1	Note	1	C0	73	. . . .
1	1	1	1	Note	1	F5	90	. . . 1
1	1	1	1	Note	1	D#6	89	. . . 1
1	1	1	1	Note	1	D#7	112	. . . 1
1	1	1	11	Note	1	F#1	92	. . . 1
1	1	3	5	Note	1	F#1	57	. . . 1
1	1	4	1	Note	1	G-1	98	. . . 1

All the note lengths are set to one tick. In the Piano Roll Editor, you can see that all the notes have the same length. A single tick can be a little short for viewing and manipulating notes in the Piano Roll Editor, so you should lengthen them.

5   Double-click the length of one of the selected notes.

A text field appears.

6   Type *200* and press Enter.

Position				Status	Ch	Num	Val	Length/Info
1	1	1	1	Note	1	G-1	108	200
1	1	1	1	Note	1	A-1	108	. . . 1
1	1	1	1	Note	1	C0	73	. . . 1

All note lengths are set to 200 ticks, which is a little shorter than a sixteenth note (a sixteenth note equals 240 ticks). Since the drum pattern is a sixteenth-note pattern, this ensures that you won't have overlapping notes.

The result sounds the same as before, but is visually clearer in the Piano Roll Editor.

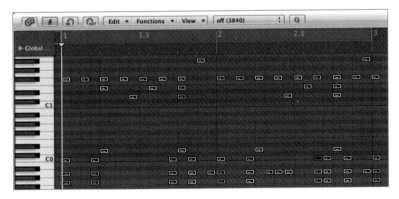

7   Go to the beginning and listen to the project.

Position				Status	Ch	Num	Val	Length/Info	
2	1	2	237	Note	1	F#1	72	. . . 200	Playhead position
2	1	4	1	Note	1	G-1	84	. . . 200	
2	1	4	1	Note	1	A-1	84	. . . 200	
2	1	4	1	Note	1	C0	49	. . . 200	
2	1	4	235	Note	1	F#1	89	. . . 200	
2	2	1	1	Note	1	D0	86	. . . 200	
2	2	1	1	Note	1	F#6	74	. . . 200	

In the Event List, the events scroll as they are played, and a white horizontal line indicates the playhead position.

In this lesson, you have used all the MIDI editors included in Logic, performing different tasks in each one. You have used the basic functions of each editor to create or edit simple sequences, but don't be fooled! The MIDI editors in Logic are powerful tools that include numerous options and features. When trying to perform a specific task, don't hesitate to look through an editor's local menu, or to Control-click an event or the editor's background area to access shortcut menus. Chances are, you will find the feature you are looking for and discover even more useful features you wouldn't have imagined.

Lesson Review

1.   In the Piano Roll Editor, what can you do with the Pencil tool?

2.   What does the MIDI Out button do?

3.   How do you resize overlapped notes?

4.   Can you quantize individual notes? How?

5.   How can you edit notes with a MIDI keyboard?

6.   How can you edit MIDI continuous controller events in the Piano Roll Editor or Score Editor?

7.   How do you insert nodes in Hyper Draw?

8.   How do you curve a line in Hyper Draw?

9.   How do you use the Line tool in Hyper Draw (when editing note velocities) or in the Hyper Editor?

10. How do you select automation in Hyper Draw?

11. How do you change the grid resolution of an event definition?

12. How do you draw automation in the Hyper Editor?

13. How do you hide a type of event in the Event List?

Answers

1.   You can insert, resize, delete, move, and copy notes.

2.   When the MIDI Out button is on, MIDI notes are triggered as you edit them.

3.   With the Finger tool.

4.   Yes, you click the notes with the Quantize tool and choose a quantize setting from the pop-up menu.

5.   Double-click the MIDI In button at the top of the MIDI editor, select the note you want to edit, and play a note on your MIDI keyboard.

6.   Click the Hyper Draw button at the lower left of the editor.

7.   Click in the Hyper Draw area to insert a node. You can also hold down the mouse button so a help tag appears, then drag the node to the desired position while looking at the help tag.

8.   Control-Option-drag the line.

9. Drag to find your Start Line position, release the mouse button, find your End Line position, and click to end the line.

10. Shift-drag around the desired nodes.

11. In the Inspector, in the Event Definition Parameter box, adjust the Grid parameter.

12. With the Pencil or Line tool.

13. When the Filter button is on, click an event type button to filter the corresponding events.

6

Time

Goals

This lesson takes approximately 60 minutes to complete.

Program a drum pattern in Ultrabeat

Add rhythmic accents

Randomize note velocity and position

Create drum rolls

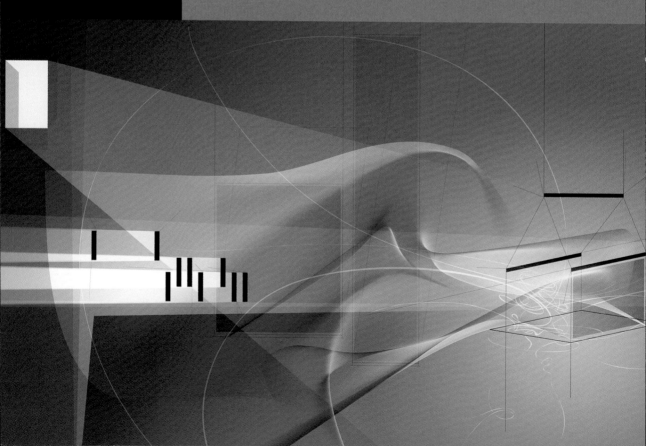

Programming Drums

In most popular modern music genres, drums are the backbone of the instrumentation. They provide the foundation for the tempo and the groove of the piece. In recording sessions, when not all of the instruments are tracked at the same time, drums are usually recorded or programmed first, so the other musicians can record to their rhythmic reference.

With today's high production standards, producing drum tracks usually involves using several techniques such as live recording, programming, sampling, audio quantizing, and sound replacement. For that reason, music producers and composers must develop drum programming skills.

In this lesson, you will program a pattern in Ultrabeat, Logic's dedicated drum production plug-in. You will then import the pattern to the Arrange area, and fine-tune the programming, humanize the groove, and add a snare roll using Logic's MIDI editors.

Programming a Drum Pattern in Ultrabeat

Ultrabeat is a plug-in designed specifically to create drum sounds and to program drum patterns. It integrates all the classic drum synthesis techniques (phase oscillators, frequency modulation, ring modulation, noise generation, and physical modeling) with sample playback and a step sequencer.

In the next exercises, you will choose an existing drum kit and program a drum pattern using Ultrabeat's interface.

Choosing a Drum Kit and Previewing Drum Sounds

Before you start programming a pattern, you need to choose the drum sounds you will be using. In Ultrabeat, you can load a drum kit made up of 24 drum sounds, plus one bass sound that you can play chromatically.

Let's insert Ultrabeat on a software instrument's channel strip, choose a drum kit, get to know the layout of Ultrabeat's interface, and preview the individual drum sounds.

1   Choose File > New (or press Command-N).

2   In the Templates dialog, click the Empty Project template.

3   Create a software instrument track, and select Open Library.

   A software instrument track is created, and its channel strip appears in the Inspector. The Library opens, displaying collections of software instrument channel strip settings.

   You will insert the Ultrabeat plug-in directly into the software instrument channel strip.

4   Click the channel strip's Instrument slot, and choose Ultrabeat (Drum Synth) from the pop-up menu.

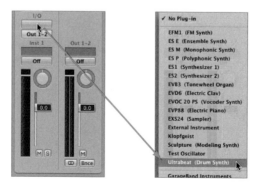

Ultrabeat is inserted, a default drum kit is loaded, and the Ultrabeat interface opens. The Library updates to display Ultrabeat settings.

All plug-in windows have a black header that contains buttons and menus to access plug-in settings and to navigate between plug-ins. For now, you can close that section to reduce screen clutter. You will use the Library to access the plug-in settings.

5 At the right of the plug-in window title bar, click the button.

The plug-in header is hidden.

Ultrabeat's interface comprises three parts:

▶   The Assignment section, where you can assign drum sounds to MIDI notes and adjust each sound's volume, pan, mute, and solo settings. The currently selected sound is highlighted in white.

▶   The Synthesizer section, occupying most of the window, where you can tweak the parameters of the selected sound.

▶   The step sequencer, where you can program a sequence for the selected sound.

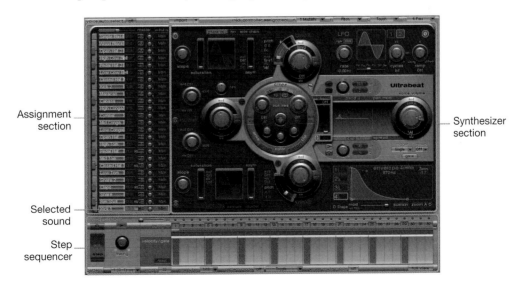

To the left of the Assignment section, a thin keyboard extends vertically. In front of each key appears the name of the sound assigned to it, and the sound's number. Sounds are numbered 01 through 25, from bottom to top. Each sound area also has a blue volume slider, a red Mute button, a yellow Solo button, and a Pan knob.

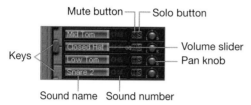

Let's listen to those drum sounds. You can click the keys of the vertical keyboard to preview individual sounds.

6   Click a key on the vertical keyboard.

The key is depressed and highlighted in blue, and the corresponding sound is played.

Using a MIDI keyboard is the best way to preview a drum kit, as you can play a little groove to get the feel of the sounds. MIDI notes C1 through B2 trigger sounds 01 through 24, used for drum sounds, while MIDI notes C3 and above play sound 25 chromatically, usually used for a bass sound.

7   Play the lowest C on your MIDI keyboard, while watching the MIDI Activity display in the Transport bar.

If the MIDI In display doesn't show a C1, press your external MIDI controller keyboard's Octave Up or Down buttons until the lowest C triggers a C1.

In Ultrabeat, you can see the lowest key light up (in blue) and you'll hear sound 01, a kick drum.

8   Play a C♯1, and keep going up chromatically on your keyboard.

You see the corresponding Ultrabeat key light up, and the sound assigned to that key is played. When you reach C3 and up, you can play the bass sound chromatically.

Are you feeling adventurous? Try alternating two fingers of your left hand on C1 and E1 to play the kick and snare, while using your right hand to play the hi-hat on F♯1. Skilled keyboard players can even play a drum groove with the left hand while the right hand plays a bass line!

Notice that sound 01 is highlighted in white. That's the currently selected sound. Its Synthesiszer parameters are displayed in the Synthesiszer section, and its sequence in the step sequencer.

9   Click the name of sound 02, Rim Shot.

Sound 02 is highlighted. The Synthesizer section and the step sequencer update to display the rim shot's Synthesiszer parameters and sequence.

Let's try using other drum kits.

10   In the Library, select 01 Drum Kits.

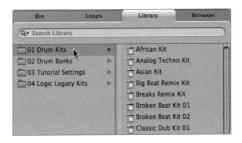

A collection of drum kits opens in the right column of the Library.

11   Select Big Beat Remix Kit.

After the kit opens, the parameters update in Ultrabeat's interface. The name of the kit appears in the plug-in window's title bar and on the track header.

Inst 1: Big Beat Remix Kit

12 Use the mouse and the vertical keyboard, or play your MIDI keyboard, to preview the kit.

13 Make sure the Library has key focus, and press Down Arrow.

The next drum kit is loaded, and you can preview it.

14 Press Up Arrow.

The previous drum kit is reloaded. For this exercise, you are going to use a rock drum kit located in the Legacy folder.

15 In the Library, select 04 Logic Legacy Kits, then Rock Kit.

LOGIC EXPRESS ▶ Close the current project, and open Logic 8_Files > Lessons > 06 Programming Drums, where Ultrabeat is preloaded with that Rock Kit.

A Progress window pops up, showing samples loading into RAM. Drum kits using a lot of samples can take a while to load, so wait until the Progress window disappears.

When the name of the drum kit (Rock Kit) appears in the plug-in window's title bar and on the track header, the kit is loaded and you can preview its drum sounds.

Using the Step Sequencer

You can use the step sequencer at the bottom of the Ultrabeat interface to program or edit patterns. In Ultrabeat, you can save up to 24 patterns with each drum kit. Most factory settings include some pre-recorded patterns, so let's listen to one and see what it sounds like.

1   At the upper left of the step sequencer, click the power button.

The power button icon turns blue and the step sequencer becomes active.

2   Click the Play button next to the power button.

The Play button turns into a green Stop button. The step sequencer starts and you can hear the first pattern. The notes on the keyboard in the Assignment section are highlighted as the sounds are played.

Ultrabeat's step sequencer is synchronized to the project and its tempo. To toggle the step sequencer playback on and off, you can also press the Spacebar to toggle the project playback, and the step sequencer will follow. Don't hesitate to leave playback on for the rest of this exercise, or to toggle it on and off frequently to listen to your results. If you choose to play the project, the playback will eventually stop when the playhead reaches the end of the project. When this happens, go to the beginning and start playback again.

3   In the Assignment section, click Hi-Hat Half (sound 09).

Hi-Hat Half is selected and the step sequencer updates to show you the hi-hat sequence. Seeing the sequence of a single drum sound at a time can be useful for precise editing, but does not give you an overview of the whole pattern.

4   At the lower right of the step sequencer, click the Full View button.

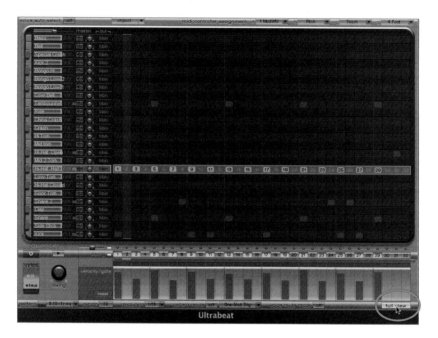

Now you can see the sequences for each sound directly across from the Assignment section. You can click anywhere on the grid to insert a new note.

5   Click step 1 on the Crash lane (sound 14).

A blue square is highlighted where you clicked, indicating that a crash cymbal is added on the first downbeat of the pattern. In the full-view grid, notice that down-beats are indicated by white vertical grid lines (on steps 1, 5, 9, 13, and so on).

You can also click an existing note to delete it.

6 On the Kick lane (sound 01), click the blue square on step 11.

The kick note is deleted.

You can access the setting's patterns in the Pattern menu at the lower left of the step sequencer.

7 Click the Pattern menu and scroll all the way down so you can see the entire menu.

The menu lists 24 available patterns. The *sq* indicates that a sequence is programmed for that pattern. For the Rock Kit, patterns 1 through 9 already have a programmed sequence, while 10 through 24 do not.

MORE INFO ► Ultrabeat also has a Pattern mode that allows you to switch patterns in real time using a MIDI keyboard. The MIDI note in parentheses indicates the note that triggers each pattern when pattern mode is on.

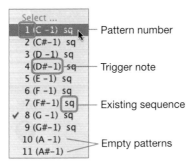

8 Choose pattern 1 and click Play.

You can hear pattern 1 and see it displayed in Ultrabeat's full-view step sequencer. You can choose from the Pattern menu to preview other patterns while the step sequencer is playing.

9   Choose pattern 2.

The step sequencer instantly updates to display pattern 2, and you can hear the pattern.

10 Stop playback.

Programming a Pattern

You are now ready to program your own pattern. You need to choose an empty Pattern from the Pattern menu so you can build your own groove from scratch.

1   From the Pattern menu, choose pattern 10.

The grid is empty and ready for a new pattern. In the menus to the right of the pattern menu, you can set the number of steps in the pattern and the step resolution. For now, you should keep the default settings: 32 steps with a sixteenth-note resolution, to create a two-bar pattern.

2   On the Kick lane (sound 01), click step 1.

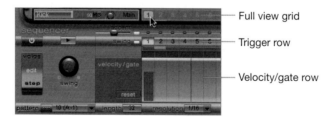

A kick note is added to the full-view grid. Since the kick sound is highlighted in the Assignment section, the step sequencer displays the kick sequence, and a blue vertical bar also appears on step 1 in the velocity/gate row. A blue square is also highlighted in the trigger row.

> **TIP**   Drag the mouse pointer in the trigger row to quickly add notes on every step, or to delete several existing notes at a time.

3 Continue entering kick notes every other beat (on steps 9, 17, and 25).

The step sequencer displays the entire kick sequence. Remember to regularly press the Spacebar to listen to the pattern as you build it. You can even choose to play the pattern continuously as you build it.

4 On the Snare lane (sound 03), click step 5.

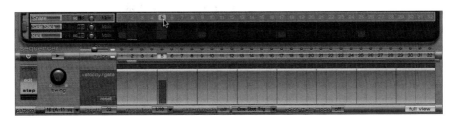

The snare sound is selected in the Assignment section, and the step sequencer displays the snare sequence, with the snare you just entered in step 5.

5 Continue entering snare notes every other beat (on steps 13, 21, and 29).

6 Control-click anywhere in the Hi-Hat Open lane (sound 11).

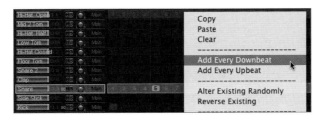

A shortcut menu opens.

TIP ▶ Logic includes a number of shortcut menus that can be accessed by Control-clicking (or right-clicking) in various parts of the interface. When you are looking for a function, try Control-clicking!

7 From the shortcut menu, choose Add Every Downbeat.

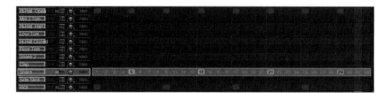

Open hi-hat notes are inserted on every downbeat (indicated by the white vertical grid lines).

8 Control-click the Hi-Hat Half lane (sound 09) and choose Add Every Upbeat.

Half-open hi-hat notes are inserted on every upbeat, between every open hi-hat note.

Often drummers will open the last hi-hat of a pattern to lead back into the first downbeat of the next pattern. Let's do just that!

9 Click the Hi-Hat Half lane (sound 09) on step 31.

The last half-open hi-hat is deleted.

10 Click the Hi-Hat Open lane (sound 11) on step 31.

The last hi-hat note is now an open hi-hat.

Editing Velocities and Accents

At this point, you have a basic rock pattern going. It sounds OK, but a little mechanical. You can make it more exciting. Editing note velocities allows you to add variations in dynamics and make the sequence sound more human. You can also accomplish this using several randomization options available in a shortcut menu.

In the following exercise, you will insert a couple of softer kick notes, add accents to the hi-hat, and subtly randomize their velocities.

1   In the Kick lane (sound 01), click step 11 to add a new Kick at that step.

In the velocity/gate row, the blue bar's height represents the velocity of a note. The blue bar's width represents the length (or *gate time*) of a note.

2   In the velocity/gate row, drag down the top left of the new kick's vertical bar until the help tag reads *Velo: 60*.

MORE INFO ▶ Dragging a note's vertical bar horizontally adjusts the note length (or *gate time*), which only affects gated sounds.

The new kick note on step 11 sounds a little softer than the others.

You can also create notes and adjust their velocity and gate time in one operation by dragging directly in the velocity/gate row.

3   In the velocity/gate row, hold down the mouse on step 27 to create a Kick note, drag vertically to adjust the velocity to 60, and drag horizontally to adjust the gate time to 4.

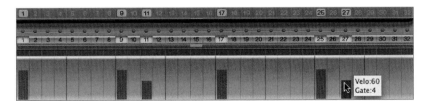

Now let's work with accents. Accents can emphasize specific steps by raising the volume of multiple sounds in the kit. Whereas changing the velocity of a note can change the sound sample that it triggers, adding an accent only changes the volume of the sound.

At the top of the step sequencer, just above the trigger row, is a row of LEDs where you can select steps to accent. The Accent slider to the left adjusts the volume increase of the accents in decibels (dB). Although the selected steps and the slider settings are the same for all the sounds in the drum kit, the accent switch (the blue LED to the right of the Accent slider) lets you toggle the accents on and off for each drum sound.

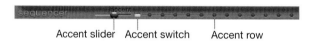

Accent slider   Accent switch   Accent row

4   In the accent row, click steps 1 and 17, and start playback, if necessary.

Listen to your pattern. Both the kick and the open hi-hat are accented on the first downbeat of each bar. The effect sounds good on the hi-hat, but not so good on the kick. Since the Kick lane is still selected, the step sequencer currently displays the kick sound parameters.

5   In front of the accent row, click the accent switch.

The kick is no longer accented, but the hi-hat is. The accent on the hi-hat is still a little too strong.

6   Drag the Accent slider to the left until the help tag reads *4.0dB*.

The difference in volume between the accented notes and the normal notes is now a little more subtle and natural.

Now let's adjust the velocities of the hi-hat notes and add a little randomness to make the pattern come alive.

7 In the Assignment section, click the Hi-Hat Half name (sound 09).

The Hi-Hat Half sound is selected and the step sequencer displays its sequence.

8 Control-click in the velocity/gate row and, from the shortcut menu, choose Alter Vel.

The velocities of all half-open hi-hat notes are randomly offset by a small amount.

Listen to the effect, and if the randomization is too subtle for your taste, repeat the procedure. If you went too far and velocity variations sound too drastic, you can reset all note velocities to their default values.

9 Click the Reset button to the left of the sequence.

All the half-open hi-hat notes are reset to the default velocity of 95.

10 Repeat the procedure to randomize the velocities of both the half-open hi-hat and the open hi-hat notes.

Remember that you made the last hi-hat an open one? Drummers like to accent that last open hi-hat to pull the groove back into the first downbeat of the next bar. Raising the velocity of the last hi-hat will accentuate that effect.

11 In the Assignment section, click the Hi-Hat Open name (sound 11).

12 In the velocity/gate row, drag the last note (step 31) up to a velocity of 121.

While dragging a note, notice that the velocity changes in increments of 2 or 3. To access every degree of velocity, you have to Shift-drag the note.

13 Shift-drag the same note to a velocity of 120.

The last open hi-hat is louder, which helps lead back into the downbeat of the next pattern.

Great job! You have programmed your first drum groove in Ultrabeat. Now you will import that groove as a MIDI region in the Arrange area and use Logic's MIDI editors to fine-tune the groove and create a snare roll.

Humanizing the Groove in the MIDI Editors

Musicians put many subtle timing and velocity variations in their playing, adding a human feeling to their performance that drum machines lack. If you reproduce those subtle inconsistencies when programming drums, your results will sound closer to a real performance.

In the previous exercises, you altered note velocities in Ultrabeat, helping make the pattern sound more natural. While Ultrabeat's step sequencer is a powerful tool to program drum patterns, it lacks some of the advanced capabilities of Logic's other MIDI editors.

In the following exercises, you will import the Ultrabeat pattern to the Arrange window, open it in the Piano Roll Editor to change the feel of the snare, and randomize the timing of the hi-hat using the Transform window.

Dragging the Pattern to the Arrange Area

You can insert the Ultrabeat pattern as a MIDI region in the Arrange area by dragging the button to the left of the Pattern menu in Ultrabeat's step sequencer. You will then be able to edit the MIDI region in Logic's MIDI editors.

1   Go to the beginning of the project.

You may have to move the Ultrabeat window to the right to see the first few bars of the Arrange area.

2   In Ultrabeat's step sequencer, position the mouse cursor on top of the Pattern button.

A help tag appears that reads, "Drag to Arrange Window."

3   Drag the pattern to bar 1 below the track in the Arrange area.

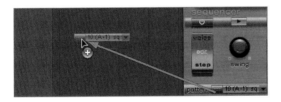

NOTE ► As you drag the pattern to the Arrange area, a green + icon appears, indicating that you can drop the pattern. You can drag the pattern to a specific track, or drag it below the last track. If you drag the pattern below the last track, it will automatically create the MIDI region on the last track.

A MIDI region is created, containing your two-bar drum groove. It is called Ultrabeat.

You can now turn off Ultrabeat's step sequencer so it doesn't play along with the MIDI region on the Rock Kit track.

4   In Ultrabeat's step sequencer, click the power button.

The step sequencer is turned off and will no longer play along when you play the project.

5   Close Ultrabeat's window (or press Command-W).

6   In the Toolbar, click the Set Locators button.

Cycle mode is turned on and the cycle area matches the length of the MIDI region.

7   At the bottom of the Arrange window, click the Piano Roll button (or press P).

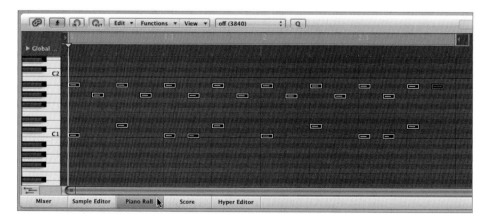

The Piano Roll Editor opens and displays the drum groove in the Ultrabeat MIDI region. (You may have to scroll down to see the notes between C1 and C2.)

Let's open the Event List to see a detail of all the events in the Ultrabeat MIDI region.

8   In the Toolbar, click the Lists button (or press E).

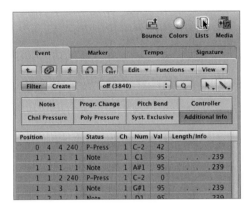

The Event List opens. If the Event List does not show the contents of the Ultrabeat MIDI region, double-click the Ultrabeat MIDI region. Notice the polyphonic pressure (P-Press) events in the Status column. They turn the volume up and down just before and after the first downbeat of each bar to reproduce the accents you programmed in Ultrabeat.

You can now edit the contents of the MIDI region in both the Piano Roll Editor and the Event List. When editing MIDI data, it is a good idea to keep the Event List open to monitor how individual MIDI events are updated as you edit them in another editor.

With Cycle mode turned on, you will press the Spacebar in all the upcoming exercises to toggle playback on and off. Playback will always start at the beginning of the pattern and will continuously loop until you stop it.

Applying a Laid-Back Feel to the Snare

An interesting characteristic of a human performance is that a drummer never hits all the drums precisely on the time grid.

You can approach the qualities of a human performance by slightly changing the position of certain drum notes, either by dragging them or by using Logic's humanization functions.

First, you will give the groove a more laid-back feel by delaying the snare notes.

1 In the Piano Roll Editor, click the D1 key (one white note above C1) on the vertical keyboard.

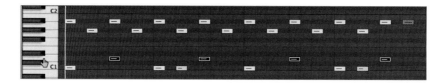

All D1 MIDI notes (all snare notes) are selected. Note the functional similarity to the Arrange area in which clicking a track header selects all the regions on that track.

2 Slowly drag the selection to the right while watching the help tag.

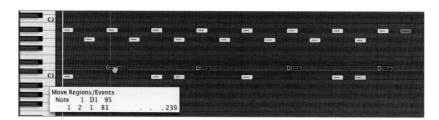

The notes snap to another position. The help tag shows that they are dragged from 1 2 1 1 to 1 2 1 81 (or another value depending on your zoom level). That's an 80-tick delay.

3 Press the Spacebar to start playback and listen to the new groove.

The snare notes are much too late and create a flam with the hi-hat notes. This almost sounds like a very bad human drummer. You need to delay the snare by a smaller amount. By pressing Control-Shift as you drag, you will have access to a higher degree of precision.

4 Choose Edit > Undo Drag (or press Command-Z).

The snares return to their original positions.

5 Hold down the first snare note, then Control-Shift-drag the note to the right.

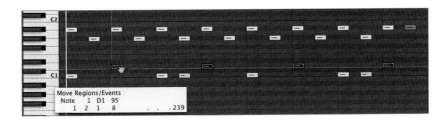

Snapping is disabled, and you can now drag with tick precision.

6   Watch the help tag and drag the selection to 1 2 1 8.

Listen to the groove; the difference is very subtle.

NOTE ▶ If you hear a flange sound on the snare, you probably forgot to turn off Ultrabeat's step sequencer in the previous exercise. Turn it off now.

Let's keep the first snare note where it is and delay the other three a little more.

7   Shift-click the first snare note.

The Shift-clicked note is deselected, and the others remain selected.

TIP ▶ When multiple notes are selected, you can Shift-click one of the selected notes to deselect it, while leaving the other notes selected. You can also Shift-click a deselected note to add it to the selection.

8   Hold down the mouse button on the first selected note, and Control-Shift-drag the selection to 1 4 1 20 to delay the three selected notes by 20 ticks.

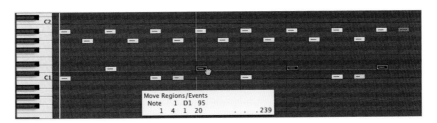

The first snare note is now 8 ticks later, and the three remaining snare notes are 20 ticks later.

Your groove already has a more laid-back feel. The difference in feel between the quantized snare and the new, laid-back snare is subtle, so let's compare the two.

Comparing the Quantized and Laid-Back Patterns

To compare the feel of the original quantized and the laid-back patterns, you are going to toggle the Quantize parameter on and off in the Inspector's Region Parameter box. In the current pattern, the fastest notes are the eighth notes in the hi-hats. So, eighth note is the quantization value you should choose for the region.

The Region Parameter box displays the parameters of the selected region, so make sure that the Ultrabeat region is selected. The name of the region, Ultrabeat, should appear at the top of the Region Parameter box.

1   In the Inspector's Region Parameter box, set the Ultrabeat's region Quantize parameter to 1/8-Note.

In the Piano Roll Editor, all four snare notes snap to the grid.

2   Press the Spacebar to start playback, if necessary.

You are listening to the rigid groove, with the snare sounding right on the grid.

3   Choose Edit > Undo Parameter Change (or press Command-Z).

The Quantize parameter turns off, and the snare notes jump off the grid. You now are listening to the laid-back groove you created.

4   Choose Edit > Redo Parameter Change (or press Shift-Command-Z).

The Quantize parameter returns to 1/8-Note.

Keep pressing the Undo and Redo key commands to switch the quantization off and on while listening to the playback. Remember, because the last thing you did with your mouse was to turn the quantization on (by choosing the 1/8-Note value), the keys behave like this:

▶ Undo (Command-Z): The Quantize parameter turns off quantization (and plays the laid-back groove)

▶ Redo (Shift-Command-Z): The Quantize parameter turns on 1/8-Note quantization (and plays the quantized groove)

The difference is subtle, so focus your attention on the timing of the snare. After a while the laid-back groove almost sounds normal, while the rigid groove sounds rushed!

If you still can't hear the difference, you can try dragging the snare notes further off the grid to make the effect more obvious. You can also turn on the metronome to listen to the snare against the metronome click.

5   In the Transport bar, click the Metronome button.

   NOTE ▶ On smaller displays, the Metronome button may not be visible. To access it, click the chevron (>>) in the Transport bar and select Click from the pop-up menu.

6   Set Quantize to 1/8-Note.

You are listening to the rigid groove, and the snare plays precisely on the grid, as do the metronome clicks. In fact, the snare sound overlaps the sound of the metronome, and it almost sounds like the metronome is not playing when the snare is playing.

7   Set Quantize to Off.

You are listening to the laid-back groove, and the snare is a little off the grid. If you focus your attention on the metronome and the snare, you can hear them *flam*; that is, they hit almost, but not quite, at the same time.

While the difference is subtle, this is the kind of detail that can breathe life into drum programming, so experiment with different amounts of delay for the snare until you get the feel you want.

Randomizing Timing

Now let's humanize the hi-hat. This time you will use Logic's Humanize function to randomize the position of the hi-hat notes by a small amount.

1   In the Piano Roll Editor, click the black key in front of the half-open hi-hat notes.

All half-open hi-hat notes are selected in that lane.

2   Shift-click the black key in front of the open hi-hats.

All open hi-hat notes in that lane are added to the selection.

3   In the Piano Roll Editor's local menu bar, choose Functions > Transform > Humanize.

The Transform window opens with the Humanize preset selected.

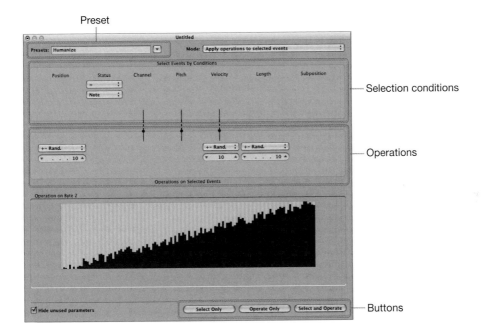

In the Transform window, you can select MIDI events based on a set of conditions (in the "Select Events by Conditions" area), and then transform those MIDI events (according to operations defined in the "Operations on Selected Events" area).

You then execute your choices by clicking one of the three buttons at the bottom of the window:

▶ Select Only (executing the settings in Select Events by Conditions)

▶ Operate Only (executing the settings in Operations on Selected Events)

▶ Select and Operate (executing both sets of settings)

In this case, you've already selected the hi-hat notes in the Piano Roll Editor, and all you need to do is randomize their positions, so you will later click the Operate Only button. But first, look at the Operations on Selected Events area in the Humanize preset. From left to right, you can see that the operations are:

▶ Randomize the positions of notes by ±10 ticks.

▶ Randomize their velocities by ±10 values.

▶ Randomize their lengths by ±10 ticks.

In this case, you want to randomize only the positions of the hi-hat notes, leaving their velocities and lengths unchanged.

4   Click the Velocity pop-up menu and choose Thru.

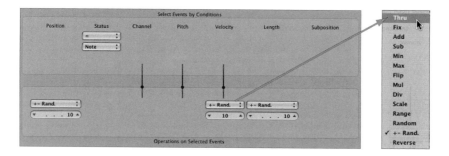

The menu disappears, indicating that no operation will be carried out on the note velocity.

NOTE ▶ At the bottom of the Transform window, the *Operation on Byte 2* graphic map area also disappears. The map area can be used to exercise advanced control over the operation carried out on MIDI events.

5   Click the Length pop-up menu and choose Thru.

That menu also disappears.

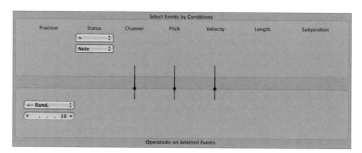

The only remaining operation is randomizing the note positions by ±10 ticks, which is what you wanted.

6   At the bottom of the Transform window, click Operate Only.

The selected hi-hat note positions are randomized and you can see them jump slightly off the grid in the Piano Roll Editor. You can also see the positions being altered randomly in the Event List.

Listen to the hi-hat. Since the operation is random, you may or may not hear or like it!

7 Keep playing the song and, in the Transform window, click Operate Only a few times, listening to the results each time you click.

Every time you click Operate Only, the hi-hat note positions are randomized again. Don't hesitate to click Operate Only quite a few times to really hear the effect. If it starts to sound like sloppy drumming, you can always undo the randomization.

8 Choose Edit > Undo Transform (or press Command-Z).

The most recent randomization is undone. You can keep pressing Command-Z to undo more randomization operations, going back in the history of randomization steps.

9 When you're happy with the results, close the Transform window.

10 In the Piano Roll Editor, click the background to deselect all the notes.

This step is important for the next exercise, so make sure that all notes are deselected before you move on.

Now you really have a good rock drum groove going. With careful manipulation of accents, note velocities, note placements, and a little randomization, you have transformed machine-like drum programming into a human-sounding groove.

Creating a Snare Roll Using the Hyper Editor

In the previous lesson, you used the Hyper Editor to draw and edit MIDI CC pan events. You can also use the Hyper Editor to create and edit MIDI note events. Its ability to adjust grid resolution independently for each lane makes the Hyper Editor a great choice for drum programming.

The Hyper Editor allows you to quickly enter many MIDI events at once, drawing them on the grid using the Pencil tool. This makes it easy to quickly draw a snare roll.

Creating a Custom Hyper Set

When you're programming a basic drum pattern, creating your own hyper set with just the MIDI notes you need will make the Hyper Editor easier to navigate.

In this exercise, you will create a custom hyper set that includes an event definition for each drum sound used in the pattern. You will then draw a snare roll using the Pencil tool and adjust velocities using the Line tool.

1   At the bottom of the Piano Roll Editor, click the Hyper Editor button (or press Y).

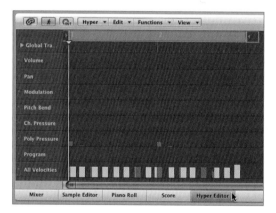

The Hyper Editor opens, and the Inspector updates to show you the Hyper Set menu, a couple of checkboxes, and the Event Definition Parameter box, which displays the parameters of the selected event definition lane.

There are two factory hyper sets in the Hyper Set menu: MIDI Controls, which you used in the previous lesson to add pan automation, and GM Drum Kit, which is used for drum programming.

2   In the Inspector, click the Hyper Set menu and choose GM Drum Kit.

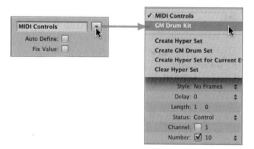

The Hyper Editor now shows event definitions for all the MIDI drum notes defined by the GM (General MIDI) standard.

MORE INFO ▶ The General MIDI standard defines many MIDI events left undefined in the MIDI standard. For example, it defines which sounds a MIDI note should trigger when playing a drum instrument: C1 is a kick drum, D1 is a snare drum, and so on.

3   Place the mouse cursor between the Hyper Editor and the Arrange area, and drag up.

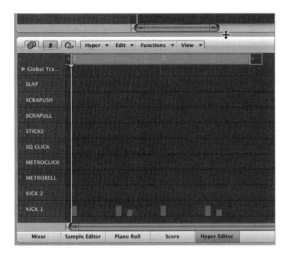

The Hyper Editor is resized and you can see more event definitions.

Scroll vertically to see the whole set of GM drum sounds. When you have numerous event definitions for a variety of drum and percussion sounds that you don't need, the Hyper Editor can be difficult to navigate. Let's create a custom hyper set.

4   In the Inspector, click the Hyper Set menu and choose "Create Hyper Set for Current Events."

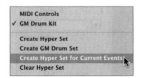

A new hyper set is displayed, called Ultrabeat, the name of the MIDI region. It contains event definitions only for the four drum sounds used in the region, plus an additional event definition, Display off, that corresponds to the accents used earlier in Ultrabeat (the polyphonic pressure events seen in the Event List).

To tidy up the display, you can delete the accent lane, then reorder and name the drum lanes.

5 Click the header of the "Display off" lane.

The lane is selected.

6 Choose Hyper > Delete Event Definition (or press Control-Delete).

The event definition is deleted from the hyper set. The accents events are not deleted from the MIDI region, and they remain visible in the Event List.

Now that you are working with a stripped-down hyper set, zoom in so the four lanes fill the Hyper Editor display.

7 Click the first A♯1 note.

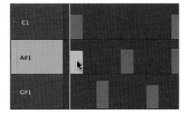

The open hi-hat note is played, and the A♯1 lane is selected. You can click the notes to trigger the sounds and determine which lane corresponds to which instrument, then rename the event definition. Even without clicking the notes, you should be able to visually identify the instruments by remembering their positions on the grid: the open hi-hat plays on every downbeat, the half-open hi-hat on every upbeat.

8 In the Inspector's Event Definition Parameter box, click A♯1.

A text field opens, and you can rename the event definition.

9   In the text field, type *Open HH*.

10   Use the same techniques to rename:

▶   G♯1 to *Half HH*

▶   C1 to *Kick*

▶   D1 to *Snare*

You can drag the Kick lane to the bottom of the Hyper Editor so the drums are in the same order as they are in Ultrabeat's step sequencer.

11   Drag the Kick event definition to the bottom of the window, below the snare.

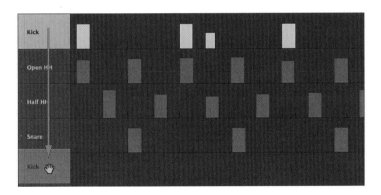

This new custom hyper set is much cleaner looking. You have event definitions only for the four current drum sounds. With the event definitions renamed and reordered, you can tell at a glance which drum sound you are editing.

Drawing a Snare Roll

Now you're ready to draw that snare roll. First, you'll adjust the grid resolution of the snare lane and add a single snare note in the first bar. Then you will draw the snare roll at the end of the second bar.

In the Hyper Editor, the Pencil tool is assigned to the Command-click tool.

1 In the Snare lane, Command-click the grid line just before the second kick.

As in Ultrabeat's step sequencer, the height of the note represents its velocity. When using the Pencil tool, click higher to insert louder notes, or click lower to insert softer notes. You can also drag up and down with the Pencil tool to adjust the velocity of the note as you insert it, and drag with the Pencil or Pointer tool to adjust the velocity of an existing note.

Listen to the pattern. Let's make that snare softer than the other snares.

2 Drag down the new snare note to a lower velocity.

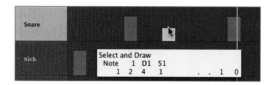

Listen to the pattern. Sounds good.

Drummers don't usually hit the hi-hat in the middle of a snare roll; so, before you add the snare roll at the end of the pattern, you will delete the last hi-hat note.

3 On the Open HH lane, click the last open hi-hat note to select it.

4   Press Delete.

The selected open hi-hat note is deleted.

You're ready to draw a snare roll at the end of the pattern. You first need to increase the resolution of the snare event definition grid so you can draw the fast snare roll.

5   Select the Snare lane.

6   In the Event Definition Parameter box, set the Grid parameter to 1/48-Note.

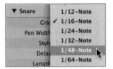

The higher-resolution grid is displayed on the Snare lane.

You will now adjust the pen width on the snare lane to make the vertical bars representing the snare notes visually narrower, making it easier to see each step on the finer grid resolution.

7   Set the Pen Width parameter to 2.

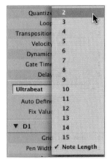

The vertical bars on the snare lane are now narrower, and you can see all the grid lines. In the Event List, note that the MIDI events represented by the vertical bars are unchanged, and the snare notes still have the same length.

You should shorten the new snare note lengths so that the notes don't overlap when you look at them later in the Piano Roll Editor.

8   Double-click the Length parameter and enter *20* to change the note length to 20 ticks.

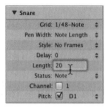

Now you can draw the snare roll.

9   Zoom in on the area after the last snare.

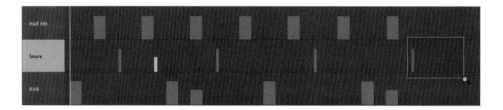

10   After the last snare, drag the Pencil tool to draw the snare roll, ending the roll just before the end of the region (indicated in the bar ruler by the cycle area).

You can adjust the vertical position of the Pencil tool as you drag it to create notes of different velocities and generate decrescendos and crescendos.

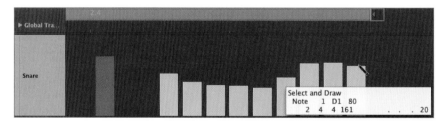

You can now use the Line tool to create a perfect crescendo.

11   Press Esc and choose the Line tool.

12   Hold down the Line tool and place it just before the first note in the snare roll, watching the help tag to ensure that the velocity is at 35.

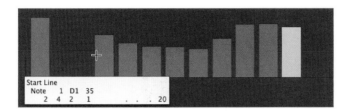

13 Release the mouse button, and position the cursor just after the last note of the snare roll, so that the velocity reads 100 in the help tag.

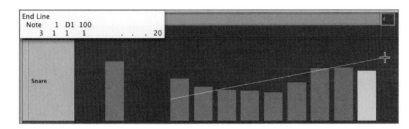

14 Click to end the line.

The note heights are adjusted to the green line, forming a perfect crescendo.

Listen to the pattern. The snare roll is a little loud. Scroll to the end of the pattern to examine the snare roll. All the notes from the roll are still selected. You will lower the velocities of the whole selection using the Pointer tool.

15 Press Esc twice.

16 Drag the last note down to a velocity of 79.

The velocities of all the selected notes are lowered. Listen to the drum pattern. If the snare roll starts a little too early, you can delete the first few notes of the snare roll.

17 Click in the background of the Hyper Editor to deselect all the notes.

18 Shift-drag the Pencil tool over the first couple of notes you want to delete to select them.

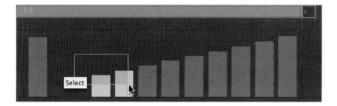

19 Press Delete.

20 In the Arrange area, make sure the Ultrabeat region is still selected, and at the bottom of the editing area, click the Piano Roll button (or press P).

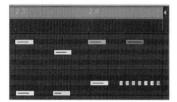

You can see the snare roll on the right. Imagine creating the snare roll in the Piano Roll Editor, one note at a time, and you will understand how powerful the Hyper Editor can be for that kind of job.

With the snare roll still selected, take a couple of minutes to open the Transform window's Humanize preset and randomize the velocities and the positions of the selected snare notes to humanize the snare roll.

Programming drums is a skill that requires you to use your ears, not just to create the pattern, but also to add the little nuances that make the difference between a machinelike drum pattern and a drum pattern that will fool the listeners into thinking a real drummer performed the part. Listen to live drummers, or recordings of live drummers, and focus on the dynamic variations, the use of accents to create the groove, and the timing of the snare and hi-hat. Then, use the tools and techniques you have learned in this lesson to incorporate those dynamic and timing subtleties into your drum programming.

Lesson Review

1. Name the three main sections of the Ultrabeat interface.

2. In Ultrabeat, what sounds are triggered by which MIDI notes?

3. How do you insert a note on every downbeat?

4. How can you add accents to a pattern?

5. How can you add accents at different positions for different drum sounds?

6. In Ultrabeat, how can you randomize a sound's note velocities?

7. How can you view an Ultrabeat pattern as a MIDI region in the Arrange area?

8. In the Piano Roll Editor, how can you deselect a single note from a multiple note selection?

9. In what window do you randomize note positions, and how can you open that window?

10. What editor is the best choice for creating a snare roll?

11. How do you create a custom hyper set containing event definitions only for the existing notes in the region?

Answers

1. The Assignment section, the Synthesiszer section, and the step sequencer.

2. Notes C1 through B2 play the 24 drum sounds; C3 and above play the bass sound chromatically.

3. Control-click the full view grid, and choose Add Every Downbeat from the shortcut menu.

4. By selecting steps in the accent row.

5. You can't. Accent positions are the same for all sounds. You can turn the accents on and off for individual sounds using the accent switch.

6. Control-click the step sequencer and, from the shortcut menu, choose Alter Vel.

7. Drag the Pattern button to the Arrange area.

8. Shift-click the note you want to deselect.

9. The Transform window. You access it in the Piano Roll Editor's local menu bar by choosing Functions > Transform > Humanize.

10. The Hyper Editor.

11. Make sure that all notes are deselected inside the region and, from the Hyper Set menu, choose Create Hyper Set for Current Events.

7

Lesson Files   Logic 8_Files > Lessons > 07 New Day_start

Media   Logic 8_Files > Media > New Day > Audio Files

Logic 8_Files > Media > Additional Media

Time   This lesson takes approximately 45 minutes to complete.

Goals   Match a project tempo to an audio file's tempo

Use and customize the Loop Browser

Create Apple Loops

Make an audio region follow the project tempo

Insert tempo changes and tempo curves

Time stretch an audio region to match the project tempo

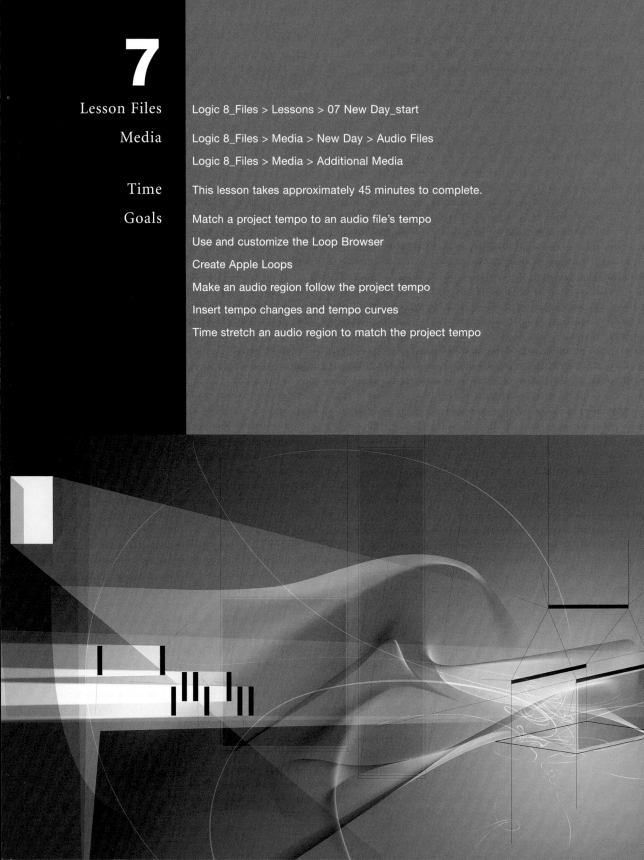

Manipulating Tempo and Time Stretching

Modern music genres have seen the use of loops and samples increase exponentially over the last few years. New technologies encourage experimentation, and it is more and more common to find, say, a sample of a Middle Eastern instrument in a modern rock song, a sample of classical music in a pop song, or a sample of a pop song in a hip-hop track.

Mixing pre-recorded material into a project can lead to exciting results, but the material must be carefully selected to ensure that it seamlessly blends into the project. The first challenge is to match the tempo of the pre-recorded musical material and the tempo of a project.

In this lesson, you will import an audio file into a new project, changing the project tempo to match the audio file's tempo. You will work with the Loop Browser to add Apple Loops to the project, customize the Loop Browser to suit your needs, and create your own Apple Loops. Finally, you will manipulate an existing project's tempo and use different techniques to make audio files match the project's tempo.

Matching the Project Tempo to an Audio Region's Tempo

Sometimes you start a new project with pre-recorded material and want to use the tempo of that material for the new project. For example, you find a drum loop that you like because of the way it grooves at its original tempo. You need to adjust the project tempo to match that loop. When the project tempo matches the loop, you can use the grid to edit regions, program and quantize MIDI regions, or add Apple Loops while keeping everything synchronized with the pre-recorded drum loop.

In Lesson 3, you selected a two-bar drum pattern from a drum recording and edited it to loop perfectly in the Arrange area. In the next exercise, you will import that two-bar audio file into a new project and adjust the project tempo so that it matches the tempo of the audio file.

1 Choose File > New (or press Command-N).

2 In the Templates dialog, click the Empty Project template.

3 Create a stereo audio track, and select Open Library.

4 In the Media area, click the Browser tab.

5 At the top of the Browser, click the Home button.

All the folders contained in your home folder are displayed in the Browser.

6 Click the Browser View button.

7 In the left column, click the Desktop folder.

The contents of your desktop appear in the right column.

8   Navigate to Logic 8_Files > Media > Additional Media.

Locate the file named **My Rock Drums Loop.aif**.

When you double-click an audio file in the Browser, an audio region is created on the selected track at the playhead position. Make sure that the playhead is placed at the beginning of the project.

9   Double-click **My Rock Drums Loop.aif**.

The audio file is imported into the project and an audio region representing the entire audio file is inserted on the selected track, at the beginning of the project.

10   In the Arrange area, click the My Rock Drums Loop region to give the area key focus, and press L to loop the region.

On the Arrange area's grid, you can see that the loop repeats don't fall on downbeats. You can use the metronome to compare the project tempo to the audio file's tempo.

11   In the Transport bar, click the Metronome button.

12   In the Arrange area, start playback.

You can immediately tell that the drum loop is out of sync with the project.

Before you can adjust the project tempo, you need to create a cycle area of the length that you want your audio file to match when the tempo is adjusted. My Rock Drums Loop is a two-bar audio file, so you need to create a two-bar cycle area.

13   In the Bar ruler, click the cycle area.

Cycle mode turns on.

14   Adjust the cycle area so it is two bars long.

Now you will instruct Logic to automatically calculate the new project tempo so that the cycle area's length matches the selected region's length.

15 Make sure that the region is still selected and, in the main menu bar, choose Options > Tempo > Adjust Tempo using Region Length and Locators (or press Command-T).

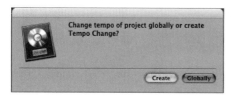

An alert message appears asking whether you want to create a tempo change, or change the global tempo of the project. In this exercise, you want to change the tempo for the entire project.

16 Click Globally.

The project tempo is adjusted to 90.6733 bpm, and the My Rock Drums Loop region is exactly two bars at the new tempo.

17 Listen to the project.

The project tempo now matches the tempo of the audio file that you just imported, and the metronome now plays in time with the drums.

18 Turn off the metronome.

You have matched the project's tempo to the audio file's tempo, and now you can start building the project using the grid. You can also add Apple Loops, and they will now automatically play in sync with your drums.

Working with Apple Loops

Apple Loops are AIFF or CAF format audio files containing additional information that allows them to automatically match the tempo and key of a Logic project. They also contain descriptive information—including instrument, genre, mood, and scale—that helps you search large libraries of Apple Loops using the Loop Browser.

> **MORE INFO** ▶ Apple Loops are also supported by the GarageBand and Soundtrack Pro applications. When Apple Loops are imported into an application that does not support them, they behave like regular AIFF audio files.

Using the Loop Browser

You were introduced to the Loop Browser in Lesson 1, when you previewed and chose loops to create a project. Now, you'll take a closer look at the Loop Browser.

1   In the Media area, click the Loops tab.

The Loop Browser opens. You are going to search for a major-scale acoustic guitar loop in the pop genre.

At the top of the Loop Browser, three menus—View, Signature, and Scale—allow you to filter searches of Apple Loops by collection (Jam Pack, GarageBand, or other), time signature, and type of scale (minor or major).

2   In the Scale menu, choose Major.

This will filter your next search to display only loops that work with a major scale. The Loop Browser needs a little more information and doesn't display any results yet.

At the upper right of the Loop Browser, you can choose one of three views: Column, Music, or Sound Effects. Each view enables a different way to filter the loops as they are organized in the Search Results list.

Music view

Column view | Sound Effects view

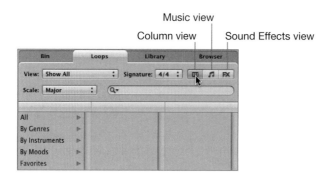

3 Click the Column View button.

While the Music and Sound Effects views display only a selection of category buttons, the Column view lets you access all the existing descriptors: By Genres, By Instruments, and By Moods.

4 Choose By Instruments > Acoustic Guitar > Acousti...ar (229) (the last category, *Acoustic Guitar (229)* is abbreviated).

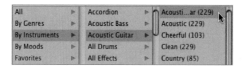

The number in parentheses (229) represents the number of results that match your search and may be different depending on the number of loops installed on your computer. The 229 major-scale acoustic guitar loops are displayed in the Search Results list at the bottom of the Loop Browser.

At the top of the Loop Browser, you can enter text in the search field and further filter the search results to display only the loops containing the search text in their names.

5 In the search field, type *pop* and press Enter.

The Search Results list now shows the 17 major-scale acoustic guitar loops that have *pop* in their names.

6 Click **Alt Pop Acoustic 01**.

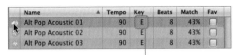

Original loop key

The loop starts playing. It sounds like a detuned acoustic guitar, and you may hear some weird artifacts. In fact, in the Key column, you can see the loop's original key. This loop was performed in E major. When previewing a loop, it is transposed to match the key of the project (the default key signature for a project is C major—you will change the project's key signature in the next exercise). The further the playback key and tempo are from the loop's original key and tempo, the more artifacts are introduced.

At the bottom of the Loop Browser, the preview settings let you adjust the volume and key at which you preview the loops.

7   In the "Play in" pop-up menu, choose C♯.

The loop plays in C♯, one semitone higher than the project's default key.

8   In the "Play in" pop-up menu, choose Original Key.

The loop plays in its original key, E major. It now sounds like an acoustic guitar playing in a regular tuning, and the artifacts disappear.

9   Drag Alt Pop Acoustic 01 to bar 1, below the existing track in the Arrange area.

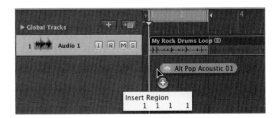

A new audio track is created, and the Alt Pop Acoustic 01 loop is inserted at bar 1.

10 Turn off Cycle mode and listen to the project.

The loop plays in the project's key, C major. In the next exercise, you will change the project's key to make that loop sound better.

Setting the Project's Key Signature

In the previous exercise, you noticed that a loop sounds more natural when it is played in its original key. It sounds closer to the sound of a regularly tuned instrument and, since there is no transposition to process, you hear fewer artifacts. It is usually preferable to choose Apple Loops with original keys and tempos that are closest to the project's key signature and tempo to reduce the amount of processing necessary to match the loops to the project, thereby reducing audible artifacts.

Let's change the key of the project to E major, the original key of the acoustic guitar.

1 In the Arrange area, make sure the Alt Pop Acoustic 01 region is still selected and press L.

The acoustic guitar region is looped throughout the project.

2 Start playback.

The loop plays in C major, the key of the project.

3 Stop playback.

To change the project's key signature you need to access the global Signature track.

4 At the top left of the Arrange area, click the Global Tracks disclosure triangle.

Project key signature

The global Marker, Signature, and Tempo tracks are displayed. In the global Signature track you can see the time signature (4/4) and the key signature (C).

5   Double-click the key signature (C).

The Key Signature window opens.

6   In the Key pop-up menu, choose E. Keep Major selected.

7   Click OK (or press Enter).

On the global Signature track, the new key signature is *E*.

8   Listen to the project.

The loop plays in the new key signature, E major. It now sounds much more natural, and matches the drums quite well.

You used the global Signature track to set the key of your project, making sure that all Apple Loops in the project will now play at the new project key. If you want to go further and create an arrangement using Apple Loops, you can also insert key signature changes on the Signature track to build a chord progression, and all Apple Loops will change key according to the Signature track.

Customizing the Loop Browser

In the Loop Browser, the Music and Sound Effects views show only a selection of category buttons. However, you can customize the button arrangement and the category that each button displays. When previewing loops, you can mark the loops you like as favorites to access them more quickly later.

1   In the Loop Browser, click the Music view button.

The Music category buttons are displayed. In the first row, the buttons are Acoustic, Bass, and All Drums. Let's assume you work mainly with vocal loops. First, you will move the Vocals button currently located at the bottom right to the top of the view, swapping its position with the Acoustic button.

2   Drag the Vocals button to the Acoustic button at the top of the view.

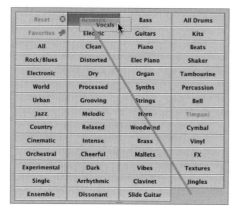

NOTE ▸ If you can't see the Vocals button, drag down the two small horizontal lines between the buttons area and the search result list to expand the buttons area.

The two buttons exchange positions.

Now you'll customize the second and third buttons to display categories not currently visible in Music View.

3   Control-click the Bass button.

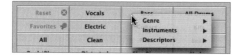

A shortcut menu appears allowing you to choose any available category, as in the Column view.

4   Choose Instruments > Vocals > Male.

The button now shows the Male descriptor.

5   Control-click the All Drums button and choose Instruments > Vocals > Female.

Your three top buttons are now Vocals, Male, and Female. You can use them to browse vocal loops.

6   In the Scale menu, choose Any.

7   Click the Female button.

All female voice loops are displayed in the Search Results list.

8   Preview the loops and find one that you like.

When searching for the perfect loop for a project, you can spend a considerable amount of time previewing loops. Often, you may find loops that you like but then decide that they won't work with the project at hand. Instead of just moving to the next loop and forgetting about those loops, you can mark them as favorites.

9   Select the Fav checkbox for the loop you like.

	Name	▲	Tempo	Key	Beats	Match	Fav
	Brazilian Sun Voice 01		115	E	16	95%	☐
	Brazilian Sun Voice 02		115	E	16	95%	☐
	Eastern Gold Voice 01		85	C	8	38%	☐
	Eastern Gold Voice 02		85	C	4	37%	☐
	Eastern Gold Voice 03		85	C	4	37%	☑
	Eastern Gold Voice 04		85	C	8	38%	☐

If there are other loops you like, mark them as favorites, too.

Now you can access all the loops you have marked as favorites.

10 At the upper left of the category buttons, click the Reset button.

All search terms are reset and the Search Results list is emptied.

11 Click the Favorites button.

	Name	▲	Tempo	Key	Beats	Match	Fav
	Eastern Gold Voice 03		85	C	4	37%	☑

All your favorite loops are displayed.

After you customize the top category buttons to suit your needs, you may not need to display so many category buttons, and you can resize the buttons area to see more loops in the Search Results list.

12 Drag up the two small horizontal lines between the buttons area and the Search Results list.

The buttons area is smaller, making the Search Results list taller; and, at the bottom right of the buttons area, a new button with the >> icon allows you to access the hidden buttons.

In the next exercises, you will open a new project, so you need to save this project.

13 Choose File > Save (or press Command-S) to save the project to the desktop, naming it *Pop Song.*

By now you should understand the power and flexibility of Apple Loops. They will automatically match the tempos and key signatures of a project. You will now create your own blue and green Apple Loops.

Creating Blue Apple Loops

When you are using audio regions to create Apple Loops, you are creating blue Apple Loops. Blue Apple Loops can be used only as audio regions on audio tracks.

In the following exercise, you will open an existing project you worked on in earlier lessons, New Day, while keeping the current project open. You will create Apple Loops using material from New Day, and then return to the current project to preview and use the new Apple Loops.

1 Keep the current project open, and open Logic 8_Files > Lessons > **07 New Day_start**.

An alert appears, asking you whether to close the current project.

2   Click Don't Close.

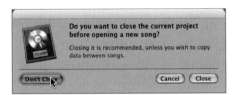

07 New Day_start opens, and the current project stays open in the background.

TIP ▶ If the new project's Arrange window does not fill the screen, you can click the window's zoom button, the third button from the left of the title bar, to make the window full screen.

Feel free to listen to New Day if you need to refresh your memory. You will now use the Marquee tool to cut the two first bars of the High Arpeggio guitar region, and turn that two-bar arpeggio into a blue Apple Loops file. The Marquee tool is your current Command-click tool.

3   Drag the Marquee tool over the High Arpeggio region from bar 5 to bar 7.

If you want, you can solo the Acoustic track and press the Spacebar to preview the Marquee selection.

4   Click the Marquee selection with the Pointer tool.

The marquee selection is divided into a new region, and the new region is selected. You will now turn that new two-bar audio region into a blue Apple Loops file.

5   In the Arrange area's local menu bar, choose Region > Add to Apple Loops Library.

The Add Region to Apple Loops Library dialog appears. All the information you enter in this window will be used by the Loop Browser to index the loop. It is the same information you will use to search for that loop in the Loop Browser.

Enter or choose the following information:

► Name: *High Arpeggio*

► Type: *Loop*

► Scale: *Minor*

► Genre: *Rock/Blues*

► Instrument Descriptors: Guitars > Acoustic Guitar

Click the tags Single, Clean, Acoustic, Relaxed, Dark, Dry, Grooving, Melodic, and Part.

MORE INFO ▶ Using Region > Add to Apple Loops Library, you can create blue Apple Loops only when the number of bars in a selected region is a whole integer. This function uses the project tempo to tag the transient positions and works best for audio files that match the project tempo. If the selected region length is not an integer, the Type parameter will be set to One-shot and dimmed.

To create blue Apple Loops with material that does not match the current project tempo, and to see a more refined transient analysis of your audio file, choose Audio > Open in Apple Loops Utility and use the Apple Loops Utility, as explained in *Logic Pro: Beyond the Basics* by David Dvorin.

6 Click Create (or press Enter).

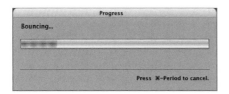

A Progress indicator shows that the audio region is bounced as a new audio file.

A second Progress indicator shows that the loop is indexed in the Loop Browser. Be patient. This process can take some time, depending upon the number of loops present on your system.

When the second Progress window closes, your Apple Loops file has been created and indexed and is available in the Loop Browser. You can now access it from any project as you can any other Apple Loops file.

7 In the Media area, click the Loops tab.

8 At the top of the Loop Browser, in the search field, type *High Arpeggio* and press Enter.

Your new acoustic guitar loop is displayed in the search results. You can click it to preview it, and play it in different keys using the "Play in" menu at the lower right of the Loop Browser.

You will now mark High Arpeggio as a favorite so that you can easily find it when you need it later in this lesson.

9   Select the Fav checkbox for High Arpeggio.

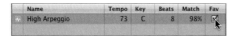

In the Arrange area, you will now heal the High Arpeggio region.

10   From the main menu bar, choose Edit > Undo Split Regions (or press Command-Z).

In the Arrange area, the High Arpeggio regions are healed back to a single region.

11   In the Arrange area, click the background to undo the marquee selection.

You have created a blue Apple Loops file from a portion of an audio region, and restored the project to its original state so that you can continue to work in it later in this lesson.

Creating Green Apple Loops

When you use MIDI regions on a software instrument track to create Apple Loops, you are creating green Apple Loops. Like the blue loops, the green Apple Loops are AIFF or CAF audio files that can be used as audio regions on an audio track; but they also contain the original MIDI region and software instrument channel strip settings that were used to create them, so you can also use them as MIDI regions on software instrument tracks.

You will use the same process as in the previous exercise to create a green Apple Loops file using the High Pitch Synth on track 8.

1   In the Arrange area, select the High Pitch Synth region on track 8, at bar 15.

2 In the Arrange area's local menu bar, choose Region > Add to Apple Loops Library.

The Add Region to Apple Loops Library dialog appears.

Enter or choose the following information:

▶ Name: *High Pitch Synth*

▶ Type: *Loop*

▶ Scale: *Minor*

▶ Genre: *Electronic*

▶ Instrument Descriptors: Keyboards > Synths

Click the tags Single, Distorted, Electric, Intense, Dark, Processed, Grooving, Melodic, and Part.

3 Click Create (or press Enter).

Wait for the two Progress windows to disappear, indicating that your Apple Loops file has been created and indexed in the Loop Browser. You will use that loop in the next exercise.

Using the New Apple Loops in Another Project

You will now switch to the Pop Song project you were working on before you opened New Day, use the Loop Browser to find your new Apple Loops, and add one of them to the project.

1 From the main menu bar, choose Window > Pop Song – Arrange (at the bottom of the Window menu).

Now preview your new High Arpeggio Apple Loops file in the Loop Browser. The Loop Browser is currently displaying your favorites, but you may have to refresh it to see the loop you just marked as a favorite.

2 Click the Favorites button to disable it, then click it again to enable it.

The list of favorites is refreshed, and you should now see your High Arpeggio loop.

3 At the bottom of the Loop Browser, in the "Play in" pop-up menu, choose Song Key.

4 Start playing the project.

5 In the Loop Browser, click the High Arpeggio loop to preview it while the song is playing.

High Arpeggio plays in E (the project's key). However, the loop was performed in a minor key and doesn't work well with the major acoustic guitar loop. Let's try the High Pitch Synth green loop.

6 In the Loop Browser, resize the buttons area to see all the category buttons.

7 Click the Reset button to clear your current search.

8 Click the following category buttons:

▶ Distorted

▶ Electronic

▶ Melodic

▶ Dark

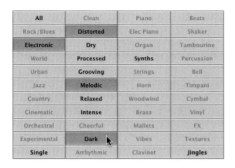

A few loops appear in the Search Results list, including your new green Apple Loops file, **High Pitch Synth**.

9   Click your loop to preview it along with the project.

If necessary, adjust the volume slider at the bottom of the Loops browser to hear the High Pitch Synth loop. That loop works pretty well.

10   Stop playback.

11   Drag High Pitch Synth to bar 1 in the Arrange area, below track 2.

A new software instrument track is created, the loop's channel strip setting is loaded, and the loop's MIDI region is inserted on the new track.

12   Select the new software instrument track header (track 3), and in the Inspector, reduce the Arrange channel strip fader level to −17(dB).

13   Press L to loop the High Pitch Synth region.

14   Start playback.

The new loop adds an interesting sound to the song, but its rhythm doesn't work well with the drum groove. However, green Apple Loops have a big advantage over blue loops: when you insert a green loop into a software instrument track, you can still edit the MIDI region or tweak the channel strip setting. In this case, you could use that new software instrument channel strip settings, and program or record a new MIDI region that works better with the song.

15 Save the Pop Song project and close it.

The project closes, and you can see the New Day project again. You will work in New Day for the remainder of this lesson, so keep it open.

Remember the distinction between blue and green Apple Loops when you preview loops in the Loop Browser. When you like the sound of a green loop, you can add it to your project just to use the software instrument channel strip setting. Then, delete the MIDI region and record or program your own MIDI region. (That's a good way to preview channel strip settings without loading them.) In contrast, if you like the melodic or the rhythmic pattern played by a green loop, you can add it to the Arrange area and keep only the MIDI region, using another software instrument channel strip setting.

Making Audio Files Follow the Project Tempo

When producing a song, choosing a tempo is usually one of the first decisions you make, before you do any audio recording. When a tempo is set, you can start building the project, record audio files, and match any imported audio to the project's tempo.

However, in some cases you might decide late in the process that you want to experiment with the tempo. Maybe you realize that the song was produced too slow and it needs a little speed bump. Or maybe you want to add tempo nuances and have certain sections subtly speed up or slow down.

While all MIDI regions and Apple Loops will automatically follow any tempo changes or variations you place in your project, audio recordings won't follow along unless you force them to do so. When an audio file is played in the same project in which it was recorded, you can use Logic's Follow Tempo feature. The audio file is loaded into RAM and automatically matched to the project tempo.

1 In the Transport bar, double-click the Tempo display, type *77*, and press Enter.

2   Go to the beginning and start playback.

During the introduction, the drums and bass Apple Loops play at the new tempo. As soon as the playhead reaches bar 5, you can hear the acoustic guitar still playing at the old tempo, out of sync with the project.

3   Stop playback and click the Acoustic track header.

All the acoustic guitar regions are selected.

Notice that the Inspector's Region Parameter box now reads "4 selected." Adjusting parameters in the Region Parameter box will adjust the same parameters for all four selected regions.

4   In the Region Parameter box, select the Follow Tempo checkbox.

The selected audio regions' lengths are adjusted, and the icon next to each region's name turns into a double arrow, indicating that the regions now follow the project tempo.

You can't apply fades or crossfades to a region that follows tempo, so the fades disappear.

5   Start playback.

This time the acoustic guitar regions match the tempo of the project, and everything is in sync.

Depending on the type of audio material and the difference between the audio file's original tempo and the project's tempo, you may hear artifacts when using the Follow Tempo function. But even if you have to record some parts again, Follow Tempo is a useful feature for experimenting with tempos. For example, the guitar player may already have recorded his parts, but the vocalist feels the song was recorded too slowly. Instead of waiting until the guitarist can get back into the recording studio, set the guitar recordings to follow tempo, increase the song tempo, record the vocals, and later record the guitar player at the new tempo.

Inserting Tempo Changes and Curves

When you want to vary the tempo throughout a project, you can use the global Tempo track to insert tempo changes and tempo curves. All MIDI regions, Apple Loops, and audio regions that are set to follow tempo will automatically follow the project tempo, even when tempo variations occur in the middle of regions.

1   At the upper left of the Arrange area, click the Global Tracks disclosure triangle.

    The global Marker, Signature, and Tempo tracks are displayed.

2   Click the global Tempo track disclosure triangle.

The Tempo track expands vertically. The Tempo track displays tempo changes as nodes. Lines connect the nodes, similar to the Hyper Draw automation of MIDI controllers that you explored in Lesson 5. Right now, because the entire project plays at one tempo, only one node is placed at the beginning of the project, and one horizontal line follows that node. You can see the tempo value displayed next to the node (77 bpm).

In the Tempo track header, you can choose up to nine Alternative tempo maps. Let's leave Alternative 1 set to 77 bpm, and choose Alternative 2. This will allow you to experiment with tempo changes in Alternative 2 while leaving Alternative 1 available at the original tempo if you are not happy with the new results.

3   In the Tempo track header, click the Alternative menu and choose 2.

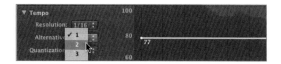

Tempo Alternative 2 is displayed, and the whole project is set to the default 120 bpm tempo. (Try playing the song at 120 bpm if you want a good laugh.)

You'll continue by adjusting the tempo to 71 bpm.

4   In the Tempo track, position your mouse pointer over the tempo line.

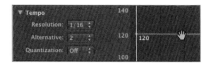

The mouse pointer turns into the Hand tool, indicating that you can move the line.

5   Drag the line down to 71 bpm.

Even though the line has to be dragged below the bottom of the Tempo track and seems to disappear, keep dragging down and watch the help tag to set the tempo to 71.

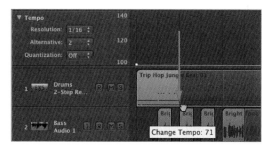

When you release the mouse button, the scale in the Tempo track header readjusts and the line is visible again, with the new value (71 bpm) visible next to the node.

Now insert a tempo change on bar 5.

6 At bar 5, double-click slightly below the tempo line.

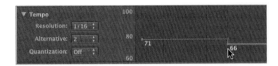

A new node is inserted at bar 5, and you can see the value of the new tempo displayed next to the node. Adjust the new tempo to 69 bpm.

7 To the right of bar 5, drag the new line vertically to a value of 69.

When you know that you are not going to use tempos outside a certain range, you can adjust the vertical scale of the Tempo track to make it visually easier to edit tempos within that range. In this song, you won't use tempos faster than 80 bpm or slower than 60 bpm.

8 In the Tempo track header, drag the maximum value (100) down to 80.

9 Drag the minimum value up to 60.

The new tempo scale ranges from 60 bpm to 80 bpm.

You will now create an accelerando during the first electric piano and acoustic guitar section. The goal is to increase the tempo slowly from 69 bpm to 77 bpm. First, you have to insert a tempo change at the end of the section. Use the Pencil tool to do so. It lets you insert a tempo change and adjust its value in one operation.

10 Press Esc and, from the Tool menu, choose the Pencil tool.

11 At bar 9, drag the Pencil tool vertically so the tempo in the help tag reads 77.

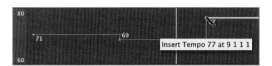

To create a tempo curve between two nodes, you need to drag the deep blue node located above or below the second node.

12 At bar 9, drag the deep blue node below the new 77 bpm tempo change, and then drag it toward the left and up.

 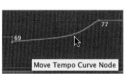

You can precisely adjust the tempo curve by dragging the node farther to the left, farther up, or both.

13 Go to the beginning of the song and start playback.

The whole project follows the new tempo map. Depending on the Apple Loops you are using or the type of audio recordings that follow the tempo, your results may vary. Here again, drastic tempo variations may create artifacts, so let your ear be the judge. Note that percussive material usually reacts better to tempo variations than melodic and harmonic material.

If you are not happy with your tempo experimentations, you can now revert to the first tempo alternative.

14 In the Tempo track header, click the Alternative menu and choose 1.

The first tempo alternative (a single tempo at 77 bpm throughout the project) is displayed in the Tempo track. The song actually sounded better at its original tempo, 73 bpm.

15 Press Esc twice to revert the left-click tool back to the Pointer tool.

16 Drag the tempo line down to 73 bpm.

17 Press Esc twice to revert the left-click tool to the Pointer tool.

18 Close the global tracks (or press G).

Time Stretching an Audio Region

In the first exercise, you used a drum audio file at its original tempo and matched the project's tempo to the tempo of the drum region. That's useful when you use pre-recorded material in a new project. But what if you wanted to add that drum loop to an existing project? Most of the time, you want to keep the original project tempo and adjust the loop tempo to match the project.

While Apple Loops automatically match the project tempo when you import them, other audio files always play at their original tempos. You have to time stretch an audio file to make it match the project tempo.

In this exercise, you will import the same drum audio file, and time stretch it to match the tempo of the project.

1   In the Arrange area, select the last track (track 8) and create a new stereo audio track.

The new stereo audio track is created in the Arrange area, below the selected track.

You will import the drum audio file to that new track using the Browser, and use it for the end section of the song that starts on bar 15. Since double-clicking a file in the Browser inserts a region on the selected track at the playhead position, you need to position the playhead on bar 15.

2   On your main keypad, press / (slash), the Go to Position command. In the Go To Position dialog, type *15*, and press Enter.

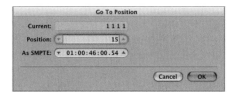

The playhead moves to bar 15.

3   In the Media area, click the Browser tab.

4   In the Browser, click the Project button.

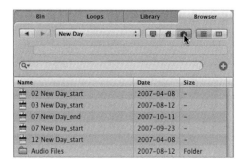

The Browser displays the contents of the New Day project folder.

5   Double-click the Audio Files folder.

You can see the project's audio files and the file **My Rock Drums Loop.aif** you saved in Lesson 3.

NOTE ▶ If you didn't save My Rock Drums Loop in Lesson 3, go to Logic 8_Files > Media > Additional Media, and you will find an equivalent **My Rock Drums Loop.aif** file to use.

6   Double-click **My Rock DrumsLoop.aif**.

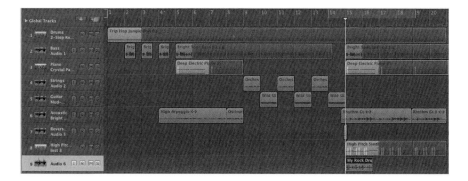

The My Rock Drums loop is inserted on the selected track, at bar 15. When working with audio files it's a good idea to open the Audio Bin to keep track of the audio files added to the project.

7   In the Media area, click the Bin tab.

You can see **My Rock Drums Loop.aif** in the project's Audio Bin.

8   Listen to the project starting at the current playhead position, bar 15.

The new drum audio region plays too fast. To get the best results when time stretch-ing an audio region, select the best time-stretching algorithm for the type of material to process before you time stretch the region.

9   In the Arrange area's local menu bar, choose Audio > Time Machine Algorithm > Percussive.

MORE INFO ▸ You can also purchase high-quality time-stretching algorithms like iZotope Radius or Serato Pitch 'n Time. When they are installed on your computer, those algorithms can be accessed from the same menu.

You will now time stretch the My Rock Drums Loop region to make it exactly two bars long. To time stretch a region, hold down Option as you resize the region.

TIP▸ You can time stretch MIDI regions using the same technique.

You may want to zoom in on the region before time stretching it.

10 Position the mouse pointer over the lower-right corner of the My Rock Drums Loop region.

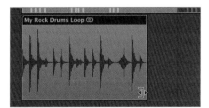

The mouse pointer turns into a Resize pointer.

11 Option-drag the Resize pointer toward the right until the help tag indicates a region length of two bars, 2 0 0 0.

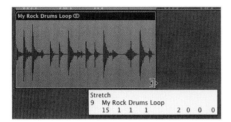

As you Option-drag the Resize pointer, it snaps to the grid, making it easy to stretch the region to exactly two bars. The help tag indicates that you are stretching the region, and you can see the audio waveform inside the region being stretched.

When you release the mouse button, an alert message appears asking you to confirm the operation.

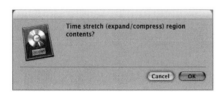

12 Click OK (or press Enter).

Another alert message appears, asking for confirmation that you want to destructively time stretch the audio file **My Rock Drums Loop.1.aif**. Look at the Audio Bin. Logic automatically duplicated the original audio file, and appended *.1* to the copy's filename. Time stretching is a destructive operation, so Logic will perform the time stretch on the copy, leaving the original file unaltered.

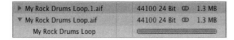

13 Click Process (or press Enter).

Samples to process:233488

At the top of the Arrange area, a help tag appears displaying the number of samples being processed.

When the processing is completed, the region in the Arrange area is replaced with the time-stretched copy, **My Rock Drums Loop.1**.

14 Position the mouse pointer at the upper right of **My Rock Drums Loop.1** to get the Loop tool and drag out two repeats to fill the last section of the song.

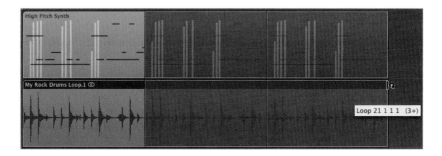

15 Position the playhead before the last section and start playback.

The My Rock Drums Loop.1 region now perfectly matches the tempo of the project.

Listen to the last section. The new drum loop is a good fit for the song, but at the moment, it is overpowering the original drum beat and the other instruments. You can mix it with the song so that it blends better.

The High Pitch Synth on track 8 is panned to the left, so you will pan the loop to the right to balance it with the synth.

16 Make sure the Audio 6 track containing the new drum loop is selected, and drag its balance knob up to about +20.

The drum loop is positioned to the right, leaving the center space available to place the other instruments, which no longer sound as though they are buried underneath the drum loop.

Now you will use a channel strip setting to give that loop some texture.

17 At the top of the Audio 6 Channel Strip, click the Setting button, and choose 02 Electric Guitar > 06 Distorted (Effects) > Distorted – Filter > Pig Wah.

That creates too much distortion, and the drum loop is much too loud. Also, the wah effect is a little exaggerated. You should bypass the Fuzz-Wah plug-in.

18 Option-click the Fuzz-Wah plug-in.

The plug-in is bypassed.

19 Drag down the Audio 6 channel strip volume fader to about –6 (dB).

Position the playhead around bar 13 and listen to the end section. Now the new drum loop adds an interesting texture to the section without blurring the other instruments.

To put your new time-stretching skills to work, try time stretching the reversed hi-hat on track 7 to lengthen it two to three times. Then open it in the Sample Editor and readjust the anchor position to its maximum amplitude peak, as you did in Lesson 3. A longer reversed hi-hat sample will build up even more tension to announce the ending of the song.

You now have a large repertoire of techniques to ensure that any audio file recorded or imported in a project will play back at the project tempo. Mastering these techniques will give you the freedom to use almost any pre-recorded material in your projects, so keep your ears out for interesting material you hear that you think could be sampled and looped for one of your future songs.

Lesson Review

1. In the Loop Browser, how do you customize a category button?
2. How can you change a project's key signature?
3. How do you match the project tempo to an audio file's tempo?
4. How do you time stretch a MIDI or an audio region?
5. How do you make an audio region follow the tempo of the project?
6. How do you insert tempo changes?
7. Which region types will always follow the project's tempo map?
8. How do you create an Apple Loops file from a region?
9. What are Apple Loops? Describe the difference between blue and green Apple Loops.

Answers

1. Control-click the button and choose another category.
2. Open the global tracks, and double-click the key signature on the global Signature track. Choose a new key from the Key Signature window.
3. Drag a cycle of the same number of bars as the audio file. Then, in the main menu, choose Options > Tempo > Adjust Tempo using Region Length and Locators.
4. Press Option as you resize the region.
5. In the Inspector's Region Parameter box, select Follow Tempo.
6. In the global Tempo track, double-click above or below the tempo line.
7. MIDI regions, Apple Loops, and audio regions set to follow tempo.
8. Select the region and, in the Arrange area's local menu bar, choose Region > Add to Apple Loops Library.
9. Apple Loops are AIFF or CAF audio files that automatically match the project's tempo and key. Unlike blue Apple Loops, green Apple Loops also contain the MIDI region and software instrument channel strips used to create them, and they can be used on software instrument tracks.

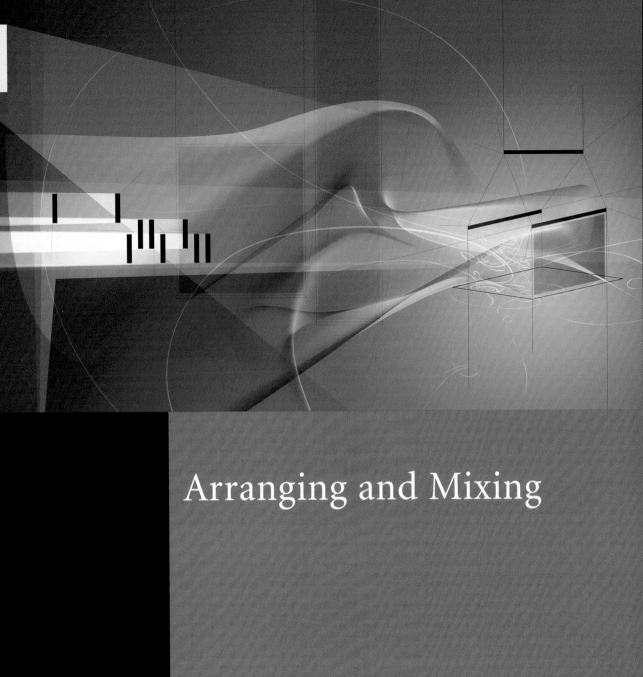

Arranging and Mixing

8

Lesson Files   Logic 8_Files > Lessons > 08 Darkside_start

Time   This lesson takes approximately 60 minutes to complete.

Goals   Experiment with the order of regions in Shuffle mode

Pack regions into folders

Cut and insert sections into a project

Divide a region into multiple slices

Clean up a noisy recording

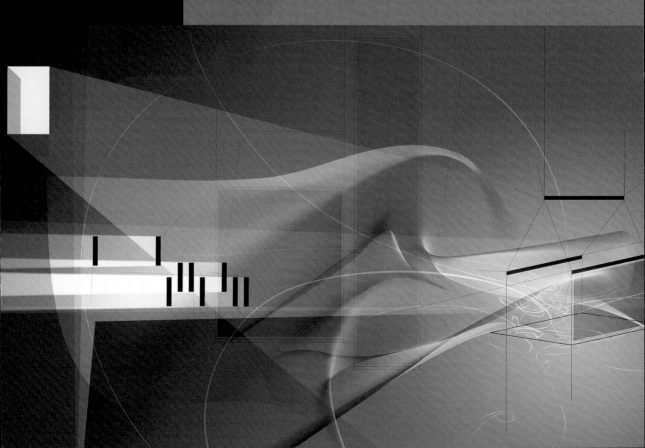

Arranging and Preparing for the Mix

In previous lessons, you recorded and edited audio and MIDI regions of raw musical material. The next step is to arrange all that material into a song: copying and repeating some elements, removing others, and assembling only those elements that communicate the message of your song.

In this lesson, you will start with a song in which all the basic elements have been recorded, and you'll make that song come to life. You will use existing material to fill in missing elements, and employ clever editing to make a simple handclap sound more exciting. You will also suppress some musical elements when the arrangement sounds too busy, add an introduction, and clean up noisy recordings in preparation for the mixing stage.

Previewing the Song

Before you start arranging a song, you need to get to know its structure and instrumentation.

You can use markers in the global Marker track to visually identify different sections in a project. In this first exercise, you will listen to a song and navigate using existing markers to familiarize yourself with its structure. Using the Solo mode, you'll identify and audition the individual tracks.

1   Go to Logic 8_Files > Lessons and open **08 Darkside_start**.

At the top of the Arrange area, in the global Marker track, the markers identify the different sections of the song (Verse, Chorus, and Bridge). You will use the markers as a visual aid as you copy, move, and loop regions.

TIP   To create your own markers, choose the Pencil tool and click in the Marker track. To choose which global tracks are displayed, Control-click the Global Tracks header and choose Configure Global Tracks from the shortcut menu.

2   Click the Global Tracks disclosure triangle to close the global tracks.

The Marker track disappears, and the markers are now displayed in the lower half of the Bar ruler. The markers are translucent; but if you need to see the grid lines more clearly in the Bar ruler, you can reopen the Marker track.

TIP   To toggle the global tracks, you don't have to precisely click the Global Tracks disclosure triangle. Clicking the words *Global Tracks* has the same effect.

3   Start playback.

Listen to the song and examine its structure. The song starts on bar 2, allowing space for guitar and clavinet pickup notes at the end of bar 1. The whole song is composed of eight-bar sections. It first alternates choruses and verses; then a bridge section starts on bar 42, followed by four choruses.

In popular music, it is common to work with eight-bar sections. This makes the Fast Forward and Fast Rewind key commands very useful for navigating a song, since they allow you to jump forward or back eight bars at a time.

4   As you listen to the song, press Shift-> (Fast Forward) to jump to the next eight-bar section and Shift-< (Fast Rewind) to jump to the previous one.

You can also press > (Forward) and < (Rewind) to jump ahead or back one bar at a time.

Use the key commands to listen to each verse, the different choruses, and the bridge. Except for the first chorus, the choruses feel empty. Later, you will add backup vocals in the choruses to give them substance.

To identify the material you are going to edit in the arrangement, you have to listen to individual instruments. You could use the Solo buttons on the track headers to keep a track selected as you edit any regions in the arrangement. However, soloing and unsoloing one instrument after another to preview them is inefficient. In the next steps, you'll use Solo mode as a faster alternative for soloing the selected region(s).

5   Click the Kick track header.

The Kick audio region is selected.

6   In the Transport bar, click the Solo button (or press S).

The Bar ruler is shaded yellow, indicating that you are in Solo mode. The selected Kick region is outlined in yellow, indicating that it is soloed.

7   Start playback.

You are hearing the Kick audio region.

8   Click the Snare track header (or press Down Arrow).

The Snare region is selected, and after a little delay, you can hear the Snare region.

To avoid the delayed reaction of the Solo mode when changing the selection, you can stop playback, select a new region, and restart playback. If you press the Spacebar to toggle playback and press the Down Arrow to select the next track, you can become very effective at quickly switching the soloed tracks.

9   Press the Spacebar.

Playback stops.

10   Press the Down Arrow twice to select the Hi Hat track.

The Hi Hat region is selected and soloed.

11   Press the Spacebar.

You can hear the Hi Hat region.

You can also select and listen to multiple regions.

12   Drag to select all the backup vocal regions in the first chorus.

All selected regions are soloed.

13   Position the playhead at the beginning of the first chorus and press the Spacebar.

You hear all the backup vocals.

14   In the Transport bar, click the Solo button (or press S).

Solo mode is turned off.

By now you should be a little more familiar with the song, and you're ready to start arranging it.

Using Existing Material to Fill In Parts

A good arrangement carefully balances between introducing new elements to keep listeners excited, and repeating sections to return listeners to familiar territory and motivate them to hum along.

Often the structure of the song is not set during the recording sessions. When you change the structure of the song during the arrangement process, you can use elements that were recorded only once and copy or repeat them to flesh out the arrangement.

Filling In the Bass Track

Two regions are present on the Bass track. You will work with the Bridge region shortly; but, for now, you will use the first region to fill in the rest of the track and use the same bass line for verses and choruses.

1   Zoom in on the first Bass region on track 7.

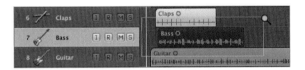

2   Go to the beginning and start playback.

Listen to the bass. The bass player missed the first downbeat, so you can't use the bass recording in the first bar of the chorus. However, he played an extra bar at the beginning of the following verse. You can cut the Bass region to create a loop that starts on the second bar of the chorus (bar 3) and ends on the second bar of the verse (bar 11).

You can scroll down the Arrange area to bring the Bass region just below the Bar ruler, and use the markers and the Bar ruler as visual help.

At the top right of the Arrange area, look at the Tool menus: the Command-click tool is the Marquee tool.

3   Hold down Command to get the Marquee tool and drag to select a section of the Bass region from bar 3 to bar 11.

The highlighted marquee selection includes all you need to fill in every chorus and verse in the song. You will now crop the marquee selection using the Crop Regions Outside Marquee Selection key command (Control-C).

4   Press Control-C.

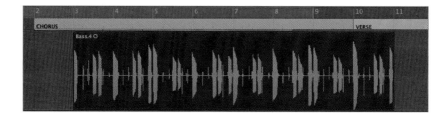

The cropping occurs right before your eyes! First, the marquee selection is divided, then the two regions outside the marquee selection are deleted. A region corresponding to the marquee selection remains.

You will now copy the first bar of the verse (bar 10) to the beginning of the chorus (bar 2) to fill the missing first bar.

5   Using the Marquee tool, select the first bar of the verse.

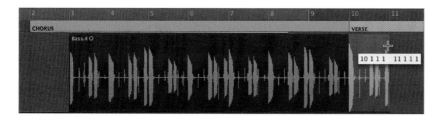

6   Option-drag the marquee selection to the beginning of the chorus (bar 2).

The marquee selection is pasted as a new one-bar region at the beginning of the chorus. You can now loop the eight-bar Bass region until the bridge comes in.

7   Click the eight-bar Bass region to select it and press L.

The eight-bar Bass region is looped until the next region on the track, the Bass Bridge region. Since the Bass region starts one bar after the beginning of the first chorus, all the repeats start one bar after the beginning of a section, and the last repeat is only 7 bar long.

8   Control-Option-click anywhere in the Arrange area to zoom out.

9   Go to the beginning of the song and press the Spacebar.

The bass sounds good. You can now copy the Bass regions to the four choruses near the end of the song.

10   Select both Bass regions at the beginning of the song.

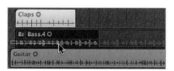

11   Hold down the mouse button on the first region and Option-drag the selection after the bridge (on bar 50).

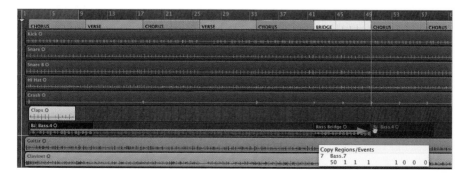

Both regions are copied, and the second Bass region of the copy is looped like the original. You still need to adjust the number of repeats at the end of the song.

12   Click in the background of the Arrange area to deselect all regions.

This will ensure that you will edit only one region when you zoom in on the end of the Bass region repeats, and not the two selected regions.

13   Scroll to the end of the song, at the end of the last chorus, and zoom in on the Bass track and the three tracks below.

When you Control-Option-drag the green selection rectangle to zoom in, make sure that the rectangle is high enough to cover the four tracks, but only about two or three bars wide. This will zoom in vertically so you can see all four tracks, and horizontally so you can see about three bars, allowing you to read the waveform and identify the bass notes.

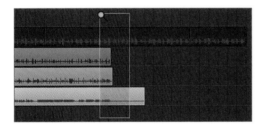

Notice that the guitar and clavinet still play one final note on the downbeat of bar 82, after the last chorus. You want the bass to stop right after playing that last note along with the other instruments.

14   Position the mouse over the upper part of the Bass loop repeats so that the mouse pointer turns into the Loop tool, and drag the Loop tool to stop the repeats after that last note.

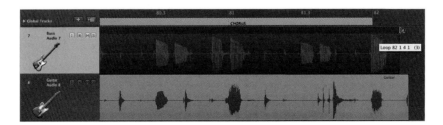

15 Listen to the ending of the song and make sure that the bass plays the last note along with the drums, the guitar, and the clavinet.

16 Control-Option-click anywhere in the Arrange area to zoom out.

Experimenting with the Order of Regions

Now you will experiment with the bass line in the bridge as you make an artistic decision. You will cut the Bass Bridge region into two four-bar regions and shuffle their order to determine which arrangement works best.

1 Position the playhead around bar 37 and listen to the transition from the chorus to the bridge.

The root note of the bass is changing when the bridge starts, making the transition strong.

Keep playing and listen to the transition from the bridge into the next chorus. The root note of the bass remains the same for the second half of the bridge and the first half of the next chorus, making the transition a little boring.

2 Zoom in on the Bass track so you can see one chorus, the bridge, and the following chorus.

You are going to cut the Bass Bridge region in two with the Scissors tool.

3 Press Esc and choose the Scissors tool (or press Esc-5).

4 Drag the Scissors tool over the Bass Bridge region, and do not release the mouse button yet.

As you drag, the region is selected, Solo mode is automatically turned on, and the Scissors tool allows you to scrub the audio region. When you locate the perfect position (when the help tag reads 46 1 1 1) for your edit, release the mouse button. The region is cut at that position.

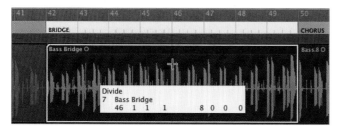

You now have two four-bar regions, Bass Bridge.1 and Bass Bridge.2. You will now shuffle the order of those regions.

5   At the top right of the Arrange area, click the Drag pop-up menu and choose Shuffle R.

The shuffle modes allow you to swap the positions of regions by dragging one over the other. You don't have to be precise when dragging regions in a shuffle mode. Even if you barely drag a region over the other, the two will be shuffled.

NOTE ▶ In this situation it doesn't matter whether you choose Shuffle R or Shuffle L. You will experience a different behavior between the two drag modes only when you delete a region or a marquee selection.

6   Press Esc twice.

The left-click tool is reset to the Pointer tool.

7   Drag Bass Bridge.2 toward the left over Bass Bridge.1.

When you release the mouse, the two regions swap positions.

8   Position the playhead around bar 38 and listen to the transition from the chorus to the bridge.

The root note of the bass changes.

Then listen to the transition from the bridge to the chorus. The root note of the bass changes again, making the transition more exciting than it was before you swapped the regions.

9   Zoom out to see the whole song again.

10 At the top right of the Arrange area, in the Drag menu, choose Overlap.

Packing Regions into Folders

Folders are regions that can contain other regions. They are a powerful arrangement tool because once you pack multiple regions into a folder, you can edit the entire contents of the folder by editing the folder.

In this exercise, you will pack the backup vocal regions into folders and use those folders to flesh out the choruses that are lacking backup vocals. When folders are packed, a folder track is created above the selected track, so you must first select the desired track, depending on where you want your folder track to be placed.

1   Click the BU Mid L track header (the first backup vocal track).

The track is selected.

2   Select all backup vocal regions in the first chorus.

You are now ready to pack the selected regions into a folder.

3   From the Arrange area's local menu bar, choose Region > Folder > Pack Folder (or press Command-F).

A folder track is created above the selected track, and all the selected regions are packed into a folder.

NOTE ▸ You will navigate in and out of a folder later in this lesson.

Let's rename the folder track and the folder.

4   Double-click the folder track name, and enter *Chorus BU*.

5   Press Esc to open the Tool menu, then Command-click the Text tool.

The Text tool is now the Command-click tool.

6   Command-click the Backup Mid L folder and enter *Chorus Backups*.

Now let's copy that Chorus Backups folder to the other choruses.

NOTE ▸ Make sure that you changed the drag mode to Overlap in step 10 of the previous exercise. If the drag mode is still Shuffle R, the folder region will not be copied to the correct position.

7   Option-drag the Chorus Backups folder to the second chorus (bar 18).

Copy the folder to the third and fourth chorus (bar 34 and bar 50).

8   Use the Loop tool to repeat the last Chorus Backups folder once.

The repeat stops where the next backup vocal regions begin.

Let's pack the remaining backup vocal regions into a new folder and use it for the two last choruses. When a folder track is selected, packing a folder inserts the new folder region onto the selected folder track.

9   Select the remaining backup vocal regions in the chorus just before the final chorus.

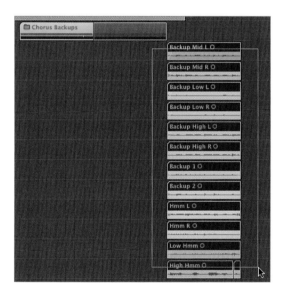

10   From the Arrange area's local menu bar, choose Region > Folder > Pack Folder (or press Command-F).

The regions are packed into a new folder. The folder is inserted into the selected folder track.

11   Command-click the new folder and rename it *Chorus Hmm*.

12 Use the Loop tool to repeat the Chorus Hmm folder once.

All the choruses in the song now have backup vocals. Since all the backup vocal tracks are now empty, you can delete them and clean up the track list.

13 From the Arrange area's local menu bar, choose Track > Delete Unused.

All empty tracks are deleted.

Listen to the whole song, or use the Forward, Rewind, Fast Forward, and Fast Rewind key commands to jump to the choruses to hear the backup vocals.

You now have a sense of how useful folders can be. There are many more applications for folders, so try to keep them in mind when you organize your Arrange area. You can also divide folders and edit them the same way you edit a region. For example, a lot of producers pack an entire song into a folder, then cut the folder into sections to experiment with changing the section order.

Slicing and Doubling a Percussion Part

On the Claps track (track 6), you'll find a recording of a few handclaps. It works well, but you can make it more exciting. You will use that audio region to create a stereo handclap part for the entire song.

You will divide the region into single handclap hits and rearrange the handclaps on two tracks, panned left and right, to create a stereo effect. Slicing the handclaps will prepare you for the next exercise, in which you will shuffle the order of the individual slices.

1 Go to the beginning of track 6 and start playback.

Listen to the handclaps. The musician claps along with the snare, on the second and fourth beats of each bar.

First, you will slice the Claps region into two-beat regions, each containing one clap.

2 Press Esc and choose the Scissors tool.

3   Zoom in on the Claps region.

You'll use the Scissors tool to divide the region into multiple regions of equal length.

4   Position the Scissors tool after the first clap, and hold down Option.

The mouse cursor turns into a scissors icon with a little plus sign, indicating that you are about to divide the region into multiple regions.

5   Option-drag the Scissors tool and release the mouse button when the help tag reads *2 3 1 1.*

Notice that when you hold down Option, the help tag reads *Divide Multiple.* The mouse cursor turns into a crosshair so you can pinpoint the exact cutting position on the waveform. In this Claps region, the waveform is easy to read!

When you release the mouse button, the region is divided into 12 two-beat regions, each containing a single handclap.

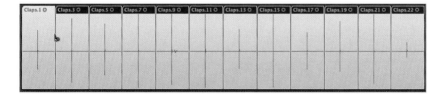

You will now prepare to create a stereo effect from these regions by panning the existing Claps track hard left (all the way to the left), then creating another track and panning it hard right.

6   Select the Claps track header.

In the Inspector, the first channel strip on the left (Audio 6) controls the selected track.

7   Drag the Pan control down until it reads –64.

The audio signal on that track will now be heard only in the left speaker.

8   At the top left of the Arrange area, click the Duplicate Track button.

The Duplicate Track button creates a new track with the same channel strip setting as the selected track's channel strip. In this case, there are no plug-ins on the Claps track's channel strip, but using that button is a quick way to create a new audio track.

9   Double-click the names in the track headers and rename the tracks *Claps L* and *Claps R*.

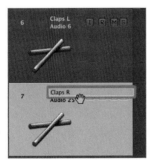

10 With the Claps R track selected, drag the Pan control all the way up to pan the channel strip hard right.

Now let's move some of the Claps regions to the new track.

11 Press Esc twice.

The left-click tool is reset to the Pointer tool.

12 In the Arrange area, select the last six Claps regions and drag them below the first six Claps regions.

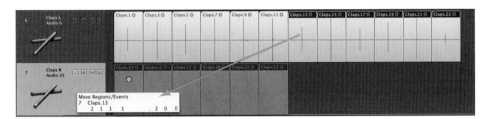

13 Go to the beginning and start playback.

You may want to solo the two Claps tracks to hear the results. You can now hear a nice stereo effect on the claps. It sounds like two musicians clapping their hands together, one on the left and the other on the right.

Let's fill in the whole song with claps.

14 Zoom out to see the whole song.

15 Select all Claps regions on both tracks and choose Region > Repeat Regions (or press Command-R). Set the Number of Copies to *26* and click OK.

NOTE ▶ If you get an alert saying "Unused occupied memory block detected," click Delete and keep going.

Copies of the selected regions fill the whole song. However, you will need to delete a few extra Claps regions at the end.

16 Zoom in on the last Claps regions, drag to select the last two Claps regions on both tracks, and press Delete.

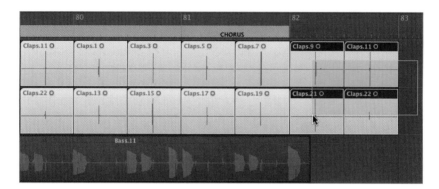

You just took a simple six-bar mono recording of a few handclaps and turned it into a stereo handclap part spanning the whole song. Slicing the original region into single-hit Claps regions will now allow you to rearrange the order of individual hits.

Humanizing a Percussion Part

In the previous exercise, you sliced the handclaps into regions of one handclap each. This allows you to swap the positions of individual handclaps, thereby randomizing the pattern to give the claps a more natural feel.

In this exercise, you will first pack all the handclap regions into a folder. Inside the folder, you will shuffle the regions to randomize them and to create accents by moving the louder handclaps to the beginning of verses and choruses.

1 Click the Claps L track header.

All the regions on the Claps L track are selected.

2 Shift-click the Claps R track header.

All Claps regions on both tracks are selected.

3 Choose Region > Folder > Pack Folder (or press Command-F).

All Claps regions are packed into a folder region.

4 From the Arrange area's local menu bar, choose Track > Delete Unused.

The two empty Claps tracks are deleted.

5 Double-click the new folder track header and enter *Claps*.

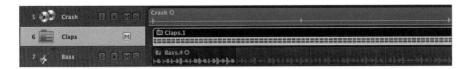

6 Double-click the folder to open it.

The folder opens, and the Arrange area displays the contents of the folder you double-clicked, which includes all the Claps regions.

TIP ▶ To unpack the folder and display its contents at the top level of the Arrange area, choose Region > Folder > Unpack Folder (or press Command-U).

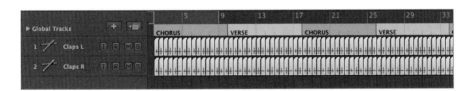

Now you can shuffle the individual handclaps to randomize their positions.

7 At the top right of the Arrange area, set the drag mode to Shuffle R.

8 Zoom in on the first chorus.

Notice how some of the claps are louder than others (their waveforms show a taller transient). Try swapping the louder claps with the first regions in each eight-bar section.

9 Drag one of the louder Claps regions over a region at the beginning of a section to swap their positions.

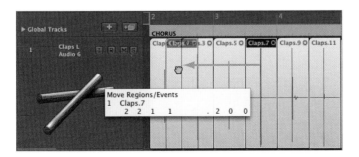

Don't try to drag a region on the other track, or you will insert that region on the track you're dragging to, and you'll end up with an unequal number of regions on each track.

Take a few minutes and swap a few claps here and there, occasionally listening to your results. You only need to randomize a few claps for the part to sound more natural. You can experiment with the placements of louder claps to accent beats, and determine which placements work the best for the song.

As you prepared to drag a Claps region, you may have noticed that the Arrange area would update its content before you had a chance to drag the region. This is due to the Catch mode, which is turned on by default when you start playback. The Catch mode makes the visible part of the Arrange area (or other editors) update to follow the playhead position. The Catch button is blue when in Catch mode.

Catch button

While the song is playing, when you see Claps regions that you want to shuffle, you can disable the Arrange area's Catch mode to stop it from following the playhead. This will allow you to keep the project playing as you work in a section of the Arrange area where the playhead is no longer visible.

10 Zoom in horizontally until about six Claps regions fill the Arrange area.

11 Start playback.

Verify that area's content Catch mode is on (the Catch button is blue). Each time the playhead reaches the end of the visible section, the Arrange area's content automatically jumps to the right to follow the playhead.

Wait to find a section where you would like to swap the position of a couple of Claps regions.

12 At the top left of the Arrange area, click the Catch button.

Catch mode is turned off. Playback continues, but the Arrange area stops automatically updating its content to follow the playhead.

> **TIP** ▶ When you use the Zoom tool or scroll horizontally during playback, Catch mode is automatically turned off.

13 Drag one Claps region over another to swap their positions.

When you are done working in the visible section of the Arrange area, you can turn on Catch mode again to see the playhead position.

14 Click the Catch button.

Catch mode is on, and the Arrange area updates to display the playhead position.

Toggling Catch mode off and on, you were able to stop the Arrange area from following the playhead position automatically, perform your edit without interrupting playback, and finally catch up with the playhead position in the Arrange area.

When you are happy with the Claps part, it is time to close the folder.

15 Zoom out to see the whole folder.

16 At the top left of the Arrange area, click the Hierarchy button.

The folder closes and you can see the top-level Arrange area again.

> **TIP** ▶ You can also close a folder by double-clicking the background of the Arrange area.

17 At the top right of the Arrange area, set the drag mode to Overlap.

Adding and Deleting Sections

Artists often get so involved in the creative process of writing a song that they may not see the big picture and arrive at an ideal structure for their song. Producers and A&R representatives may suggest adding an introduction or may want to shorten the song so the chorus comes in earlier and the length of the song is more suitable for radio play. Sometimes a shorter radio mix will be produced while a longer mix is produced for the album.

In the following exercises, you will insert and cut sections in the project to add an introduction and cut a chorus.

Adding an Introduction

To create an introduction, you will insert eight bars at the top of the song and fill the new eight bars with the desired material. The position of the playhead determines where the new section will be inserted, and the length of the cycle area determines the length of the new section. Before you insert a section, you need to position the playhead and adjust your cycle area.

1 Position the playhead on 1 1 1 1.

The new section will be inserted at 1 1 1 1.

2 In the Bar ruler, click the cycle area.

For the introduction, you need to insert eight bars. Unless you have changed the cycle area since you opened the project, the cycle area should already be eight bars in length. If you have changed the cycle area, adjust it now.

NOTE ▶ When inserting a section, the contents of the clipboard are pasted in the new section. To make sure the new section you insert is empty, click the background of the Arrange area to deselect all regions, and choose Edit > Copy (or press Command-C) to copy "nothing" into the clipboard.

3 In the Toolbar, click the Insert Section button.

An eight-bar section is added at 1 1 1 1.

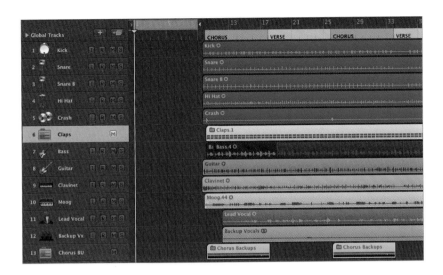

You can now create your introduction. You will copy the Chorus Hmm folder to add backup vocals to the introduction, then add a lead vocal audio file that is stored in the project's Audio Bin.

4   Scroll to the end of the song and Option-drag the Chorus Hmm folder to 2 1 1 1.

Remember that when a region is looped, the loop repeats will end automatically at the beginning of the next region on that track. When copying the looped Chorus Hmm region, the repeats are automatically trimmed at the beginning of the Chorus Backups region after it.

Now let's add the lead vocal audio file located in the Audio Bin.

5   In the Toolbar on the right, click Media (or press B).

The Media area opens and displays the Audio Bin.

In the Audio Bin, scroll all the way down to find the Intro Lead Vocal audio region.

6   Drag Intro Lead Vocal to the Lead Vocal track on 2 1 1 1.

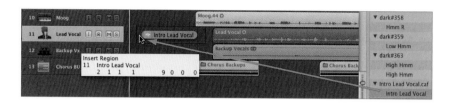

7   In the Toolbar, click the Media button (or press B).

The Media area closes.

8   In the Bar ruler, click the cycle area to turn off Cycle mode.

9   Start playback.

Listen to the new a cappella introduction. It really commands your attention, pulls you into the first chorus, and sounds great!

Cutting a Section

Now you will cut a section from the song, first playing the song while skipping sections until you find which section you want to cut. To do this, you'll use a skip cycle area, which you define by dragging a cycle area, but from right to left.

1   In the upper half of the Bar ruler, drag right to left from bar 50 to bar 42.

A skip cycle area (represented by a green candy-striped area) is created that corresponds to the chorus before the bridge. Notice the help tag, which indicates that at bar 42, playback skips eight bars.

2   Start playback a few bars before the skip cycle area.

When the playhead reaches the skip cycle area, it jumps to the bridge, skipping the whole eight-bar chorus.

The new transition from the verse to the bridge is not very pleasing. Let's try something else.

3   Drag the skip cycle area to the next chorus, just after the bridge.

4   Start playback in the middle of the bridge.

Skipping the chorus right after the bridge sounds great, and it allows you to shorten the ending of the song, reach the Chorus Hmm regions faster, and introduce that new element before the listener has a chance to get bored.

Since the cycle area (or skip cycle area) defines both the length and position of the section to cut, you are now ready to cut the section.

5   In the Toolbar, click the Cut Section button.

The regions below the skip cycle area are cut, and all the regions to the right of the skip cycle area are moved eight bars to the left to eliminate the gap. On the Bass track, the two regions in the section you cut are copied to the next chorus before the section is cut, and the number of repeats is automatically updated so the bass ends at the same place after the last chorus. The four-chorus ending is turned into a shorter three-chorus ending.

6   Click the skip cycle area to turn it off.

7   Listen to the bridge and the new, shorter ending section.

Muting Elements

Arranging is not always about layering instruments and adding elements to a project. Sometimes the creative process can lead to too many tracks, or an improvising musician can play too many notes. When you recognize those situations, you'll find that removing elements from a song will improve the final results.

Muting Sections of an Instrument

You will work on the Moog keyboard track in this exercise, listening to how the performance of the keyboardist affects the vocal tracks. You will mute sections of the Moog where it overlaps the vocals, allowing space in the mix for the vocals to naturally stand out.

1   In the first chorus and first verse, zoom in on the Moog and Lead Vocal tracks.

2   Start playback at the beginning of the first chorus.

Listen to the Moog, the vocals, and the backup vocals. You will notice that sometimes the Moog complements the vocals nicely, answering them by playing a little melody, but sometimes it clearly overlaps the vocal performance.

This happens in bar 15, where the Moog plays a busy rhythm while the vocals and backup vocals are already singing intricate parts.

You will use the Marquee tool to select portions of the Moog region to mute.

3   Press Esc and Command-click the Marquee tool.

4   Command-drag the Marquee tool over the whole musical phrase starting before bar 15 and ending after bar 16.

Don't bother looking at the help tag. For this exercise, you will rely solely on your waveform-reading skills and your ears.

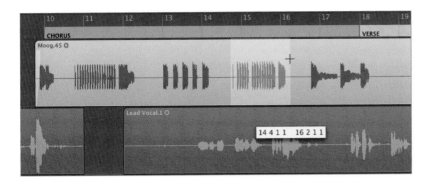

5   Press M (Mute).

The marquee selection is divided into a new region and the region is muted.

> **TIP** ▸ You can also click a marquee selection with the Mute tool to divide it into a new region and mute it.

6   Start playback at the beginning of the chorus.

Listen to the vocals and backup vocals where the Moog region is muted. Muting that melodic phrase really opened space in the mix and gave more importance to the vocals. You can press the M key to toggle the mute status of the selected region and listen again to compare the section with and without the Moog.

The next melodic phrase played by the Moog sounds good and really answers the vocals that conclude the chorus; but, in bar 18, the first note at the beginning of the verse jumps out and steals attention from the lead vocals. Let's mute that note.

7   Command-drag the Marquee tool over the Moog note in bar 18.

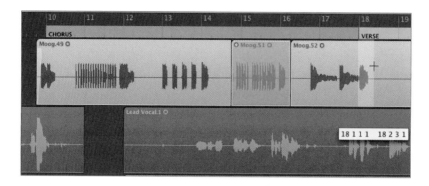

8 Press M.

The Marquee selection is divided into a region and the region is muted.

Continue listening to the entire Moog track and mute all the sections of the Moog track that in your judgment are taking away from the vocals. You may find that you will want to mute a large amount of the Moog performance, starting with all the repeated notes between bars 19 and 22.

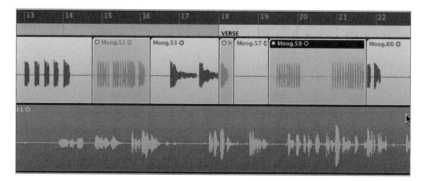

Developing the rare skill of knowing what to mute and when to mute it will help make your song breathe and later make the mixing process easier. While you acquire that skill, you'll also learn to listen to the ways instruments interact with each other, making sure they aren't fighting for a listener's attention.

Cleaning Up Noisy Recordings

At the end of the arranging process, you have to make sure that your song is ready for the next step, the mixing stage. You want to avoid unnecessary noises that could blur the mix. You already learned how to clean up edit points and avoid audible clicks in Lesson 3. You will now clean up the Kick track and the Guitar track using two additional techniques.

Removing Snare Leakage from the Kick Track

To prepare your song for mixing, you will edit the Kick track to cut the leakage from the snare drum sound into the kick drum microphone. Instead of performing the edit manually, you will use a feature called Strip Silence that automatically cuts out portions of a recording that fall below a specific volume threshold.

It is easier to use Strip Silence on a shorter audio region, so you will first cut a small portion from the Kick region.

1   Zoom out to see the whole song, and zoom in on the Kick track to see the first chorus.

2   Command-drag the Marquee tool over the first half of the first chorus, from before the Kick region starts to just after the first downbeat of bar 14.

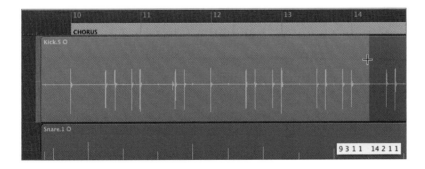

3   Using the Pointer tool, click the marquee selection to divide it into a new region.

4   In the Transport bar, click the Solo button (or press S).

The selected Kick region is soloed.

5   Start playback at the beginning of the soloed Kick region.

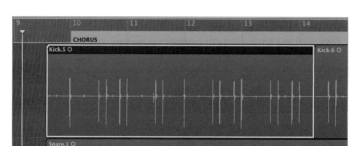

Listen to the soloed Kick region and pay attention to the snare drum in the background. Count the number of kick drum hits in the region, using both your ears and your eyes to read the waveform. You should count 16 hits.

You will use Strip Silence to cut the selected region into 16 regions, each containing one kick drum hit and, in so doing, remove the snare drum hits.

6   From the Arrange area's local menu bar, choose Audio > Strip Silence (or press Control-X).

The Strip Silence window opens, showing you how the region will be edited.

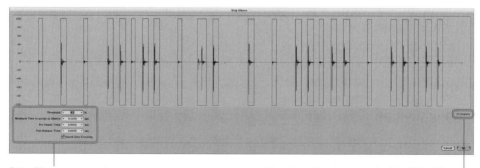

Strip Silence parameters   Number of regions created by Strip Silence

You can see the number of regions that Strip Silence will create displayed near the bottom right of the waveform. Using the default parameter settings, Strip Silence will create 24 regions. Looking at the waveform, you can see that some of the resulting regions (for example, the first and third regions) consist of snare drum hits.

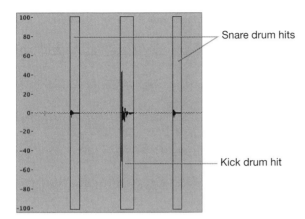

Snare drum hits

Kick drum hit

You will need to adjust the parameters at the bottom left of the Strip Silence window until Strip Silence creates only 16 regions containing the kick drums.

The Threshold parameter adjusts the minimum volume that Strip Silence detects to create a region. You need to raise the threshold so the snare drum hits don't create regions.

7 Drag the Threshold value up to 5.0%.

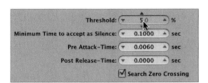

Strip Silence now creates 16 regions, and all the regions are kick drum hits.

Leave the default settings for the other parameters, but notice that the Pre Attack-Time is set to 0.0060 sec. The Pre Attack-Time is set to 0.0060 sec. This makes sure each region starts 6 ms (milliseconds) before the attack detected by Strip Silence.

8 Click OK (or press Enter).

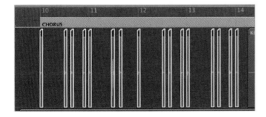

In the Arrange area, the selected region is replaced by the 16 individual kick drum regions created by Strip Silence.

Since the regions are selected and Solo mode is still turned on, the regions are soloed and you can listen to your results.

9   Start playback just before the first chorus.

You can hear all the kick drums, but you no longer hear any snare drums on the Kick track.

The regions are so short you can barely see a waveform. Let's zoom in on one of the kick drums.

10   Zoom in on the first kick drum region.

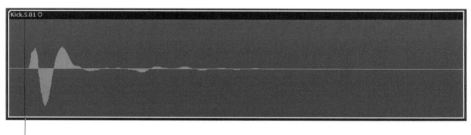

Anchor position

Notice the black vertical line that indicates the position of the anchor in the audio region. Although Strip Silence places the region start 6 ms before the attack, it auto-matically positions the anchor on the attack of the sound. This is helpful if you need to reposition the audio region on the grid.

11   Zoom out and turn off Solo mode.

Take a moment to use Strip Silence on another portion of the Kick track, or on the whole track, if you want. It is easier to use Strip Silence on smaller regions because you can count the kicks and check your work as you progress through the track.

Reducing a Wah Noise from the Guitar Track

You will now use a processing plug-in called Denoiser to reduce the noise of the guitarist's wah-wah effect pedal on the Guitar track.

1   On the Guitar track header, click the Solo button.

2   Start playback anywhere in the song.

You can clearly hear the noise of the guitarist's wah-wah pedal. In fact you can hear the wah modulate the frequency of the noise when the guitar is not playing.

You can use the Denoiser plug-in to reduce that noise.

3   Click the Guitar track header.

The Guitar track is selected and the Guitar channel strip (Audio 8) is displayed in the Inspector.

4   Click the first Insert slot on the Audio 8 channel strip and choose Specialized > Denoiser.

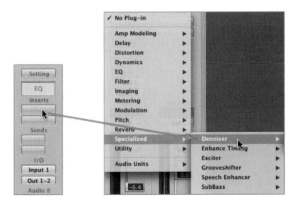

The Denoiser plug-in window opens.

5   At the top right of the Denoiser plug-in window, click the Settings field and choose Effect Wah-Wah Denoiser.

6   Close the plug-in window (or press Command-W).

7   As you listen to the soloed Guitar track, Option-click the Denoiser plug-in insert on the channel strip to toggle it on and off.

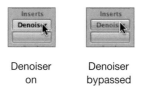

Denoiser   Denoiser
   on   bypassed

Compare the sound of the Guitar track with the Denoiser on (blue Insert slot) and with the Denoiser bypassed (gray Insert slot). The Denoiser is efficient at reducing the noise from the wah-wah pedal, so leave it on.

You now have a few tools and techniques in your arsenal to arrange a song in Logic. Remember that a successful arrangement balances repeated elements and new elements. Repeating melodies and grooves gives the listener a chance to get familiar with the song, sometimes to the point of singing along or dancing. The new elements are like ear candy that keep the listener excited and curious to hear what's coming up.

As you produce more music, you will become increasingly acute in determining what makes a good arrangement. Try to analyze the arrangements of the songs you love, and incorporate some of those ideas into your own compositions.

Lesson Review

1. How do you use the Solo mode?

2. How can you swap the positions of regions?

3. How do you pack regions into a folder?

4. How do you open and close a folder?

5. How do you slice a region into regions of equal length?

6. How do you insert a new section into a project?

7. How do you skip a section when playing back a project?

8. How can you remove background noises on a track?

Answers

1. In the Transport bar, click the Solo button (or press S), then select the region(s) you want to solo.

2. At the top right of the Arrange area, set the Drag menu to one of the shuffle modes.

3. Select the regions to pack, and choose Region > Folder > Pack Folder (or press Command-F).

4. Double-click a folder to open it. Double-click the background of the Arrange area, or click the Hierarchy button, to close a folder.

5. Hold down Option as you cut the first slice with the Scissors tool.

6. Adjust the cycle area to identify the length of the section to insert, and position the playhead where you want to insert the section.

7. Create a skip cycle area by dragging in the upper half of the Bar ruler from right to left.

8. You can use Strip Silence to remove all the portions of a region that fall below a specific level threshold. You can use the Denoiser plug-in to reduce the noise level of a track.

9

Lesson Files	Logic 8_Files > Lessons > 09 Mitral Valve Prolapse_start
Media	Logic 8_Files > Media > Mitral Valve Prolapse
Time	This lesson takes approximately 60 minutes to complete.
Goals	Navigate the Mixer and use effect plug-ins
	Adjust volume levels and use groups
	Adjust pan positions
	Filter frequencies with the Channel EQ plug-in
	Process with aux sends and aux channel strips
	Add depth with delay and reverberation plug-ins

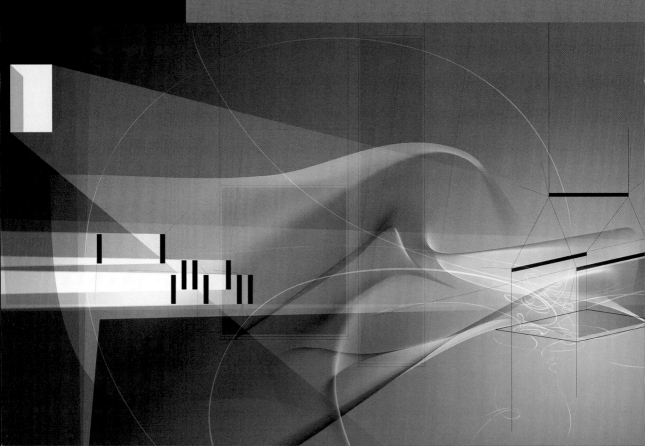

Mixing

Mixing is the art of blending all the instruments and sounds in a stereo sound field. A good mix can make the difference between an amateur demo and a professional production. Mixing should carefully balance two goals: blending all the elements into a cohesive whole and, at the same time, keeping them sufficiently defined so that listeners can distinguish between them. In other words, make the musicians sound as if they are playing in the same room, while ensuring that they don't mask each other and muddy the mix. A good mix is like a completed puzzle, in which all the pieces (all the instruments) fill their proper places in the sound field without overlapping each other.

With those goals in mind, you can adjust four parameters of an instrument to define its space in the stereo sound field. You can adjust the instrument's volume, its position in the stereo field (from left to right), its distance and depth, and its frequency spectrum. Those parameters are interrelated, and changing one often means that you will need to readjust the others.

In mixing, it is also fundamental to be consistent with the genre of the song. In the previous lesson, you worked with a mix that was really dry because the song genre didn't call for many effects, and the simple instrumentation didn't require much processing to get the desired results. In this lesson, you will work with a modern pop rock song that will benefit from a variety of processing effects. A more complex arrangement with more layered instruments also means that more attention must be paid to each instrument's place in the mix.

Previewing the Final Mix

Before you open the project and start mixing the song, watch a QuickTime clip of the music video to get familiar with the song and its final mix.

1   Go to Logic 8_Files > Media > Mitral Valve Prolapse and open **Mitral.mp4**.

The music video opens in QuickTime.

2   At the bottom of the QuickTime Player window, click the Play button (or press the Spacebar).

Watch the whole music video, and listen to the mix, trying to identify the effects it uses and the position of each instrument in the stereo sound field.

In the following exercise, you will open a project file that has been partially mixed, but it requires that some of the instruments receive additional polish. You will use techniques that will help you achieve a mix like the one you just heard.

Adding Effects

You can use effects-processing plug-ins to sculpt the sound of the instruments and help certain instruments find their places in the mix. These plug-ins will also give those instruments a different timbre and, later, influence the way you adjust their levels or EQs (equalization).

To start your mix, you'll apply an amp modeling plug-in to the bass to give it a distinctive character, and a rotor tremolo effect to both electric guitars to help distinguish them from the lead vocal.

1   Go to Logic 8_Files > Lessons and open **09 Mitral Valve Prolapse_start**.

2   Listen to the beginning of the song.

The intro starts on bar 3 playing only the bass. The bass was recorded without a bass amplifier and sounds a little raw. You will add a bass amp modeling plug-in to simulate the sound of a bass amplifier.

3   In the Arrange area, select the Bass track (track 15).

In the Inspector, the channel strip on the left is the channel strip of the selected track, while the right channel strip is the Output 1-2 channel strip, the one on which you are mixing your tracks.

4   In the left Arrange channel strip, click the first Insert slot and choose Amp Modeling > Bass Amp from the pop-up menu.

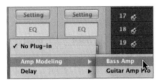

The Bass Amp plug-in is inserted and its window opens. The bass sounds a little edgier now.

5   Play the song starting before bar 3.

6   In the plug-in header, click the Bypass button.

The Bass Amp plug-in is bypassed, and you can hear the sound of the bass without the amp modeling plug-in applied. The bass sounds louder without the plug-in, so you will need to raise the output level of the plug-in to return the bass to its original level.

7   Click the Bypass button again to turn the Bass Amp plug-in back on.

8   At the bottom of the plug-in, raise the output level to 0 dB.

The bass now has the same level that it did before you added the Bass Amp plug-in; but now it sounds a little edgier, as if it were playing through a bass amp. When the vocals start, you can continue comparing the sound of the bass with and without the Bass Amp plug-in. The plug-in makes the bass sound sharper and more prominent against the vocals.

9 Close the Bass Amp plug-in window.

You will now apply a rotor tremolo effect to the first electric guitar.

10 In the Arrange area, select the Elec 1 track (track 22).

11 Start playback at the beginning of the first Elec 1 region (around bar 21).

Listen to the electric guitars, and note the way they influence the perception of the lead vocal when they start playing. The guitars are really present and occupy a large frequency range, slightly masking the lead vocal.

Adding a rotor tremolo effect to the guitars will give them a narrower frequency spectrum and free up some of the frequency range occupied by the lead vocal.

12 In the Elec 1 track header, click the Solo button.

In the Arrange channel strip, you can see that a compressor plug-in has already been inserted. You will later use a compressor plug-in on an acoustic guitar track.

The order in which processing plug-ins are placed on a channel strip changes their combined effect on the instrument's sound, just as the order of a guitarist's effects pedals change his guitar's sound. Remember that the signal flow of a channel strip is from top to bottom. The audio signal in the track's audio region is routed to the first plug-in at the top of the Inserts section, then to the next plug-in below it, and so on. After it is processed by the final plug-in, the signal level is routed to the volume fader, then the Pan control, and finally to the output selected in the I/O section—in this case, the Output 1-2 channel strip. In this exercise, you want to insert the tremolo effect before the compressor, so you first need to move the compressor plug-in down one slot.

In the Arrange channel strips, you can move plug-ins to a different Insert slot by holding down Command to use the Hand tool.

13 Command-drag the Compressor plug-in down one slot.

The first Insert slot is now available, and you can insert the rotor plug-in before the compressor.

14 Click the first Insert slot and choose Modulation > Rotor Cabinet.

The Rotor Cabinet plug-in is inserted and its window opens. The guitar sounds a little piercing now, so you will change the plug-in parameters to create a more rounded tremolo effect.

15 In the Rotor Cabinet plug-in window, click Tremolo.

16 Click the Cabinet Type parameter and choose Single.

You can bypass the plug-in to compare the dry guitar sound with the tremolo sound. The tremolo sound gives the guitar sound a more focused frequency range with fewer high frequencies.

You will now copy the Elec 1 channel strip setting to the Elec 2 channel strip.

17 Close the plug-in window.

18 In the left Arrange channel strip, click the Setting button and choose Copy Channel Strip Setting.

19 In the Arrange area, select the Elec 2 track.

20 In the left Arrange channel strip, click the Setting button and choose Paste Channel Strip Setting.

Both the Rotor and the Compressor plug-ins and their settings are copied to the Elec 2 channel strip, and both electric guitars now have the same sound.

21 In the Arrange area, unsolo the Elec 1 track and start playback around bar 21.

Notice that the new guitar sound doesn't mask the vocals as it did before you added the rotor tremolo effect. Although the guitars now have a narrower frequency range, the modulation effect gives them character, so you can easily distinguish the guitars in the mix. You have separated the electric guitars from the vocals by giving the guitars their own space in the frequency spectrum.

Adjusting Levels

Adjusting the level of each instrument may seem like the most obvious part of the mixing process. You will usually start setting levels while you build the song. However, the perception of an instrument's loudness will change during the mixing process, and you will often have to readjust the level of an instrument after you change its pan position or EQ settings, or as you mix other instruments that influence the perception of the first instrument.

Another consideration when adjusting levels is to avoid distortion. If an instrument is too loud, it will start clipping the signal (the clip detector indicates this by turning red) and you may hear distortion. Although clipping a channel does not always result in audible distortion, it is usually best to follow good mixing practice and ensure that all track level meters stay below 0 dBFS and the clip detectors don't turn red.

Adjusting the Levels of the Drum Tracks

In this exercise, you will solo all the drum tracks and adjust their levels to get a good balance among all the drums in the drum kit.

1   At the bottom of the Arrange area, click the Mixer button (or press X).

   The Mixer opens, and you can see the channel strips for all the tracks you have in the Arrange area.

   NOTE ▶ If you have a small screen resolution, the Mixer area may not show the entire height of the channel strips, and may be hiding the Arrange area. To perform the exercises in this lesson, you may need to resize the Mixer area to see a few tracks in the Arrange area, and you may need to scroll the Mixer area vertically to see the channel strip names at the bottom, or Setting button and EQ display at the top.

   The first nine channel strips from Kick to Room are the drum channel strips. (You may have to scroll to the left to see them.) You should solo all the drum channel strips to focus on them while adjusting their levels. In the Mixer, selecting multiple channel strips will temporarily link their settings, allowing you to solo all nine channel strips at once.

2   Starting with the Kick channel strip, drag across the bottom of the first nine channel strip labels.

All nine channel strips are highlighted, indicating that they are selected.

3   On one of the selected channel strips, click the Solo button.

All selected channel strips are soloed.

A good way to find the right level for each drum is to use the kick as a reference, setting it at 0 dB, turning the other drums all the way down, then slowly raising each drum individually, stopping when you find the level you prefer.

4   On one of the selected channel strips, drag the volume fader all the way down.

All the faders in the drum channel strips are turned all the way down.

Now you need to deselect the channel strips to unlink their parameters, so you can adjust their volume levels independently.

5   At the bottom of the Kick channel strip, click the Kick label.

The Kick channel strip remains selected and all other channel strips are deselected. While you could click anywhere in the background of a channel strip to select it, clicking its label is the best way to ensure that you're not going to change one of its settings accidentally.

6   Option-click the Kick volume fader to set it to 0 dB.

You can loop the pre-chorus section as you mix the drums.

7   In the Arrange area, drag to create a cycle area from bar 25 to 31.

8   Start playback.

You are now ready to adjust the level of the drum channel strips in relation to the Kick.

9   Slowly drag the Snare volume fader until you find the appropriate level.

Set the Snare fader to about –11 dB.

Before you can adjust the levels of the other drums, you should find the right level for the overhead microphones (the stereo pair of microphones placed above the kick to pick up the sound of the cymbals) and the room microphones (a pair of microphones placed farther away from the kick to pick up the sound of the whole drum kit in the room).

10 Slowly raise the Overhead fader to –11 dB.

11 Slowly raise the Room fader to –27 dB.

You can experiment with the Room fader by raising it a little higher if you want your drums to have a roomier sound.

12 Continue adjusting the drum track levels as follows:

▶ Set Snare B (the microphone placed at the bottom of the snare) to –13 dB.

▶ Set Hats to –13 dB.

You now need to find a section of the song in which the drummer hits the toms. Since the drummer plays the toms only a few times in the song, you need to loop one of those sections as you adjust the toms' volume levels.

One way to adjust the cycle area is to use the Marquee tool to select a section, and set the cycle area to match the marquee selection.

13 Zoom in on the three tom hits in the second chorus, around bar 41.

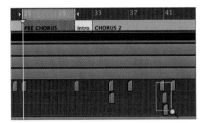

14 Drag the Marquee tool (your current Command-click tool) over the three tom hits to select them.

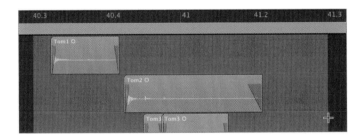

15 In the Toolbar, click the Set Locators button.

Cycle mode is turned on, and the cycle area matches your marquee selection, encompassing the three tom hits.

16 Start playback.

17 Adjust the three toms track levels as follows:

▶ Set the Tom1 fader to –7.9 dB.

▶ Set the Tom2 fader to –7.3 dB.

▶ Set the Tom3 fader to –7.3 dB.

You now have a good balance between all the drum tracks. In the next exercise, you will make sure the whole drum kit is at the right level when you listen to it in the context of the song.

18 Turn off Cycle mode and click in the background of the Arrange area to undo your marquee selection.

Grouping Tracks

Some channel strips are closely related to each other, such as all the drum channel strips that make up the drum kit. When you're mixing, it is useful to group those tracks and link some of their parameters, so you can adjust parameters for the whole group at once.

You'll try this by grouping all the drum tracks, then adjusting the volume level of the entire drum kit while listening to the rest of the instruments in the song, all the time preserving the relative level of each individual drum track.

1   Starting with the Kick channel strip on the left, drag across the labels of the first nine channel strips.

All nine channel strips are selected and temporarily grouped.

2   On the Kick channel strip, click the Group slot, and choose Group 1 from the pop-up menu.

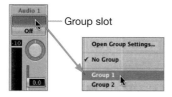

The number *1* appears in the Group slot of the selected channel strips, indicating that they are assigned to Group 1.

The drum channel strips are now permanently grouped, and you can deselect them.

3   At the bottom of the Kick channel strip, click the label to deselect the other channel strips.

You can name the group in the Group Settings window.

NOTE ▶ The first time you use a group in a project, the Group Settings window automatically opens. In this project, Group 1 was used before the project was saved, so you have to manually open the Group Settings window.

4   In one of the grouped channel strips, click the Group slot, and choose Open Group Settings.

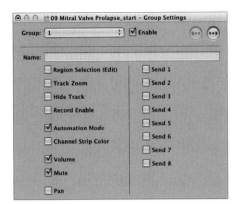

The Group Settings window opens.

All the parameters selected in the Group Settings window are linked for the whole group. The Volume parameter is selected by default, so you don't need to change any settings. You can, however, name the group to easily identify it.

5   In the Name field, type *Drums*, and press Enter.

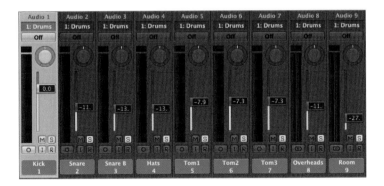

The name *1: Drums* appears in the Group slots on all the drum track channel strips.

Note that the Solo parameter is not available in the Group Settings window. However, you can Option-click the Solo button of a soloed channel strip to unsolo all the channel strips in a project.

6   On the Kick channel strip, Option-click the Solo button.

All the soloed channel strips are unsoloed.

7   Close the Group Settings window.

8   Start playback at the beginning of verse 2.

The drums are now too low, so you will raise their level.

9   Drag the Kick fader up to about +3.4 dB.

All the drum channel strip volume faders are raised by the same amount, raising the level of the whole drum kit while preserving each drum's relative level.

Choosing Pan Positions

Positioning instruments to the left or to the right of the stereo mix is a good way to separate them and make it easier for the listener to distinguish between the instruments. Panning instruments and positioning them at different places in the stereo field can also result in a wider stereo mix.

Continuing with your drum kit, you will use the Pan control knobs to reproduce the real positions of the individual drums, from the drummer's perspective. Then you will spread the guitar tracks throughout the stereo field.

First, imagine that you are the drummer, and visualize the pieces of the drum kit in front of you. The hi-hat is slightly to your left, and the toms are spread out left to right. You will recreate those positions using the Pan control knobs on the drum channel strips.

1   In the Arrange area track list, place the mouse pointer over the Kick track header's Solo button. Drag down to solo all nine drum channel strips.

Since the Mixer is open, the Arrange area is smaller, and you may have to zoom out or scroll down the Arrange area to see all nine drum tracks.

2   Start playback at the beginning of the second pre-chorus (around bar 55).

TIP▶ When mixing, you often need to repeatedly start playback from the same position. You can use the Marquee tool to indicate a playback position. First zoom in on a section, and hold down the Marquee tool (your current Command-click tool) for about a second in the Arrange area to create a thin vertical white line. Then use the Spacebar to toggle playback from that position. To clear the Marquee playback position, click the background of the Arrange area with the Pointer tool.

Marquee playback position

3   On the Hats channel strip, set the Pan control to –24.

To pan the toms, you need to find a playback position in the Arrange area where the drummer plays a tom fill—for example, toward the beginning of the last chorus. You will exaggerate the toms' panning to make the drum kit sound wider than it really is.

4   On the tom channel strips, set the Pan controls to the following values:

▶   Tom1: –57

▶   Tom2: +24

▶   Tom3: +49

Listen again to a section where the drummer hits the toms. They really sound spread out in the stereo field, widening the sound of the tom fills.

5   Option-click one of the soloed channel strips' Solo button to unsolo them all.

To spread the guitars in the stereo field, you will pan them left and right. First, solo all the guitar channel strips.

6   In the Mixer, scroll toward the right, and drag across the eight guitar channel strips labels, from V Acous 1 (channel strip 16) to Elec 2 (channel strip 23).

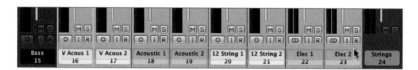

All eight channel strips are selected, and their settings are temporarily linked.

7   On one of the selected channel strips, click the Solo button.

All eight channel strips are soloed. You need to deselect the channel strips to unlink their parameters.

8   Select any channel strip to deselect the eight guitar channel strips.

Notice that the guitars were recorded in pairs. Two acoustic guitars during the verses (V Acous 1 and V Acous 2), two acoustic guitars during the choruses (Acoustic 1 and Acoustic 2), two 12-string guitars (12 String 1 and 12 String 2), and finally two electric guitars (Elec 1 and Elec 2). Focusing on one pair of guitar channel strips at a time, you will pan the first guitar to the left and the second to the right. However, on each side of the stereo field, you don't want to end up with four guitars overlapping each other in the same position. So, you will vary the amount of panning for each pair of guitars.

You may want to scroll down in the Arrange area to see all the guitar regions, so you can easily navigate to a section where the guitars you are adjusting are playing.

9   Play a verse, and pan V Acous 1 to –24 and V Acous 2 to +23.

10   Play a chorus, and pan Acoustic 1 to –53 and Acoustic 2 to +50.

11   Pan 12 Strings 1 to –64 and 12 Strings 2 to +46.

While mono channel strips include a Pan control (which determines the position of the mono signal in the stereo field), stereo channel strips include a Balance control (which determines the relative levels of the left and right signals). In other words, a stereo channel strip always sends the left signal to the left speaker and the right signal to the right speaker, but turning the Balance control to one side turns down the level of the signal sent to the speaker on the other side.

MORE INFO ▸ For true stereo panning, you can use the Direction Mixer plug-in (in the Imaging category).

12 Set the Elec 1 and Elec 2 Balance controls to –47 and +46, respectively.

Now the guitars are spread out and you have achieved better stereo separation, making it easier for the listener to distinguish each individual guitar.

13 On one of the guitar channel strips, Option-click the Solo button.

The mix sounds much wider, like an ensemble of eight guitar players placed at different positions in a room, rather than a single guitar player who layered eight guitar tracks.

Choosing EQ Settings

The sound of an instrument is composed of several frequencies mixed together in various amounts. By using an EQ plug-in to attenuate or boost certain ranges of frequency, you can alter the timbre of the sound, much as you would change the sound of your stereo by tweaking the bass or treble knobs.

EQ plug-ins can shape the sound of your instruments, focusing the sound in a specific frequency range, and helping that instrument cut through the mix without boosting the overall level of its channel strip. Equalizing (EQing) an instrument can also decrease unwanted frequencies in its recording and keep it from masking another instrument in the same frequency range.

To shape the frequency spectrum of your snare, you will use the Channel EQ plug-in to attenuate some of its low rumbling while boosting the high frequencies to make it sound snappier.

1   In the Arrange area, drag a cycle area from bar 25 to bar 31.

2   In the Mixer, scroll to the left and solo the Snare channel strip (channel strip 2).

3   On the Snare channel strip, double-click the EQ area.

A Channel EQ plug-in is inserted in the first available Insert slot below the compressor, and the Channel EQ window opens.

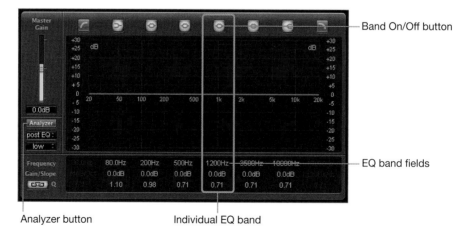

The Channel EQ plug-in allows you to adjust eight bands of EQ. You can toggle a band on and off by clicking the button at the top of the band. By default, the first and last bands are turned off, and all of the other bands are turned on. Each band's settings are shown below the graphic display in the parameter section.

Clicking the Analyzer button turns on the frequency analyzer, which displays the frequency spectrum curve of the sound on the graphic display when the track is playing.

TIP ▶ By default, the frequency analyzer displays the frequency spectrum of the sound at the output of the Channel EQ plug-in. You can click the Pre/Post EQ button below the Analyzer button to switch the frequency analyzer to pre EQ. It will then display the frequency spectrum of the sound at the input of the Channel EQ, before being adjusted by the Channel EQ.

4   Click the Analyzer button.

5   Start playback.

A curve appears in the graphic display, showing the sound's frequency spectrum curve in real time. Every time the kick hits, notice the pulsating movement in the very low range of frequencies (to the left).

You will filter out those very low frequencies to attenuate the low frequencies of the kick drum in the snare audio signal.

6   On the left, click the first Band On/Off button to turn that EQ band on.

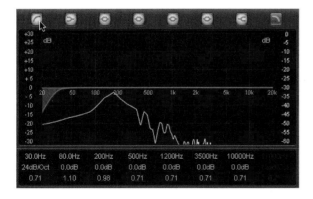

The first EQ band's shape appears on the graphic display, and you can see that the low frequencies are attenuated below 30 Hz.

7   In the parameter section below the graphic display, drag the Frequency parameter of the first band up to 70 Hz.

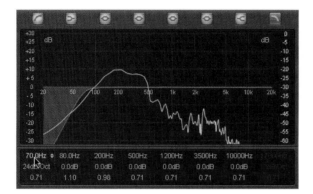

The EQ band shape updates in the graphic display. In the frequency curve displayed by the Analyzer, you can watch the low frequency content disappear from the snare signal. Not all speakers reproduce very low frequencies, and you may not hear the result, but it will make an audible difference in a system that accurately reproduces very low frequencies.

Now you will attenuate the low-mid frequencies to get the mud out of the snare sound. Instead of adjusting the numerical settings in the parameter section, you can drag the mouse pointer on the graphic display to adjust the shape of individual bands.

8   Position the mouse pointer over the graphic display and move the mouse from left to right.

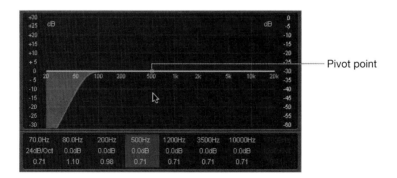

Pivot point

As you move the mouse horizontally, you can see the settings for the EQ band high-lighted in the parameter section.

You can shape the selected EQ band by dragging in the graphic display.

▶ To adjust the gain, drag vertically in the area of the EQ band.

▶ To adjust the frequency, drag horizontally in the area of the EQ band.

▶ To adjust the Q (or width, or resonance), drag the pivot point (which appears at that band's frequency) vertically.

You first need to adjust the gain of the band to see its shape on the graphic display.

9 Position the mouse pointer to select the fourth band, which is currently set to a frequency of 500 Hz.

10 Place the mouse pointer in the background of the graphic display (away from the pivot point) and drag down so the Gain parameter below reads –10.0dB.

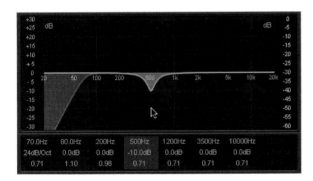

The shape of the selected EQ band appears on the graphic display, and the settings below are adjusted according to your mouse movements.

Now, while listening to the snare, you will adjust both the Q and the frequency of the EQ band you are attenuating.

11 Drag the pivot point all the way down to get a wide band of EQ.

12 Drag the band to the left to set the frequency to 450 Hz.

13 Drag down in the area of the band to set the gain to –11 dB.

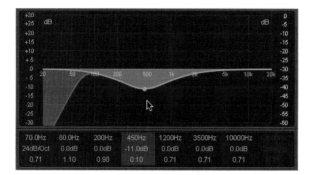

The snare sounds less muddy already. Remember to click the Bypass button to compare the snare sound before and after the EQ.

Now you can boost a high-frequency EQ band to make the snare sound snappier and have it more easily cut through the mix.

14 Adjust the sixth EQ band's parameters:

▶ Set the frequency to 5700 Hz.

▶ Set the gain to +7.5 dB.

▶ Set the Q to 0.12.

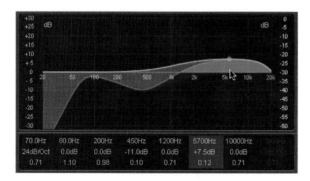

Now the snare sounds clearer and will cut through the mix.

15 Close the Channel EQ window (or press Command-W).

16 Unsolo the Snare channel strip.

17 Keep playing the song, and Option-click the Channel EQ plug-in to toggle it on and off, comparing the sound with and without the Channel EQ.

With the Channel EQ turned on, the snare volume is lower, so you need to raise its volume fader to bring it back up in the mix. First you need to temporarily disable the drums group so you can adjust the snare volume level without adjusting the whole drum kit.

18 From the Mixer's local menu bar, choose Options > Group Clutch (or press Command-G).

In the drum channel strips' Group slot, the group is dimmed.

19 Drag the Snare fader up to –3.1 dB.

20 Press Command-G again to turn the drums group back on.

By applying an EQ plug-in to the snare, you shaped its frequency spectrum to make it sound clearer and snappier, giving the snare its appropriate place in the frequency spectrum of the mix.

Using Delay and Reverberation

In a natural environment, an instrument's sound is reflected by the floor, walls, and ceiling of a room. The sounds of those reflections, combined with the direct sound of the instrument, allow listeners to determine the distance from the instrument to their ears and understand the nature of the acoustic space.

When recording instruments, you can choose to record in an absorbent studio to primarily record the direct sound of each instrument. You then use delay and reverberation plug-ins to create artificial reflections, giving you total control over the apparent placement and depth of the instruments.

Adding Delay to the Vocals

By adding delay and reverberation to vocals, you'll give them more depth. Since you are now working with a single channel strip, you can close the Mixer to get a better view of your arrangement.

1   Close the Mixer.

2   Select the Lead Vocal track (track 25).

3   Start playback at the beginning of the first verse.

Notice how dry the vocals sound. They were recorded in an absorbent studio, and you can't hear much reverberation.

First, you will add a delay plug-in to add dimension to the vocals.

4   In the left Arrange Channel Strip, click the first available Insert slot (below the DeEsser), and choose Delay > Tape Delay.

The Tape Delay plug-in is inserted and its window opens. You can hear the reflections on the vocals as an echo. By default, the tape delay is automatically synchronized to the project tempo so the reflections are produced every quarter note. That sounds fine for this song.

In the Tape Delay window, you can use the two Output sliders to the right to adjust the level balance between Dry (the sound not affected by the plug-in) and Wet (the reflections generated by the plug-in). You will bring the Dry signal all the way up to its maximum level, so you have the same level of direct sound as you had before inserting the plug-in.

5   Drag the Dry slider up to 100%.

At the lower left of the Tape Delay window, you can adjust the Low Cut and High Cut sliders to filter the sound of the reflections. Narrowing the frequency range of the reflections gives them a more rounded sound, so they are not as sharp as the dry sound. This allows you to make the echo effect less perceptible and more natural sounding.

6   Drag the Low Cut slider toward the right to 160 Hz.

7   Drag the High Cut slider toward the left to 10,000 Hz.

The reflections are now softer and don't steal attention from the dry vocal sound.

Adding Reverb Using Aux Sends

You could insert a reverb plug-in directly in the channel strip the same way you inserted a delay plug-in in the previous exercise. However, when you use reverb to place the instruments in an artificial room, using an individual reverb plug-in for each instrument would require a lot of processing power. You would also have to readjust the parameters of every reverb plug-in each time you wanted to change the sound of your artificial room.

Instead, you can use aux sends to route some of the signal from a channel strip to a new channel strip, called an *aux* (auxiliary channel). Once you have set up an aux channel strip with the desired reverb plug-in, you can add reverberation to any instrument by sending some of its signal to that aux for processing.

In this exercise, you will use an aux send to send the lead vocal to an aux, and insert the reverberation plug-in on the aux channel strip.

1   Make sure the Lead Vocal track (track 25) is still selected, and solo it.

2   In the left Arrange channel strip, click the first Send slot and choose Bus > Bus 1.

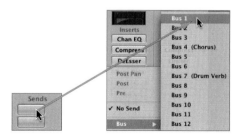

When you click on a Send slot and choose an available bus, a new aux channel strip is automatically created and added to the Mixer. In the Inspector, the right channel strip automatically shows the Aux 1 channel strip, so you can monitor the signal path from the lead vocal channel strip to the aux channel strip. In the I/O section of the Aux 1 channel strip, the input is set to Bus 1.

A bus is a virtual audio cable that allows you to route the audio signal from one channel strip to another—in this case, from the lead vocal channel strip to a new aux channel strip. By default, an aux send is positioned in the signal flow of the channel strip after the volume fader but before the pan. You will later learn to change aux send positions, but for routing vocals to a reverb, that position is perfect, as the balance between dry and wet will be preserved if you adjust the level of the vocal.

3   In the left channel strip, Option-click the Send level knob next to Bus 1.

The Bus 1 send level is set to 0.0 dB, and the Aux 1 channel strip meter displays the same signal level as the left channel strip.

By default, choosing a new bus in the Send slot of a mono channel strip creates a mono Aux channel strip. In this case, you want to make that Aux stereo have a wider stereo reverb effect, where different reflections have different positions in the stereo field. You can toggle the mono/stereo status of a channel strip by clicking its Format button below the meter.

4   Below the Aux 1 channel strip's meter, click the Format button.

The Format button now displays two interleaved circles, indicating the channel strip is stereo. Notice the channel strip now has a stereo meter.

MORE INFO ▶ You can also hold down the Format button to choose other channel strip formats such as Left, Right, or Surround.

Now you will insert a reverb plug-in.

5   On the aux channel strip, click the first Insert slot and choose Reverb > Space Designer.

You will now choose a preset for the Space Designer plug-in.

LOGIC EXPRESS ▶ Instead of Space Designer, choose Reverb > GoldVerb and in the following step, choose the Medium Room setting.

6   In the Space Designer plug-in header, click the Settings menu and choose 01 Large Spaces > 01 Rooms > 02.1s_Big Drums.

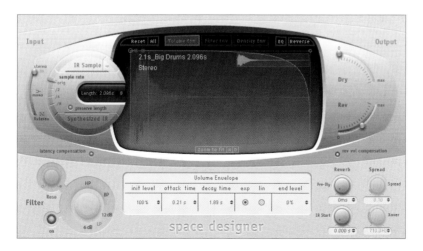

You can hear the reverb's effect on the vocals. When you solo a channel strip, any channel strip included in its signal flow is not muted. In this case, Output 1-2 and Aux 1 are not muted, so you can hear the vocals and their reverb.

At the upper right of the Space Designer plug-in window, notice the two Output sliders, Dry and Rev. When a plug-in is inserted on an aux channel strip, the Dry slider is automatically set to 0, so the aux channel strip processes 100 percent of the signal that is sent to that aux. You can adjust the balance between dry and wet signals on the left channel strip. The volume fader adjusts the dry signal, and the Bus 1 Send level knob adjusts the amount of reverb.

7   Drag the Bus 1 Send level knob down to −7.3 dB.

You can now send any channel strip to Bus 1 to route it to that aux channel strip and add the same reverb effect to its sound. Let's add some reverb to one of the guitar tracks.

8   Unsolo the vocals.

9   Open the Mixer.

10 Solo the V Acous 1 channel strip (channel strip 16).

Make sure you start playback in a verse to hear the sound of the V Acous 1 guitar.

11 On the V Acous 1 channel strip, click the first aux Send slot and choose Bus > Bus 1 (Aux 1).

12 Slowly raise the Bus 1 Send level knob to adjust the amount of reverb in the acoustic guitar.

13 Unsolo the guitar.

14 Close the Space Designer plug-in window.

Now you will add reverb to some of the drum channel strips. Scroll all the way to the right of the Mixer. One of the last channel strips is an aux channel strip called Drum Verb, with reverberation and compression plug-ins adjusted for drum sounds.

Notice that the input of that channel strip is set to Bus 7. You will use Bus 7 to route the snare and the toms to that aux channel strip.

15 Scroll to the left of the Mixer, and select both the Snare and Snare B channel strips. Then hold down Shift and select the three tom channel strips.

16 On one of the selected channel strips, click the first aux Send slot and choose Bus > Bus 7 (Drum Verb).

All the selected channel strips now send to the Drum Verb aux channel strip. By default, aux sends are placed in the signal flow before the pan, which means that even though you carefully panned the toms in an earlier exercise, their reverb sounds will be panned to the center.

To make sure that the reverb of the toms is positioned at the same place as the toms in the stereo sound field, you can change the position of the aux sends to *post pan* on the selected channel strips.

17 On one of the selected channel strips, position the mouse pointer over one of the Bus 7 aux sends, hold down the mouse button, and choose Post Pan.

The aux sends of the selected drum channel strips are placed after the pan, and the reverb on these toms will be panned to the same position as their direct sounds.

TIP ▶ You can also choose Pre, which places the aux send both pre fader and pre pan. When used with an aux channel strip with a reverb plug-in, this setting can be useful to create an effect where you progressively drown an instrument in reverb, slowly fading out the dry signal by dragging down a channel strip's level fader, while the level of the reverb remains constant.

18 In one of the selected channel strips, click the Solo button.

19 Click any channel strip to deselect the other channel strips and unlink their settings.

20 One by one, drag the aux Send level knobs on the snare and tom channel strips vertically to adjust their reverb levels to suit your taste.

21 In one of the soloed channel strips, Option-click the Solo button.

All the channel strips are unsoloed.

Listen to the drums and their reverbs in the mix, and adjust the amount of reverb on the snare and toms, if necessary.

22 Close the Mixer.

Using Dynamic Processing Plug-ins

The dynamic range of a recording is the difference between the softest and loudest parts of the recording. Sometimes too much dynamic range in a recording can be a problem, as the loudest parts become too loud, and the softest parts are barely audible. You can use dynamic processing plug-ins such as a compressor or a limiter to control the dynamic range of an audio signal, usually to make the audio signal level more consistent over time.

Dynamic processing can be applied to a single channel strip or to the entire mix.

Using the Compressor

When recording an instrument, the musician rarely plays all the notes at the same volume. This can become a challenge when mixing, as some of the notes will stick out while others are buried in the mix.

A compressor attenuates a signal when its level reaches a specific threshold. You can use it to attenuate notes that are too loud and raise the overall level of the instrument to bring up the softer notes.

You will use a compressor plug-in to make the dynamic range of the acoustic guitar in your intro more consistent, making sure you can hear all the notes at the same level.

1   Drag a cycle area from bar 5 to bar 9 (the first half of the first verse).

2   Start playback.

Listen to the acoustic guitar. The first few notes are nice and loud, but the two notes around bar 7 are too soft and get buried behind the bass and the vocals.

3   Select the V Acous 1 track (track 16).

4   In the left Arrange channel strip, click the first Insert slot below the Channel EQ, and choose Dynamics > Compressor.

While the song is playing, look at the Gain Reduction meter. It becomes active when the compressor is triggered. The first few notes trigger the compressor (you can see the meter react), but the softer notes around bar 7 barely trigger it.

Below the Compressor Threshold slider, two buttons let you choose between peak or RMS methods to analyze the incoming audio signal and determine how it should trigger the compressor. The acoustic guitar notes have strong attacks, and you want the attacks to be attenuated by the compressor, so you'll choose Peak.

5   Below the Compressor Threshold slider, click the Peak button.

On the Gain Reduction meter, you can see the attack of the notes being attenuated a little more than when RMS was selected.

You will now adjust the threshold so all the notes trigger the compressor.

6   Drag the Compressor Threshold slider down to –19.5 dB.

On the Gain Reduction meter, you can see the compressor being triggered by all the notes. The gain reduction slowly decrease as the notes sustain, and you can hear the notes sustain longer.

You can adjust the amount of compression with the Ratio slider, which adjusts the ratio by which the signal is reduced when it exceeds the threshold.

7   Drag the Ratio slider to 3.3:1.

TIP ▶ If you want to make the compression really obvious, you can experiment with more extreme settings by turning the threshold down further and raising the ratio.

Notice the Gain slider is set to 4.0 dB, raising the overall level of the guitar signal. The compressor attenuates the parts of the signal that go above the threshold, then raises the overall level to compensate for that attenuation.

The guitar sound is now more consistent. The attacks are softened, and the notes sustain longer. All the notes are closer to being the same level, and you don't hear the guitar drop in volume around bar 7 as you did before compressing it. Don't hesitate to solo the guitar track and toggle the compressor's bypass button to compare the sound with and without compression.

8   Close the Compressor window.

9   In the Bar ruler, click the cycle area to turn off Cycle mode.

Using a Compressor and a Limiter on the Master Channel Strip

On a professional project, you would usually send your final mix to a mastering engineer, who would put a final polish on the stereo audio file using subtle amounts of EQ, compression, reverb or other processing.

When you don't have the budget to hire a mastering engineer, you can master your own mix, inserting plug-ins on the Output 1-2 channel strip, as in this exercise. You will start by using a compressor to make the mix level consistent throughout the song, and then apply a limiter to make sure you're not clipping the Output 1-2 channel strip audio.

1   Start playback at the beginning of the song.

When you choose a bus in the Send slot of the left Arrange channel strip, the right Arrange channel strip automatically updates to display the Aux corresponding to that bus. You can choose to display any channel strip in the signal flow of the left Arrange channel strip by clicking the desired send or output slot.

2   On the left Arrange channel strip, click the Output slot.

The right Arrange channel strip now displays the Out 1-2 channel strip.

3   On the Out 1-2 channel strip, click the first Insert slot and choose Dynamics > Compressor.

The compressor is inserted and its window opens. This time you will use a setting designed to emulate the soft, warm compression of analog tape recorders.

4   Click the Setting button and choose 05 Compressor Tools > Analog Tape Compression.

Try playing different sections of the song. In the intro, the bass barely triggers the compressor. In the first verse, the compressor attenuates the mix by up to 2 or 3 dB. In the loudest parts of the song, like the choruses, the compressor attenuates the mix by up to 6 dB. Since the Gain parameter raises the overall gain at the output of the compressor, you end up with a louder mix with more consistent levels from section to section.

You can see the clip detector on the Out 1-2 channel strip going into the red.

You will now insert a limiter after the compressor to ensure that you don't clip the output. A limiter works in a manner similar to a compressor; but, when the signal reaches a certain threshold, it attenuates the signal so that the output signal never exceeds a specific ceiling.

5   Click the Insert slot below the compressor and choose Dynamics > Adaptive Limiter.

LOGIC EXPRESS ▶ Choose Dynamics > Limiter and keep the default settings.

At the bottom of the Adaptive Limiter plug-in window, the Out Ceiling is set to 0.0 dB, ensuring that the audio signal will never go over 0 dBFS on the Out 1-2 channel strip. The meters on the left display the signal level at the input of the plug-in; the meters on the right display the signal level at the output of the plug-in.

When adjusting the Adaptive Limiter, you should adjust the Input Scale knob to avoid having red "overs" warnings on the input meters. However, sometimes a few red overs can be OK. When in doubt, trust your ears!

6 Drag the Input Scale down to –3.4 dB.

7 At the top of the input meters, click both red over warnings to reset them.

The overs are dimmed. Keep playing the song and make sure the overs don't turn red all the time.

You can now adjust the Gain knob in the middle of the plug-in window to raise the perceived level of the mix. This is when you need to pay close attention to what you are hearing. While it is tempting to raise the Gain to produce a louder mix, high gain settings will introduce distortion.

8 Drag the Gain knob up to 10.0 dB.

You can clearly hear the distortion introduced by the Adaptive Limiter, even though the signal is not clipping on the Out 1-2 channel strip meters.

NOTE ▶ During playback and after you stop playback, the clip detector keeps displaying the last maximum peak value. When you start playback again, the clip detector is automatically reset. If you have not stopped playback since you inserted the Adaptive Limiter plug-in, remember to click the clip detector on the Out 1-2 channel strip to reset it.

TIP ▶ When you are not sure how a specific plug-in parameter affects the sound, don't hesitate to turn it all the way up and all the way down. The results are most probably not going to be good, but you will hear how that setting affects the sound, and you will know what to focus on in the sound as you adjust the parameter to a more reasonable setting.

9 Drag the Gain down to 5.9 dB.

Even though the Adaptive Limiter's output meters still display "over" warnings, the audible distortion disappears, and the Adaptive Limiter still gives you a nice gain boost on the whole mix.

10 Close the plug-in windows and click the Bypass button to turn both plug-ins on and off, comparing the mix with and without the compressor and limiter plug-ins on the Out 1-2 channel strip.

The compressor and limiter plug-ins make your mix sound more consistent.

You have finished your mix using effect plug-ins and adjusting the four main parameters of the instrument sounds (volume levels, pan position, frequency, and depth) to give each sound its own place in the stereo sound field.

To study and listen to one possible version of this final mix, go to Logic 8_Files > Media > Mitral Valve Prolapse and, depending on your version of Logic 8, open one of these Logic projects:

▶   Mitral Valve Prolapse Logic Express 8

▶   Mitral Valve Prolapse Logic Pro 8

The final mix is more complete, with additional tracks and more processing plug-ins applied. It also includes a lot of track automation, which will be the topic of the next lesson.

A Few Tips and Tricks

Like any other art, mixing requires a combination of skill, experience, and talent. It takes practice to learn to apply mixing techniques efficiently, and even more practice to learn to listen. Here are a few tips and tricks that will help you perfect your craft and become better at mixing your projects.

Take a Break

After you mix for while and listen to the same song for the hundredth time, you can lose your objectivity and experience ear fatigue. Take frequent breaks while mixing, and return to the mix with rested ears. You will then be able to better judge your results.

Listen to Your Mix Outside the Studio

When you feel your mix is pretty advanced and you are happy with the way it sounds in your studio, burn it on a CD and listen to it in a boombox in another room or, even better, in your car while driving. You will probably hear things you didn't notice in your studio, and miss things you could hear clearly in your studio. You can take notes, and go back to your studio to rework the mix. Obviously, the mix will never sound the same in the studio and in the car, but it's the mixing engineer's job to make sure that all the instruments can be heard in most situations.

Compare Your Mix with Commercial Mixes

Compare your mix with the commercial mixes you like. Build a small library of good-sounding mixes in the same genre of music as the songs you are mixing. You can open a new Logic project and place your mix on one track, and a professional mix on another track so you can solo them and compare them one after the other.

Lesson Review

1. Identify the four main instrument sound components that you can adjust to give each instrument its place in a mix.

2. For what purpose do you use an aux send?

3. How can you temporarily link the parameters of several channel strips?

4. How can you permanently link the parameters of several channel strips?

5. How can you adjust the level of an individual channel strip assigned to a group?

6. Where is an aux send positioned in the signal flow of a channel strip?

7. What does a compressor do?

8. What does a limiter do?

9. How can you choose which channel strip is displayed in the right Arrange channel strip?

10. How do you change the mono or stereo status of a channel strip?

Answers

1. Volume level, pan position, frequency spectrum, and depth.

2. You use an aux send to route some of the signal from a channel strip to an aux channel strip, usually to be processed by plug-ins.

3. Select multiple channel strips in the Mixer to temporarily link their parameters.

4. By using groups. Click the Group slot on a channel strip to choose a group to assign that channel strip to.

5. Choose Option > Group Clutch to toggle the groups on and off.

6. By default, aux sends are positioned after the volume fader but before the pan. You can also choose to position them before the volume fader or after the pan.

7. It attenuates the level of a signal after that signal goes over a certain threshold, giving the signal a more consistent level.

8. It works in a similar fashion to a compressor, but it makes sure that the signal is attenuated so it never goes over a certain output ceiling.

9. On the left Arrange channel strip, click any send slot or the output slot to display the corresponding channel strip on the right.

10. Click the format button below the meter.

10

Lesson Files   Logic 8_Files > Lessons > 10 LVL-Home_start

Time   This lesson takes approximately 40 minutes to complete.

Goals   Edit automation offline

Record live automation

Record live automation using a control surface

Export the final mix

Automating the Mix and Using Control Surfaces

When multitrack recorders first appeared in recording studios, they forever changed the way artists produced music. Having separate recordings of individual instruments opened the door for experimentation, and soon artists and producers alike placed their hands on the mixing board during the final mixdown, panning an instrument from left to right, or riding a volume fader to change the level of a track throughout a song. Soon enough, two or three pairs of hands weren't enough to perform all the changes needed throughout a mix, and a solution was needed.

Eventually, mixing consoles were designed so that moving a fader also generated a data stream. By recording those data streams onto a separate track of the multitrack tape, the console could automatically recreate the fader movements during playback. This started the era of automated consoles. Today, professional computerized mixing boards and digital audio workstations are fully automated.

In Logic, you can automate almost all the controls on a channel strip, including volume, pan, and all plug-in parameters. In this lesson, you will draw and edit offline automation to play a snare at different volume levels in verses and choruses, create a decrescendo on a pair of grouped guitars, and pan a sound effect from left to right. You will then record live automation using the mouse, bypassing a plug-in and tweaking its parameters remotely using the knobs on a control surface.

Creating and Editing Offline Automation

In Logic, the techniques used to create and edit track-based automation closely resemble Hyper Draw, the graphic editing of MIDI continuous controller events that you explored in Lesson 5, "Programming and Editing MIDI." While Hyper Draw allows you to auto-mate MIDI CC parameters in a region, track automation lets you automate almost any channel strip controls (including all plug-in sliders, knobs, and bypasses) and to do so independently of the regions on the track.

Drawing automation graphically is also known as *offline automation*, because it is inde-pendent of the playhead position and can be performed while Logic is stopped.

Creating Automation to Adjust the Volume of a Section

When you need accurate control over the volume of an instrument in specific sections of the song, drawing offline automation over the waveform gives you surgical precision with-out the pressure of performing fader movements in real time.

You will now create offline volume automation on the snare track so that it plays softer during the verses.

1   Go to Logic 8_Files > Lessons and open **10 LVL-Home_start**.

2   Play the song.

   Throughout this lesson, you may want to use the Track Solo buttons or Solo mode to listen to a track before automating it.

   Listen to the snare on track 6. It is really sharp and sounds great in busier sections such as the choruses, but it is a little too loud and distracting during the verses. You will automate the snare volume to remedy this.

3   In the Toolbar, click the Automation button.

In the Arrange area, tracks need to be tall enough to display their automation data, so the Arrange area is automatically zoomed in vertically. In the Automation Parameter menu on the track header, you can choose the parameter to be displayed in the *automation track,* a transparent gray area overlaid on the track.

Automation Parameter menu   Automation track

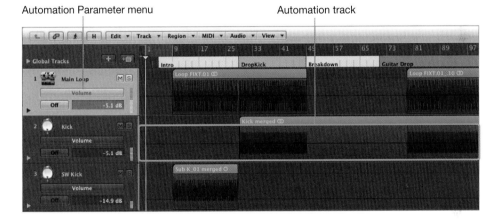

While it can be useful in some cases to view the automation tracks for all the tracks, in this case you need to automate only the snare track. You can use Auto Track Zoom to automatically expand the height of the selected track, thereby displaying the automation data only on the selected track.

4   In the Toolbar, click the Automation button to hide the automation tracks.

The Arrange area returns to its previous vertical zoom level.

5   In the Toolbar, click the Auto Zoom button (or press Z).

The selected track (Main Loop, track 1) expands vertically, while all other tracks retain their original vertical zoom levels.

6 In the Toolbar, click the Automation button (or press A).

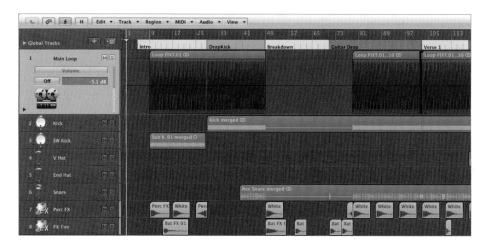

The automation track is displayed for the selected track only.

7 Click the Snare track header (track 6).

The Snare track is selected and zoomed in vertically, while the previously selected track returns to its original zoom level. You can see the snare's volume automation track and its Automation Parameter menu in the Snare track header. In the automation track, a horizontal black line indicates the current volume level of the track (–11.2 dB).

8 Control-option-drag to zoom in on the Snare track around the Verse 1 section.

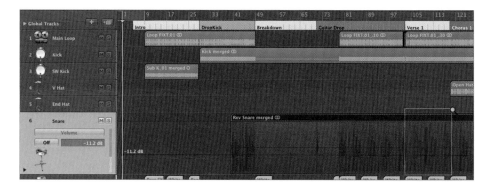

TIP If you need more horizontal space in your Arrange area, you can close the Inspector by clicking the Inspector button in the Toolbar (or by pressing I).

9 Zoom in on the first few snare hits at the beginning of the verse.

Using your waveform-reading skills, you'll notice that the last snare before the verse is a reversed snare. You will drop the snare volume level after that reversed snare plays.

You can edit track-based automation using the same drawing techniques you learned when creating Hyper Draw automation of MIDI CC events in Lesson 5.

10 Just after the reversed snare that leads into the verse, click the black line to create a node at the current volume level (–11.2 dB).

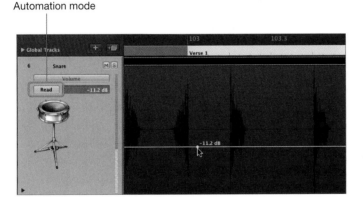

Automation mode

The node is created and the yellow volume automation line appears.

When you create the first automation node on a track, the automation mode auto-matically switches from Off to Read, so the next time you play the project, the volume automation you create will be read by the level fader. You can see the automation mode of the selected track on its channel strip and track header.

11 Hold down the mouse button slightly below the yellow automation line and to the right of the node you just created—but before the first snare in the verse—then drag the new node to −16.4 dB.

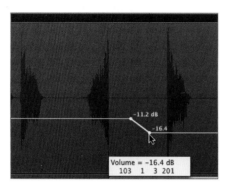

You have reduced the volume just before the verse. Now you need to create two more nodes at the end of the verse to return the volume to its original level for the following chorus.

12 Control-Option-click in the background to return to the previous zoom level.

You should now be able to see the entire Verse 1 section. Depending on your screen resolution, you may need to zoom in to perform the following steps, but if you can clearly see the individual snare hits on the waveform, try to create the automation without zooming in.

13 After the last snare in the verse (at bar 119), click the yellow automation line to create a node at −16.4 dB.

14 Place your mouse pointer slightly above and to the right of the node you just created, and drag up to position the new node at a value of −11.2 dB.

When trying to create a node close to an existing node, you may accidentally click the existing node and delete it. If this happens, hold down the mouse button a little farther to the right of the existing node, and then drag the new node to the desired position.

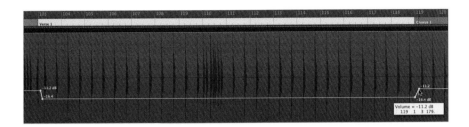

You have changed the level of the snare so that it drops to –16.4 dB during Verse 1, and then returns to –11.2 dB at the beginning of Chorus 1. You will now create the same automation in Verse 2.

15 Scroll to the right until you can see the entire Verse 2.

This time, you will use a new technique using the Marquee tool to quickly set a different volume for a section of the song. Remember to press Command to use the Marquee tool.

16 In Verse 2, drag the Marquee tool from just before the first snare to after the last snare.

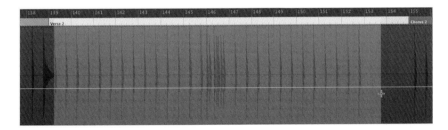

You can now adjust the volume of the section by vertically dragging the horizontal line within the Marquee selection

17 Drag down the horizontal line within the Marquee selection to –16.4 dB.

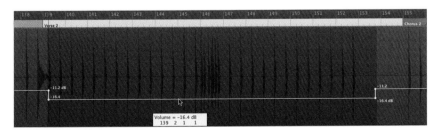

As you drag the line down, you can see two nodes created on each end of the Marquee selection, so dragging the automation line only adjusts the volume for the selected section.

18 Control-Option-click outside the Marquee selection to zoom out.

19 Start playback just before the first verse.

In the left Arrange channel strip, watch the level fader "read" the automation you just created, and notice the softer snare in the verses.

Creating a Decrescendo with Volume Automation

In this exercise, you will create a slow decrescendo on the Heavy Guitars track to evolve the timbre of the Guitar Drop section. It will start with an assault of aggressively distorted guitars; then the guitars will slowly fade out throughout the section, leaving some space in the mix for the synths that start playing a melody and, later, a chord progression.

1 Select the Heavy Guitars track (track 10).

The Heavy Guitars track expands vertically and you can see its volume automation track.

2 Listen to the Guitar Drop section (starting around bar 69).

When the guitars come in at the beginning of the Guitar Drop section, they are supported by two more guitar tracks playing an octave lower (in tracks 11 and 12), which creates a strong impact. The mix is very sparse at that point, so the guitars fill the entire sound field. Then, the drum beat and the synths return at bar 79. At bar 87, the synth starts playing a melodic riff and is joined by a dreamy high-pitch synth. You can hear an evolution from the very aggressive guitars at the beginning of the section to the more musical synths at the end. However, the guitars play the same rhythm at the same volume throughout the section, fighting with the melodic synths at the end of the section.

You will now create a decrescendo on the Heavy Guitars to slowly make space for the dreamier synth melodies at the end of the section.

3 Click the black horizontal line at the beginning of the first Heavy Guitars region to create a node at the current volume (−5.3 dB).

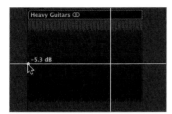

The node is created and the Heavy Guitars automation mode is set to Read.

Before you create the decrescendo, you will create another node at the current volume level before the next Heavy Guitars region on the track. This will ensure that the next regions on that track play at –5.3 dB.

4   Click the yellow volume automation line after the end of the first Heavy Guitars region, but before the next region on the track.

You can now draw the decrescendo over the first Heavy Guitars region without worrying about changing the volume automation of the remaining regions to the right.

5   Create a node at the end of the first Heavy Guitars region, before the last node you created, and drag it all the way down to negative infinity (–∞).

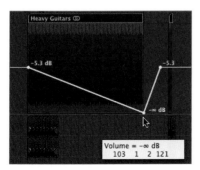

You can now add a curve to the decrescendo to make it a little slower at the beginning and faster toward the end of the Guitar Drop section. When you Control-Option-drag an automation line to create a curve, make sure you first click exactly on the line with the tip of the mouse pointer. If you Control-Option-drag in the background, you will be zooming in.

6   Control-Option-drag the sloped automation line in the Guitar Drop section upward to create a convex curve.

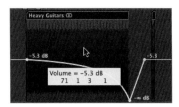

7   Listen to the Guitar Drop section.

Listen to the way the section evolves as you see the level fader slowly move down on the left Arrange channel strip. It starts with the guitars playing loudly; then they slowly fade out as the synths start playing. Later in the section, the guitars slowly disappear as the synths play melodic lines. The Guitar Drop section evolves from an aggressive rhythm guitar pattern to a melodic synth part that leads into the first verse.

Creating Pan Automation

Pan automation can be a fun way to create movement in your mix, moving a sound from one side of the stereo field to the other. It is a powerful effect that calls attention to the automated sound but, when used in moderation, can add life to a sound effect.

You will now draw offline pan automation on the first sound effect after the intro, making it move from the left speaker to a position slightly right of center.

1   Select the Perc FX track (track 7).

Automation Parameter menu

You can use the Automation Parameter menu in the track header to choose the parameter you want to automate.

2   In the Perc FX track header, click the Automation Parameter menu and choose Pan.

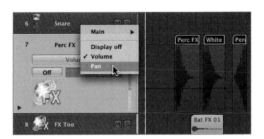

The Perc FX track now displays the pan automation track.

3   Zoom in on the first Perc FX region.

The black horizontal line at the top of the pan automation track indicates the current pan position (−64).

4   Create a node on the black horizontal line (−64) at the beginning of the region.

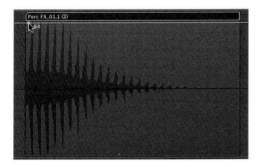

The node is created, and the green pan automation line appears. The Perc FX automation mode is automatically set to Read.

5   Create a node around the middle of the region, and drag it down to +20.

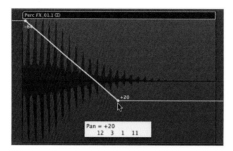

Your new pan automation will move the sound effect from the left speaker to its new pan position, slightly to the right (+20).

6   Start playback before the first Perc FX region to listen to your pan automation.

The pan automation is a little slow, but you can make it happen quickly so the effect will be more obvious.

7   Drag the second node (+20) to the left.

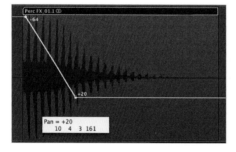

Listen while you adjust the position of the second node, or create a curve shape until you get the desired pan automation. For a more pronounced effect, try dragging the second node all the way down to +63.

8   Zoom out.

Recording Live Automation

While offline automation is a good option when you know in advance what automation movements you want to achieve, you sometimes want to hear the song playing as you adjust the controls of a channel strip (or in a plug-in window) in real time.

To record live automation, you need to choose a live automation mode for the track(s) you want to automate, start playback, and tweak the desired controls on the channel strip.

Recording Automation in Touch Mode

In Touch mode, any existing automation on the track will be read as in Read mode. As soon as you hold down the mouse button on a knob or slider, its automation is recorded. When you release the mouse button, Touch mode behaves like Read mode again, and the automation parameter returns to its original value, or reproduces any existing automation on the track.

In this exercise, you will slowly fade in a synth in the DropKick section, returning it to its original value when the snare enters.

1   Select the Virus 747 A track (track 13).

2   Listen to the beginning of the DropKick section (starting at bar 29).

The Virus synth comes in suddenly at bar 33. You will create a slow crescendo so the synth fades in slowly, reaching full volume as the snare starts on bar 41.

3   In the Virus 747 A track header, set the automation mode to Touch.

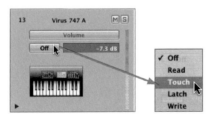

You are ready to record live automation. You don't need to put Logic in record mode to record live automation. You only need to put the track in one of the live automation modes (Touch, Latch, or Write) and start playback.

When you record automation in Touch mode, hold down the mouse button until you want the parameter to return to its original level (in this case, after you hear the first reversed snare).

4   Zoom in on the group of Virus regions in the DropKick section (bar 33 to bar 49).

Since you will now record live automation as the song is playing back, you may want to first read steps 5 through 9 before starting.

5   Start playback at the beginning of the DropKick section.

6   In the left Arrange channel strip, drag the volume fader all the way down, but don't release the mouse button.

You can see volume fader movements being recorded in the Virus 747 volume automation track.

7   When the playhead reaches the beginning of the first Virus region, slowly drag the volume fader up to create the crescendo.

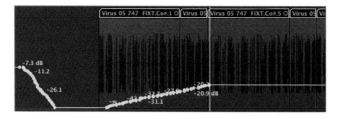

Try to time your crescendo so the level is almost back to the original level (−7.3 dB) at the beginning of the snare region.

8   When you hear the first reversed snare in bar 40, release the mouse button.

The automation line jumps back to its original level (−7.3 dB).

9   Stop playback.

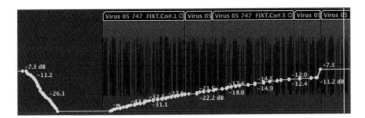

At the end of the crescendo, where you released the mouse button, you can see the volume automation jump back to the original level on the track (–7.3 dB).

If you are not entirely happy with the crescendo, or with a particular section of the crescendo, you can stay in Touch mode and correct your automation. Let's correct it now to start the crescendo a little later in the section.

10 Start playback before the first automation node on the track.

As long as you don't touch it, the level fader reproduces the volume automation on the track.

11 When the level fader is all the way down (–∞), position the mouse pointer over it and hold down the mouse button.

As soon as you start holding down the mouse button, a node is created, and the position of the fader (–∞) overwrites the existing volume automation.

12 A little later in the section, slowly start raising the level fader.

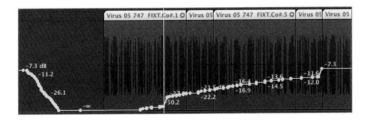

The new fader movements continue to overwrite the existing automation.

13 Continue raising the fader a little faster, trying to catch up with the level of the existing automation in the middle of the crescendo, and then release the mouse button.

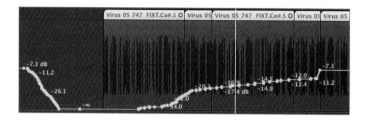

When you release the mouse button, the fader reproduces the movements of the existing volume automation on the track.

When you are done automating the track, make sure that you return its automation mode to Read, or you could accidentally record automation if you adjust any channel strip or plug-in setting while the project is playing.

14 Set the automation mode to Read.

15 Start playback at the beginning of the DropKick section to listen to the automation you created.

The Virus synth should come in slowly and jump to its original level right after the reversed snare.

Recording Automation in Latch Mode

Latch mode works the same way as Touch mode, except that when you release the mouse button, the automation continues to be recorded and the parameter stays at the same value. If automation is already present for that parameter on that track, the automation is overwritten until you stop playback.

You will now use the Latch mode to record pan automation on the Virus 747 A synth without the need to hold down the mouse button.

1 Start playback at the beginning of the DropKick section.

Listen to the Virus 747 A track. It repeats the same four-bar melody four times (although the new crescendo makes the first four-bar melody barely audible). You will try to time your Pan control movements to place each successive four-bar melody on opposite sides of the stereo sound field.

Even though you don't need to display automation tracks to record live automation, you will now display the Virus 747 A track's pan automation track to look at the pan automation as you record it.

Rather than choose Pan from the Automation Parameter menu, you can open a second automation track for the same track. That way you can still watch your volume automation as you record the pan automation.

2   In the lower-left corner of the Virus 747 A track header, click the disclosure triangle.

A separate automation sub-track opens below the track.

3   In the sub-track header's Automation Parameter menu, choose Pan.

4   In the Virus 747 A track header, choose Latch from the Automation Mode menu.

5   On the left Arrange channel strip, set the Balance control to –20 in order to pan the synth to the left.

NOTE ▶ The "Pan" automation parameter allows you to automate the Pan control of a mono channel strip or the Balance control of a stereo channel strip.

In the automation track, notice that the black horizontal line indicating the current pan position moves up to –20.

6   Start playback at the beginning of the DropKick section.

7 When you hear the synth start to fade in, wait for the end of a four-bar melody, and quickly drag up the Pan control to about +20, then release the mouse button.

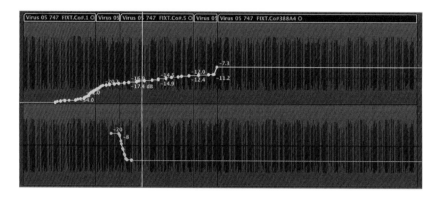

The pan automation is recorded, and the pan remains at the position it was in when you release the mouse button.

8 Wait for the end of that new four-bar melody, and drag the Pan control down to about –20, then release the mouse button.

Continue panning each four-bar melody to the opposite side of the stereo field.

9 When you have entered the last pan automation, stop playback.

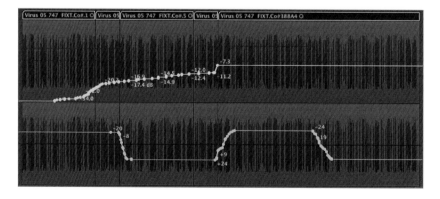

10 Listen to your result.

The synth slowly fades in during the DropKick section, reaching its full volume when the snare comes in, and the four-bar melodies alternate their pan positions from left to right.

11   In the lower-left corner of the Virus 747 A track header, click the disclosure triangle to close the pan automation sub-track.

12   Set the automation mode back to Read.

13   Zoom out.

> **NOTE** ▶ The Write automation mode is rarely used. It erases *all* automation data as the playhead passes it and records any new movements you make on the channel strip. It can be quite dangerous, as it even erases automation not currently displayed in the automation track.

Recording Plug-in Bypass Automation

Like a guitar player engaging a distortion pedal to play a solo, you'll sometimes want to use an effect plug-in for only specific sections of a song. Automating the plug-in bypass allows you to turn the effect on and off at particular positions in the song.

You will now automate the bypass of a distortion plug-in on a synth track, turning off the plug-in when the vocals enter to give them some space in the mix.

1   Select the V2 String track (track 18).

2   Zoom in on the group of regions at the end of Verse 2.

3   Start playback before the V2 String regions, around bar 145.

The first small region at the end of bar 146 sounds good as it punctuates the drum and guitar fills. Then, after bar 147, that synth starts fighting for attention with the vocals. You will bypass the Bitcrusher plug-in on the channel strip right after the first region at the end of bar 146, to bypass the distortion when the vocals enter.

4   In the left Arrange channel strip, set the automation mode to Latch.

> **NOTE** ▶ Remember that it is not necessary to choose a parameter from the track header's automation menu to record live automation.

Get ready to Option-click the Bitcrusher plug-in as soon as you've heard the distorted synth punctuating the drum fill at the end of bar 146.

5 Start playback around bar 145.

6 When you hear the end of the drum fill, Option-click the Bitcrusher plug-in to bypass it.

On the V2 String track, the Insert#1 bypass automation is automatically displayed (Bitcrusher is the first insert on the channel strip).

The bypass automation should occur on the first downbeat of bar 147, but it's OK if it's a little later, as long as you don't hear the distortion on the synth when the vocals come in.

7 On the left Arrange channel strip, set the automation mode back to Read.

8 Zoom out and listen to the result.

You still have the punctuating effect of the first synth hit at the end of the drum and guitar fill, but now the synth is not distorted during the verse, letting the vocals shine through.

Using Control Surfaces

Recording live automation by dragging onscreen sliders and knobs with the mouse can be a powerful means of expression, but nothing beats the feel of a real fader or knob under your fingers. Adding a control surface to your Logic setup allows you to map different knobs to the desired channel strip or plug-in parameters and remote-control those parameters while you record live automation.

Many supported control surfaces (such as the Mackie Control Universal) can be detected automatically by Logic, which also will automatically assign their faders and knobs.

> **MORE INFO** ▶ To learn more about supported control surfaces, choose Help > Logic Pro 8 Control Surfaces Support.

When the controls are not automatically mapped—for example, when control knobs are used on a MIDI keyboard that isn't a supported device—you can manually assign the physical knobs to the parameters you want to automate. In the following exercises, you will use two different methods for entering those assignments into Logic, then use them to automate a synth.

> **NOTE** ▶ If your only control surface is a MIDI keyboard that does not have a controller knob of any kind, you can use the pitch bend and modulation wheels as controller sliders to perform the following exercises. Any device sending MIDI CC events can be assigned to any channel strip or plug-in parameter.

Using Automation Quick Access

Automation Quick Access allows you to assign a single controller knob to the automation parameter that is currently displayed on the selected track. You need to assign the controller knob only once, and you can then use it to control any parameter on any track. You just select a track and choose the desired parameter from the Automation Parameter menu.

1   Select the ES 2 track (track 20).

2   Start playback at the beginning of the first ES 2 region (bar 79).

You may want to solo the ES 2 track to clearly hear the results of your automation.

You will use a controller knob to create wide pan automation on the ES 2 track, creating drastic movements of the synth in the stereo field to add frenzy to this aggressive part of the song.

First, you need to set up a controller knob using Automation Quick Access.

3   Choose Options > Track Automation > Automation Quick Access (or press Control-Option-Command-A).

An alert message appears asking you to assign a controller to Automation Quick Access.

NOTE ▶ If a controller has already been assigned to Automation Quick Access, this alert does not appear, and choosing Options > Track Automation > Automation Quick Access will toggle Automation Quick Access on and off. To reassign Automation Quick Access to a new controller knob, choose Logic Pro > Preferences > Automation, make sure Automation Quick Access is turned on, click Learn Message and continue with step 5 of this exercise.

4 Click Assign.

The Automation Preferences window opens, Automation Quick Access is turned on, and you can assign the controller knob that you want to use.

5 Move a knob or slider on your control surface.

A help tag appears to indicating that the controller has been assigned.

6 In the Automation Preferences window, click Done.

7 Close the Automation Preferences window (or press Command-W).

8 Move the controller knob, giving it a wide swing to cover its entire range from the minimum to the maximum positions.

In the Inspector, the volume fader of the ES 2 should follow the movements of the knob. On the ES 2 automation track, the black line representing the current volume value moves in the same way.

Since Automation Quick Access controls the displayed automation parameter, you need to display the pan parameter. First, make sure the ES 2 returns to its original volume.

9 Set the ES 2 volume back to –12 dB.

10 In the ES 2 track header, choose Pan from the Automation Parameter menu.

11 Move the controller knob until you see the pan control move on the left Arrange channel strip.

The controller knob now remotely controls the panning of the selected track, and you can use it to record live pan automation.

12 In the Automation Mode menu, choose Touch.

13 Start playback before the Guitar Drop section.

14 When the ES 2 starts, move the knob left and right to generate wide pan automation.

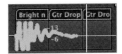

The pan automation is recorded on the track.

Feel free to go crazy with the pan automation in the first few bars, then gradually narrow the range of your controller movement to decrease the width of the pan automation, finally settling back to a center position around the middle of the Guitar Drop section. Remember, that section evolves from frantic to melodic, and you want to respect that mood progression in the panning of the ES 2 synth.

15 Set the automation mode back to Read and listen to your results.

Now that you have assigned a controller to Automation Quick Access, you can use that same controller for any parameter on any track. Try selecting another track, choosing a parameter from the Automation Parameter menu, and automating that parameter using the same controller.

16 In the main menu bar, choose Options > Track Automation > Automation Quick Access to turn it off.

Using Multiple Controller Assignments

Recording live automation with a mouse or using Automation Quick Access and a control surface allows you to automate only one parameter at a time. The fun really begins when you assign several controller knobs to different parameters so you can record their automations at the same time.

To automate multiple parameters simultaneously, you need to use a control surface with multiple knobs or sliders. In this exercise, you will assign two control surface knobs to two separate parameters of a Tape Delay plug-in, and automate both parameters at the same time.

1   With the ES 2 track selected, double-click the Tape Delay plug-in on the left Arrange channel strip.

The Tape Delay plug-in window opens. You will assign one controller knob to the Feedback parameter, and another to the High Cut parameter, so you can tweak them both at the same time. The Feedback parameter controls the number of repeats produced, and the High Cut parameter controls the cutoff frequency of the low-pass filter applied to the repeats.

2   From the main menu bar, choose Logic Pro > Preferences > Control Surfaces > Controller Assignments (or press Command-K).

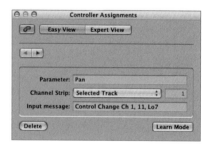

The Controller Assignments window opens.

You first need to delete the current Automation Quick Access assignment.

3   In the Controller Assignments window, click Delete.

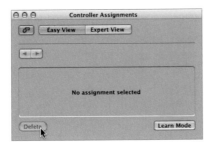

The Controller Assignments window reads "No assignment selected."

NOTE ▶ If you can still see assignments after clicking Delete, keep clicking Delete to remove all controller assignments until you see the message "No assignment selected."

Logic is now ready to learn controller assignments for the two Tape Delay parameters.

4   In the Controller Assignments window, click Learn Mode.

5   In the Tape Delay plug-in window, click the Feedback slider.

In the Controller Assignments window, the Parameter field is set to Tape Delay: Feedback.

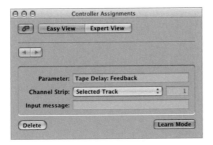

6   Move a knob on your control surface.

A help tag appears reading "Assignment Learned."

7   In the Tape Delay plug-in window, click the High Cut slider.

In the Controller Assignments window, the Parameter field is set to Tape Delay: High Cut.

8 Move another knob on your control surface.

A help tag appears reading "Assignment Learned."

9 Close the Controller Assignments window.

10 Move both knobs on the control surface.

Give both controllers a wide swing to cover their entire range until both the Feedback and the High Cut sliders react to the movements of the controllers.

11 Set the ES 2 track (or channel strip) automation mode to Latch.

NOTE ▶ When using a controller that does not have touch-sensitive faders, the Touch automation mode doesn't receive any controller information that indicates whether or not you're still touching the fader. If you stop moving such a knob or fader in Touch mode, Logic keeps writing the current position for a while, then jumps back to the original parameter value or existing automation on the track.

To really hear the effects of the Feedback and High Cut parameters, you may want to solo the ES 2 track the first time you try it. Once you know what to listen for, you will record the automation again while listening to the whole mix.

12 Solo the ES 2 track.

Once again, try to create crazier effects at the beginning of the section, using lower Feedback values as the synths become more melodic. Leaving the Feedback at its maximum value for short periods while decreasing the High Cut should create nicely distorted filtered delay effects.

Make sure you end with a Feedback value lower than 50% to avoid a runaway delay effect!

13 Start playback at the beginning of the Guitar Drop section.

14 Move both knobs on your control surface to tweak the Feedback and the High Cut sliders while the song plays.

The automation track display switches from the Feedback to the High Cut parameters as you move the knobs on the control surface.

15 Stop playback.

16 In the lower left of the ES 2 track header, click the disclosure triangle.

Another automation track opens, displaying the pan automation.

17 In the lower left of the pan automation sub-track header, click the disclosure triangle.

A third automation track opens, displaying the high cut automation. You should see the automation you just recorded on the feedback and high cut automation tracks.

You will now undo the automation you just recorded and record new automation while listening to the whole mix. You'll also be able to see the automation of both the Feedback and High Cut parameters as it is recorded on their automation tracks.

18 Choose Edit > Undo Automation Write "Feedback" (or "High Cut," depending upon which knob you moved last).

The most recent automation is deleted. The pan automation you recorded in the previous exercise is still visible.

19 Unsolo the ES 2 track.

20 Start playback at the beginning of the Guitar Drop section.

21 Manipulate the two knobs on your control surface to automate the Feedback and the High Cut parameters of the Tape Delay.

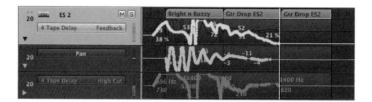

Because the automation tracks for both parameters are open this time, you can see the movements of each knob recorded live on individual tracks.

22 Return the ES 2 track's automation mode to Read.

23 Zoom out.

24 In the Toolbar, click both the Auto Zoom and Automation buttons.

> **NOTE ▶** When a controller assignment is learned, it is saved in a preference file (~/Library/Preferences/com.apple.logic.pro.cs), and the same control knob is mapped to the same channel strip or plug-in parameter in any Logic project. If you assign a knob to a parameter on a selected track, that knob will control the same parameter on any track you select. If you assign a knob to a parameter on an unselected track, that knob will only control the parameter of that track, independently of the track selection.

Using knobs on a control surface to tweak plug-in parameters in real time can be a lot of fun as you discover new ways to "play" the plug-ins as musical instruments. Make sure you keep this technique in mind when you feel an instrument or a section of a song is a little static or repetitive and could benefit from automation.

Exporting the Mix

When you finish mixing and automating a project, you need to export it—to a CD or an MP3 file, for example—so you can share it with other listeners.

You can use the cycle area to select the section of the project you are going to bounce. In this exercise, you will export the mix to an uncompressed audio file.

1   In the Arrange area, select all the regions (or press Command-A).

2   In the Toolbar, click Set Locators.

The cycle area starts at the beginning of the first region in the project and ends at the end of the last region in the project.

3   In the Toolbar, click the Bounce button.

The Bounce window opens.

4   Name the bounce file *LVL-Home* and save it to the desktop.

In the Destination area, make sure PCM is selected, so your mix is saved as an uncompressed digital audio file. At the lower right of the Bounce window, you can change the PCM file parameters.

The sample rate is set by default to the sample rate of the project, 44,100 Hz in this case, so don't change it unless you need to convert the bounced audio file to a new sample rate.

However, this project was recorded mainly with 24-bit audio files. If you intend to send the bounced file to a mastering engineer so he can put the final touches on the master before it is sent to the CD production plant, you will want to export your mix with the full dynamic range offered by 24-bit audio files.

5 In the Resolution menu, choose 24 Bit.

6 Click Bounce. A progress indicator shows that your project is bouncing. This process may take a few minutes.

7 Press Command-Tab to open the Finder, and press Option-Command-H to hide all other applications.

8 Control-click **LVL-Home.aif** and choose Open With > iTunes (or QuickTime Player) to preview your final mix.

Using automation, you have taken your song to a new level, fading instruments in and out to evolve the instrumentation and mood of a section in time. You have used offline automation to draw automation on the track, and you have recorded live automation using both the mouse and a control surface. Let your imagination run wild and try to think of other applications to automate your own projects.

To hear a more complete version of the finished automated mix, go to Logic 8_Files > Media > LVL-Home and, depending on your version of Logic, open one of the following files:

▶ LVL-Home Logic Pro 8
▶ LVL-Home Logic Express 8

Lesson Review

1. How can you view the automation track on the current track only?
2. Describe the steps needed to record live automation.
3. Compare the similarities and differences of the Touch and Latch modes.

4. When using Automation Quick Access, how many parameters can you control, and how many controller knobs can you use?

5. How do you assign different controller knobs to different parameters?

Answers

1. In the Toolbar, click the Auto Zoom button to automatically zoom in vertically on the selected track, then click the Automation button to display the selected track's automation track.

2. Choose the desired automation mode (Touch, Latch, or Write), then start playback and adjust the desired parameters.

3. In both modes, recording automation begins when you first touch a controller slider or knob (or hold down the mouse button over a slider or knob on the interface). When you release the controller knob (or the mouse button), Touch mode returns the automation to the original parameter value or existing automation on the track, while Latch mode continues recording at the current parameter level.

4. You can use only one controller knob, and control only one parameter at a time, but you can easily choose the desired parameter by displaying it on the selected automation track.

5. Open the Controller Assignments window, click Learn, click the desired parameter, then move the desired controller knob. Repeat for each parameter/knob assignment, and close the window.

Other Topics

11

Media Logic 8_Files > Media > Additional Media

Logic 8_Files > Media > Car Commercial

Time This lesson takes approximately 60 minutes to complete.

Goals Import a movie file into a project

Choose synchronization settings

Detect scene cuts

Start a musical cue on a downbeat

Export a project's audio to a video file

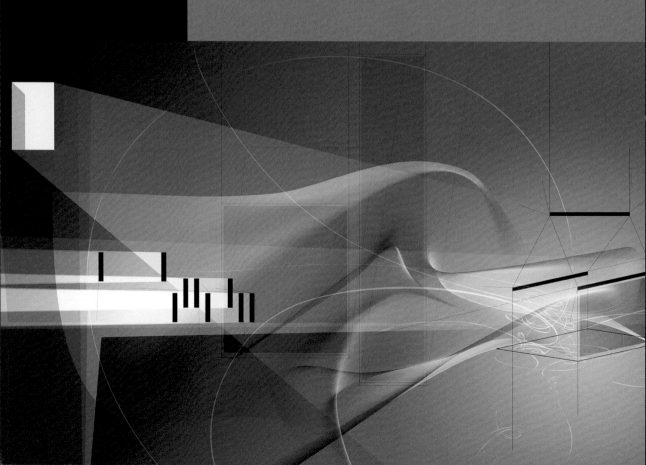

Scoring Movies

Scoring movies is an exciting creative process. Many composers make a highly successful living writing scores in a variety of music genres, not only for feature films but also for documentaries, cartoons, commercials, and video games.

Writing music to picture can present a number of challenges. You have to be ready to address last-minute changes in the movie's editing. Movie directors generally start by giving you a precise idea of the soundtrack they want from the style of music to the exact position of musical cues or sound effects, often related to scene cuts. Those ideas may change even as your writing progresses, and you'll need to rework your score to incorporate that changing feedback under harsh time constraints. This constant creative flux requires that you and your tools be prepared for a highly flexible and efficient workflow.

Logic offers many features that will facilitate the scoring process. In this lesson you will import a car commercial movie to a project, adjust the synchronization settings, compose a score to the picture, start a musical cue on a scene cut, and finally export your music to a new movie file.

Opening a Movie and Choosing Settings

Logic uses the QuickTime engine to play movies in synchronization with a project. Any movie formats supported by QuickTime can be played in a Logic project.

> **MORE INFO** ▶ Logic streams the movie file from the hard disk while it streams all the audio files used in the project. High-definition movie files can put a lot of strain on your hard drive, so it is recommended that you use a compressed copy of the movie file when working in Logic. You can use QuickTime Pro to export a movie file in a compressed format such as MP4.

Opening a Movie

When working with movies, you can use the global Video track to display frames of the QuickTime movie as thumbnails. The Video track also offers a quick way to open a movie, which you will use in this exercise.

1   Choose File > New (or press Command-N) and choose the Empty Project template.

2   In the New Tracks dialog, choose a stereo audio track and open the Library.

Let's open the Video track and import the movie.

3   At the top of the track list, Control-click the Global Tracks header and choose Configure Global Tracks (or press Option-G).

The Configure Global Tracks dialog opens. In the following exercises, you will use the global Marker, Tempo, and Video tracks.

4   Deselect Signature, select Video (keep Marker and Tempo selected), and click Done (or press Enter).

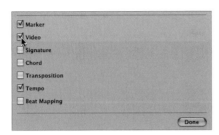

5   In the Video track header, click the disclosure triangle.

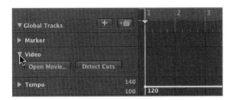

The Video track expands and two buttons appear in the header.

6   Click Open Movie.

A file selector box opens.

7   Navigate to Logic 8_Files > Media > Additional Media and double-click
    Car commercial.mov.

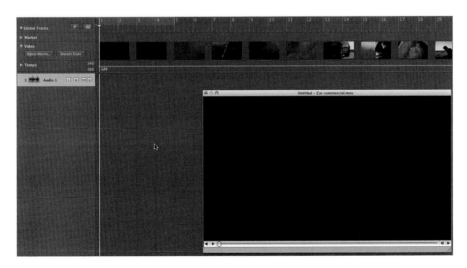

A Movie window opens, and the Video track displays movie frames as thumbnail images selected at regular intervals. Each thumbnail is left aligned, meaning that the thumbnail shows the movie frame displayed in the movie window when the playhead is positioned at the left edge of the thumbnail. The number of thumbnails shown depends upon the height of the Video track and the horizontal zoom level of the Arrange area.

8 Press the Spacebar.

Playback starts, and the movie plays in synchronization with the playhead in the project. By default, the movie's sound is muted.

You can use the QuickTime controls to navigate the movie and adjust its volume (if you need to hear the original soundtrack for reference).

9 At the lower left of the Movie window, hold down the mouse button with the pointer positioned over the speaker icon. When the volume slider appears, drag the slider to change the playback volume.

You should hear the movie's sound. The sound is routed by QuickTime, not Logic, so in the right Arrange channel strip, the Out 1-2 meters don't move. The movie's sound will be reproduced in the outputs selected in your Sound preferences (in the Apple menu).

10 Press the Spacebar to stop playback.

11 At the bottom of the Movie window, drag the position slider toward the right.

The movie scrolls forward, and in the Arrange area the playhead updates its position in the project, staying in perfect synchronization with the movie.

12 In the Arrange area, click the lower half of the Bar ruler to reposition the playhead to another location.

In the Movie window, the display updates to show the movie frame at the new playhead position, still maintaining sync with the project.

13 Drag the lower-right corner of the Movie window to resize it, and then drag the window aside so you can see the Arrange area.

Even when you resize the movie and drag it aside, it still hides a portion of the Arrange window, so you can close it for now.

14 Close the Movie window.

At the top of the Inspector, the Movie area automatically opens and displays the movie.

LOGIC EXPRESS ▶ Click the disclosure triangle to open the Movie area.

15 Choose File > Save (or press Command-S).

Name your project and save it to the desktop. Don't forget to save your project at regular intervals throughout this lesson.

TIP ▶ To copy the movie file to your project folder (for example for archiving purposes, or when you need to move the project to another location), click the Advanced Options disclosure triangle below the Include Assets checkbox in the Save As dialog and select "Copy movie files to project folder."

You can import only a single movie file into a project, and you can't edit the movie or change its playback speed in Logic. When you import a movie into a project, the movie is always synchronized with the project.

Choosing Synchronization Settings

When you're working with movies, time is expressed in SMPTE time code format. The SMPTE time code takes its name from the Society of Motion Picture and Television Engineers, the association that developed a time code format for synchronizing devices used to play movies and audio. The SMPTE time code is displayed as hours, minutes, seconds, frames, and (sometimes) subframes.

QuickTime movie files do not have time code data embedded in them. Before you can work on your project, you have to choose the correct synchronization settings to ensure that the time code you are reading in Logic reflects the frame rate of your movie and that it is the same code everyone involved in the production is using.

1   Look at the Transport bar.

The top line of the display on the left shows the current playhead position in SMPTE units. The bottom line displays the playhead position in Logic's familiar bar, beat, division, and tick format.

Since QuickTime movie files do not have embedded time code data, it is preferable whenever possible to use movie files that have burned-in time code (BITC), a visible time code superimposed onto each frame of the movie, or a *2-pop*, which is a one-frame long 1 kHz tone recorded in the soundtrack at 00:59:58:00 (2 seconds before the start of the program) and usually accompanied by a flash-frame.

For this exercise, assume that the movie production team told you that the first frame of the video file is at 01:00:00:00, and the first visual frames start slowly fading in 4 seconds into the movie, at 01:00:04:00.

MORE INFO ▶ A number of devices do not support negative SMPTE time code, so it is common to use 01:00:00:00 (1 hour) or 10:00:00:00 (10 hours) as the time code for the first frame of a movie file. In so doing, SMPTE time code can still be used to allow extra material such as movie titles and credits to be added before the first frame.

2   Click the Stop button (or press 0, or Return on a laptop).

The playhead moves to the beginning of the project. The playhead position is 1 1 1 1 (the first beat of the first bar) and 01:00:00:00.00 (exactly one hour) in SMPTE time code.

Your movie starts at the correct time code, but you still need to choose the correct frame rate to make sure Logic displays an accurate SMPTE time code. Different film and video formats have various frame rates: film is shot at 24 frames per second, the PAL video format (used in Europe) plays at 25 frames per second, and the NTSC video format plays 29.97 frames per second. The video file used in this lesson was shot on film, so it plays at 24 frames per second, the standard film frame rate.

3   In the Toolbar, click the Settings button and choose Synchronization.

The Synchronization Project Settings window opens.

4   Click the Frame Rate pop-up menu and choose 24.

You now have the correct synchronization settings, ensuring that you will see the proper SMPTE time code in your project. Keep the Project Settings window open, as you will need it throughout this exercise and the next.

When working with SMPTE time code, you can switch between a Bar ruler, a SMPTE time ruler, or a combination of both.

5   At the right of the Bar ruler, click the note icon and choose Time and Bar.

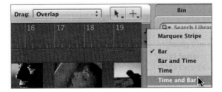

Choosing Time and Bar displays both the SMPTE ruler and the Bar ruler, but displays the SMPTE ruler below the Bar ruler, and the grid in the Arrange area now shows SMPTE time positions.

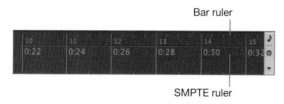

Bar ruler

SMPTE ruler

6   Play the beginning of the project.

For the first four seconds, the movie contains only black frames, and you will start writing music at 01:00:04:00.00 (1 hour, 0 minutes, 4 seconds). Let's adjust the synchronization settings so the first bar of the project plays at that time code, when you start seeing the first visual frames fade in. At the bottom of the Synchronization Project Settings window, two displays allow you to adjust which bar position plays at which SMPTE time code.

7   Leave Bar Position on 1 1 1 1, and in the "plays at SMPTE" field, drag the seconds digit to 04 so the value reads 01:00:04:00.00.

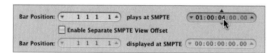

In the Video track, the movie moves toward the right.

8   Click the Stop button (or press 0).

The playhead moves to the beginning of the project.

In the Transport bar, the playhead position is shown as 01:00:04:00.00 in SMPTE units, and 1 1 1 1 in bars and beats.

9   Start playback.

The movie starts four seconds after the first frame of the movie file, and you no longer see the four seconds of black frames.

Finally, you need to set the project's sample rate to 48 kHz, which is usually the
sample rate of choice when working for picture.

10 At the top of the Project Settings window, click the Audio button to access your
Audio project settings.

11 Click the Sample Rate pop-up menu and choose 48.000 kHz.

You can adjust the time code of the first frame in the video file in your Video project
settings.

12 At the top of the Project Settings window, click the Video button to access the Video
project settings.

The Movie Start field allows you to adjust the SMPTE time code of the first movie
frame. In this exercise, the first movie frame is at the one hour time code, so leave it
at the default 01:00:00:00.00 setting.

Keep the Video Project Settings window open, as you will need it in the next exercise.

Your project is now configured with the correct SMPTE time code, frame rate, and sample
rate, and you have adjusted the position of the start of the movie to start writing music at
the desired position in the movie.

Importing the Movie's Audio Track

In the trailer and commercial industry, you will sometimes be given movie files that contain dialog or a temporary musical soundtrack. It is often quickly assembled from preexisting materials, usually by the video editor, and often reflects the expectations of the director. Such a soundtrack is called the *temp track* and can serve to guide you in your choice of tempos and genre of music.

Rather than use QuickTime's output to reproduce the temp track, you can import the track into Logic, where you can easily mute it and unmute it from the Arrange area. First, you need to mute QuickTime's output so the temp track playback isn't duplicated.

1   In the Video Project Settings window, click the Sound Output pop-up menu and choose Mute.

QuickTime sound output is now muted.

NOTE ▸ If you want to display the movie on an external video monitor, you can choose FireWire from the Video Output menu to output the video signal to a FireWire device that converts the digital signal into an analog video signal that you can connect to the external monitor.

2   Close the Project Settings window (or press Command-W).

3   From the main menu bar, choose Options > Movie > Import Audio to Arrange.

A progress indicator shows that the soundtrack is being converted to an audio file. Then, a second progress indicator shows that the audio file is being converted to the project's sample rate.

An audio region is inserted on the selected audio track at the beginning of the project. The lock icon before the region name indicates that the region is locked to SMPTE time code. When a region is locked to SMPTE, it always stays in sync with the movie. You can't drag it, and changing the tempo of the project does not affect its SMPTE position.

4   Start playback.

You can hear the temp track. If the temp track contains music reflecting the expectations of the director, you can mute it as you write your score, and listen to it once in a while as a reference for your composition. If the temp track contains dialog, you can use it to ensure that the music you write does not overpower the dialog.

You will not use the temp track in this lesson, however, so let's mute it.

5   Mute the Audio 1 track.

6   Stop playback.

Your project is now ready, and you can start writing music to the movie.

Writing the Score

The individual pieces of music used in a movie are generally referred to as *cues*. When scoring longer movies, you may want to write each cue in a separate Logic project; but for short movies, trailers or commercials, it is often easier to score the whole movie in a single project.

For this score, the director asked you to write two cues. The first one should be sparse yet emotional. The second cue should start at a specific scene cut and be modern and rhythmically driving. In the following exercises, you will score the car commercial using Apple Loops.

Writing the First Cue

You usually have a lot of liberty when writing the first cue, because you don't have to worry about transitioning from the previous cue. When writing music, you need to view the time grid in bars and beats, not in SMPTE time, so you will first swap the Bar and the SMPTE rulers.

1   At the right of the ruler, click the note and clock icons and choose Bar and Time.

The Bar ruler is now below the SMPTE time ruler, and the Arrange area grid shows bar and beat positions.

2   In the Media area, click the Loops tab.

3   In the search field, type *Emotional*.

A few piano Apple Loops appear in the Loop Browser. Preview them to choose the best one.

4   Drag **Emotional Piano 01** to the Arrange area, and place it below the audio track on 1 1 1 1.

A software instrument track is created, the green loop's channel strip setting is loaded, and the Emotional Piano 01 MIDI region is inserted at 1 1 1 1 on that track.

5   Click the new software instrument track header.

In the Inspector, you can see the Inst 1 channel strip with the piano instrument and a couple of processing plug-ins.

6   Start playback.

The cue sounds too rushed for an emotional cue. In the Loop Browser's tempo column, you can see that the loop's original tempo is 80 bpm. That's a little slow.

7   In the Transport bar, set the tempo to 90 bpm.

That's better.

You have the beginning of your first cue. Now you need to find the *scene cut* where the second cue will start so you can determine the length of the first cue.

Detecting Scene Cuts

Many directors love to accent important scene cuts with sound effects or new musical cues. In scoring movies, part of your responsibility is to locate the scene cuts and position audio elements on or near the scene cuts for the best effect.

For this movie, the director wants the second cue to start on a specific scene cut and tells you that it's around SMPTE time code 01:00:19 (1 hour and 19 seconds). This exercise will show you how to detect the scene cut.

1   Start playback from the beginning of the project.

In the Inspector, watch the Movie area. The movie starts with greenish clouds, then you see the two characters introduced, and again you see the greenish clouds. Then, around 01:00:19, the scene is flooded with sunlight, and the color tones become much brighter and warmer. That scene cut, around 01:00:19, is where you will place your second cue.

To automatically detect the scene cut, you first need to indicate which portion of the movie file should be analyzed. Your Command-click tool is the Marquee tool, and you can use it to highlight the section around the scene cut.

2   Reposition the playhead just before the scene cut on bar 6. Start playback and try to stop playback just after you see the scene cut.

The scene cut is now close to the playhead, and you can select the area around it.

3   On any one of the tracks, drag the Marquee tool around the playhead.

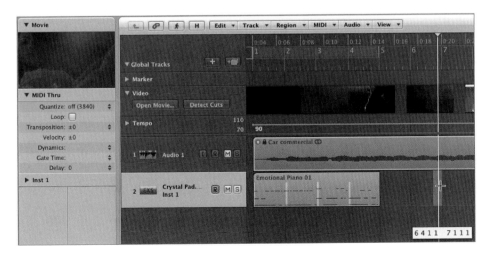

4   Press the Spacebar.

The marquee selection is played once. Watch the Movie area. You should see the scene cut within that marquee selection. If you don't see the scene cut, adjust the marquee selection until you do. Also make sure you don't see the following scene cut (when the car comes in) or you will detect that scene cut, too.

5   In the global Video track header, click the Detect Cuts button.

The portion of the movie corresponding to the marquee selection is analyzed and the scene cut is detected. A marker called Scene-1 is inserted at the scene cut position in the global Marker track. The movie frame symbol in front of the marker's name indicates that it is a scene marker. Scene markers are locked to SMPTE time code and will always stay in sync with the picture.

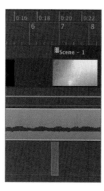

Aligning a Downbeat to a Scene Cut

Now that you have a scene marker at the scene cut position, you need to align the first beat of a bar to the scene marker, so you can start writing a new cue at the beginning of a bar and use the grid to write and arrange the cue.

You will now use the global Beat Mapping track to map the first beat of a bar to the Scene-1 marker.

1   Control-click the Global Tracks header area and choose Configure Global Tracks (or
    press Option-G).

2   Select Beat Mapping and click Done.

3   In the Beat Mapping track header, click the disclosure triangle.

    The Beat Mapping track expands vertically. In the upper half of the Beat Mapping
    track you can see white vertical lines corresponding to the bars, beats, and divisions
    in the Bar ruler.

4   Zoom around bars 6 to 8 to see your Scene-1 marker.

    You can't Control-Option-drag in the global tracks to zoom, so zoom on the tracks
    below.

    You may also want to move the playhead out of the way to clearly see the Beat
    Mapping track.

5   Click the Scene-1 marker.

    The marker is selected, and a blue vertical line indicating its position appears in the
    lower half of the global Beat Mapping track.

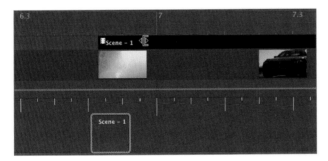

You will now map the first beat of bar 7 to the Scene-1 marker.

When you map a beat to a new SMPTE position that is identified by a scene marker,
Logic automatically adjusts the tempo of the previous section so that the beat falls
precisely at that SMPTE time. Mapping the beat closest to the scene marker will result
in the smallest tempo adjustment.

Since you haven't mapped any other beat in this project, the new tempo will be calculated from the beginning of the song, and the value of the first tempo node in the global Tempo track (at 1 1 1 1) will be adjusted.

NOTE ▶ If you had manually inserted tempo changes to the left of the beat you are mapping, they would automatically be deleted as the new tempo was calculated from the beginning of the project. If you had mapped beats earlier in the project, mapping a beat would insert the tempo change at the position of the mapped beat immediately to the left. Any tempo changes manually inserted between that beat and the one you are mapping would be deleted. Always map beats from left to right, and don't manually insert tempo changes or tempo curves if you intend to map another beat at a later position in the project.

6   In the global Beat Mapping track, drag the white line corresponding to bar 7 over the blue line corresponding to the Scene-1 marker.

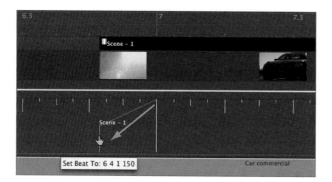

Make sure you don't accidentally *click* the white line corresponding to bar 7. Just *drag* it over the blue Scene-1 line, and don't release the mouse button until a diagonal yellow line ties the beat to the blue line.

If you make a mistake, double-click the long vertical line representing the beat that you just mapped. That will delete it, and you can start over.

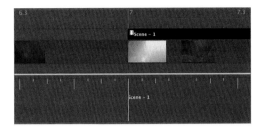

When you release the mouse button, a vertical line represents the beat you mapped, and the Scene-1 marker seems to move to 7 1 1 1. In reality, the Scene-1 marker stays exactly at the same SMPTE position, still indicating the scene cut, but the new tempo was automatically calculated and adjusted to make bar 7 fall exactly on the marker.

The tempo is adjusted to 93.2835 bpm (you may get a slightly different value). The new tempo is a little faster, so bar 7 now falls a little earlier in the movie. This means that you can't adjust the tempo before bar 7 without losing the alignment between bar 7 and the Scene-1 marker. You can, however, create a tempo change on or after the first beat of bar 7 and, in fact, you will do just that when you create the second cue.

Now you can lengthen your first cue so that it transitions nicely into the second cue.

NOTE ▶ The Emotional Piano 01 MIDI region may not match the new tempo, but it still works great for the first cue.

7   Loop the Emotional Piano 01 region so it stops a little bit before the Scene-1 marker.

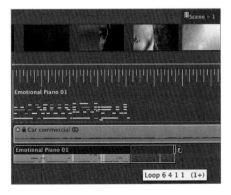

Listen to the end of the first cue and make sure it ends with softer notes. If you loop it until 7 1 1 1, you will hear loud notes just before the next cue, and the transition will not work so well.

NOTE ▶ In the lower half of the Beat Mapping track, you can see all of the MIDI notes contained in the selected MIDI region. The lower half of the Beat Mapping track always displays selected events so you can map beats to them.

Writing the Second Cue

In the previous exercise, you prepared the project for the second cue, mapping the first beat of bar 7 to the scene cut where the new cue will start. All you have left to do is choose a tempo for the new cue and start creating it on bar 7.

In the following exercise, you will add a drum loop, choose a tempo for the second cue, then add a few more Apple Loops and mix the cue.

1   In the Loops Browser's search field, enter *Basic Rock*.

2   Drag **Basic Rock Drumset 27** below the piano track at bar 7.

An audio track is created and the drum loop is inserted at bar 7.

3   In the Region Parameter box, select the Loop checkbox (or press L).

The Basic Rock Drumset 27 region is looped.

4   Start playback around bar 5.

Listen to the transition between the first cue and the new cue. A faster tempo for the new cue would definitely lift things up.

5   In the global Tempo track header, click the disclosure triangle.

The Tempo track expands vertically.

6   Double-click the Tempo track at bar 7, above the tempo line.

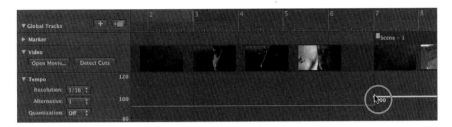

A tempo change is inserted at bar 7. The tempo of the first cue is left unchanged, and the Scene-1 marker is still exactly on bar 7.

Listen to the transition again.

7   To the right of bar 7, drag the tempo line to 105 bpm.

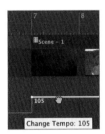

Listen to the transition. The new tempo is more effective in creating a driving groove. Let's add more Apple Loops to build the second cue.

You will no longer need the global tracks, so you can close them to reduce visual clutter in the Arrange area.

8   At the top of the track list, click the Global Tracks disclosure triangle (or press G).

The global tracks close.

9   Using the Loop Browser's search field, find the following loops. Drag each loop below the bottom track of the Arrange area into the indicated positions to create a new track for each one of them.

▶   Drag **Edgy Rock Bass 07** to bar 7.

▶   Drag **Acoustic Vamp 01** to bar 11.

▶   Drag **Orchestra Strings 02** to bar 13.

10 Select all three loops and press L.

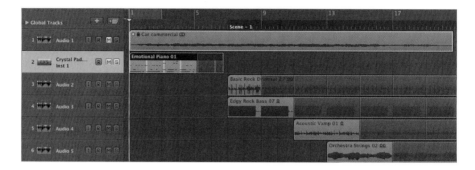

The regions are looped.

You need to quickly mix the new tracks. First, name them.

11 Double-click the new tracks' headers and rename them:

  ▶ Change Audio 2 to *Drums.*

  ▶ Change Audio 3 to *Bass.*

  ▶ Change Audio 4 to *Acoustic.*

  ▶ Change Audio 5 to *Strings.*

12 At the bottom of the Arrange area, click the Mixer button (or press X).

13 Start playback at bar 13 to hear all four new tracks and mix them as follows:

  ▶ Bass: Set the Balance control to –10, and the volume fader to –14.

  ▶ Acoustic: Set the Balance control to +22, and the volume fader to –4.6.

  ▶ Strings: Set the volume fader to –15.

When you lower the track levels to avoid audio clipping, remember to raise your speaker's volume so you are not misled into thinking the mix is now weaker.

The drums could use a little reverb to make them sound bigger.

14 Click the Drums channel strip to select it.

15 In the Media area, click the Library tab.

The Library displays audio channel strip settings for the selected channel strip.

16 In the Library, choose 01 Spaces > 01 Large Spaces > Male Vocal Hall.

> **LOGIC EXPRESS** ▶ Choose 01 Spaces > Big Detriot Room.

The drums now have a nice reverberation.

Listen from the beginning of the project. The second cue doesn't take off as it should. That's because its level is lower than the first cue's. Since the second cue is already mixed as loud as it can be, you need to turn down the piano in the first cue.

17 Drag the Inst 1 channel strip volume fader down to –12.

Listen to the transition from the first cue to the second. Now the second cue really wakes up the listener. Mission accomplished!

18 Close the Mixer (or press X).

You now have two cues, one with a simple yet emotional piano, and the other with a modern and driving groove, as requested by the director. You will create an ending to wrap up the score in the next exercise.

Placing a Sound Effect to the Picture

You will now place a sound effect on the last scene cut of the movie to punctuate your score. Then, you'll trim the loops where the sound effect starts.

1 In the Media area, click the Loops tab.

2 At the top right of the Loop Browser, click the FX button.

The Loop Browser displays a variety of sound effects category buttons.

3 Click the Impacts button.

4 Drag **Alien Impact** to bar 20 below the bottom track.

Now you need to position the Alien Impact region so it falls on the last scene cut. To do so, reopen the Movie window.

5 In the Inspector, double-click the Movie area.

The Movie area closes and the Movie window opens.

6 Drag the Movie window to the left so you can see the Alien Impact region.

Start dragging the Alien Impact region toward the left to find the beginning of the scene with the car. As you drag the region, the Movie window shows you the frame of the movie at the position of the region.

Try to get as close as possible to the scene cut between the scene with the woman and the last scene with the car.

7 Zoom in on the beginning of the Alien Impact region.

8 Drag the region to find the precise location of the scene cut.

In the Transport bar, watch the playhead's SMPTE position. If you have zoomed in enough, dragging the region allows you to see every frame of the movie.

Although you can move the region exactly onto the scene cut, experiment placing the region a few frames off to the right and listen to the result. Some directors prefer having sound effects or cues that start a few frames after a scene cut, so ask your director if you should do that, or use your ears to judge what works best.

9 Zoom out.

The last thing to do is trim the repeats of the four Apple Loops in the second cue.

10 In the second cue, drag to select all four Apple Loops.

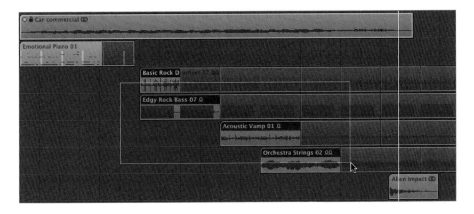

11 Position the mouse pointer on the upper part of one of the repeated regions until the Loop tool appears.

12 Drag the repeated regions until they end approximately where the Alien Impact region starts.

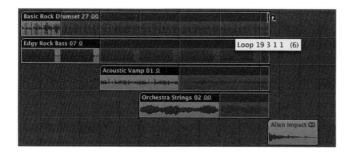

13 Go to the beginning of the project.

Now is the time to sit back and watch the movie in full screen while listening to the score.

14 Control-click the Movie window and choose Fullscreen.

The movie fills the screen.

15 Press the Spacebar.

Take advantage of the fact that Logic is hidden behind the Movie window. You have to forget about Logic, your arrangement, and your mix, and focus on the movie you are watching. If the music supports the movie, you should feel inspired and entertained. If there is an issue with the arrangement or the mix, it will most probably distract you from the movie, and you'll have to go back and fix it.

16 When you are done watching the movie, close the Movie window, or Control-click it and choose Original Size.

Feel free to compare your work with the completed score in Logic 8_Files > Media > Car Commercial > 11 Car Commercial_end. When you are happy with your score, you can export it to the movie.

Saving a Movie with the Score

At the end of the project you will probably be asked to deliver a regular uncompressed PCM audio file that you can bounce, as you learned in the previous lesson. On larger projects, it is common for composers to deliver *stems*, submixes that contain a specific category of sounds, such as a strings stem, a percussions stem, or a sound effects stem. The engineer who mixes the movie's soundtrack will mix your stems with the dialog and other sound effects.

However, as you make progress writing your score, you will need to share your work with the client, so that she can give you feedback and suggestions. To do that, you need to save a new copy of the movie that includes your project's audio. You first need to adjust the cycle area to make sure the new movie doesn't include the four seconds of black frames at the beginning, but does include the trail of the Alien Impact sound effect at the end.

1   Select all the regions in the Arrange area.

2   In the Toolbar, click Set Locators.

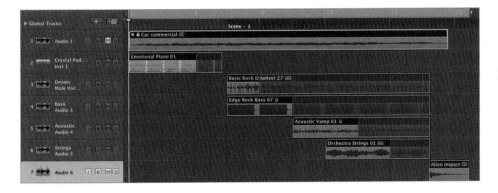

Cycle mode turns on and the cycle area matches the length of the whole soundtrack. You will now save a new movie matching the length and containing your soundtrack.

3   From the main menu bar, choose Options > Movie > Export Audio to Movie.

A Sound Settings dialog appears.

4 In the Format menu, choose AAC, and click OK.

NOTE ▶ Linear PCM will give you the best sound quality, but the resulting movie file will also be much larger than a file in which you compress the sound by choosing AAC. File size can be an issue if you need to e-mail or upload the movie file. For previewing purposes, the sound quality of AAC is usually sufficient.

A Save As dialog opens. You need a name and a location to save your new movie file.

5 Name the movie *My Car Commercial*, choose the desktop as a save location, and click OK.

One last dialog appears, allowing you to choose the audio tracks from the original movie you want to include in the new movie. Since you don't want to mix the original soundtrack with yours, you need to deselect it.

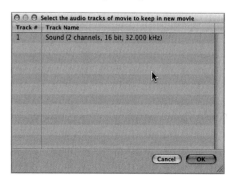

6 In the dialog, click the background to deselect the original audio track, and click OK.

A progress indicator shows that the project is being bounced as an audio file. Then, a second progress indicator shows that the audio file is being converted.

When the second progress indicator disappears, you can look for your movie on your desktop.

7 Press Command-Tab.

The Mac OS X application selector appears in the middle of the screen. Choose the Finder.

8 Press Option-Command-H.

The other applications are hidden, and you can see your desktop.

9 Find **My Car Commercial.mov** and double-click it.

The movie opens and plays in QuickTime.

And it has *your* soundtrack on it!

In this lesson you used many techniques to quickly build a car commercial soundtrack using Apple Loops. Using new tools and techniques, you also imported the movie, ensured that you had the correct synchronization settings, detected scene cuts, mapped a beat to a scene marker, and started a new cue on the scene cut. Ultimately, you exported your score to a new QuickTime movie file for previewing.

When you start writing music to picture, you will never watch a movie, cartoon, commercial, or trailer in the same way. Start focusing on the soundtracks, and a whole new world opens up that you didn't realize existed.

Lesson Review

1. How do you import a movie to a project?

2. How can you watch the movie in full screen?

3. How can you detect a scene cut?

4. How do you align a beat to a scene cut?

5. How do you place an audio region on a specific movie frame?

6. How do you display a SMPTE time ruler at the top of the Arrange area?

7. How do you export the audio from the project to a copy of the movie file?

Answers

1. On the global Video track header, click Open Movie.

2. Control-click the Movie window and choose Fullscreen.

3. Marquee select the portion of the movie to analyze, and in the global Video track, click Detect Cuts.

4. After detecting a scene cut, click the scene marker to select it. Then, in the global Beat Mapping track, drag the white vertical line representing the beat over the blue vertical line representing the scene marker.

5. Zoom in on the region and, as you drag the region to position it, the Movie window will show you the movie frame at that position.

6. Click the note icon at the right of the Bar ruler and choose from one of the three combinations of rulers containing the SMPTE time ruler.

7. Choose Options > Movie > Export Audio to Movie, choose the sound settings, choose a name and a location to save the new movie, and select the audio tracks from the original movie to keep in the new movie.

12

Lesson Files	Logic 8_Files > Lessons > 12 New Day_start
Time	This lesson takes approximately 40 minutes to complete.
Goals	Learn good backup practices
	Understand the principles of troubleshooting
	Learn basic troubleshooting steps

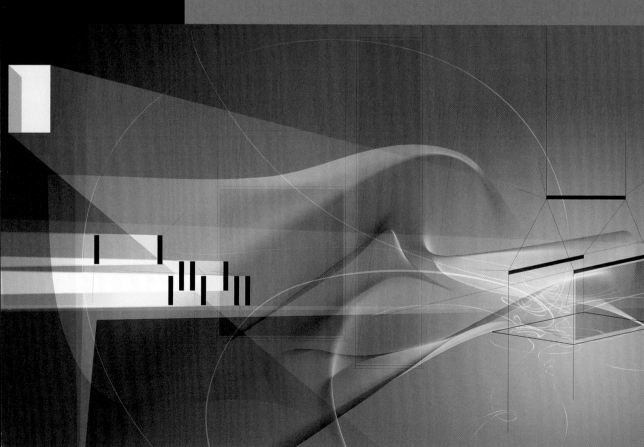

Lesson 12

Troubleshooting and Optimization

As an Apple Certified Pro, you will find yourself in situations where you are responsible for the proper functioning of several Logic systems. Whether maintaining your home studio or a professional studio, teaching in a classroom with student computer stations, or working as a technical consultant, you will often need to safely and quickly solve problems.

Problems can generally be attributed to one of three causes.

- ▶ Human errors: The user forgot to press a button, didn't connect devices properly, didn't install the proper driver, or made another mistake.

- ▶ Hardware limitations: The user reached the limitations of the computer, was trying to use too many plug-ins, or asked the system to play back more tracks than it could handle.

- ▶ Software- and hardware-related problems: Incompatible devices, corrupted preferences or project files, and other defects can result in unexpected behaviors.

In this lesson, you will explore the most common issues you may run into and will develop a sense for general troubleshooting techniques that you can apply to many situations.

Making Backups

Before starting to troubleshoot, you should make sure that you have current backups of all your critical projects. Now is a good time to learn responsible backup practices.

The importance of backing up cannot be overstressed. Backing up data is a precautionary measure that guarantees you will always have a properly working copy of your Logic projects, no matter what system problems you might encounter.

While some Logic problems can be fixed using the troubleshooting techniques described in this lesson, many problems—such as human error, data corruption, power failure, and hard drive failure—can result in data loss. The most reliable way to recover lost or corrupted data is to revert to a backup copy. Obviously, that means you must follow a strict backup routine.

Saving a Project and Making Automatic Backups

In Lesson 1, you learned the importance of saving your project at regular intervals. Now is a good time to further understand Logic's behavior when saving a project, and the way automatic backups are created.

When you open a Logic project, the project file is transferred from the hard disk to the computer's random-access memory, or RAM. RAM has a much faster access speed than hard disk storage and allows most operations to occur instantaneously. However, RAM is also volatile. In the event of a power failure, a computer crash, or unexpected program termination, your project is erased from RAM without giving you a chance to save it to the hard disk.

When you save your project, you are copying it from RAM to the hard disk. If an incident causes the project to disappear from RAM, you can always open it again from the hard disk in the same state that it was in the last time you saved it. Therefore it is important to save it frequently, or at least after any important operation has been performed. Each time you save a project, the previously saved version of the project is backed up automatically, as in the next exercise.

When switching between Logic and the Finder, remember that you can use Command-H to hide the application with key focus, and Command-Tab to switch between applications. You will first save the project to your desktop to have an easy access to the project folder and clearly see its contents.

1   Go to Logic 8_Files > Lessons, and open **12 New Day_start**.

2   Choose File > Save As.

A Save As dialog appears.

3   If a Finder window is not open, click the disclosure triangle.

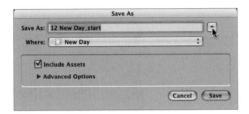

A window opens in the Finder.

4   Click the desktop icon in the sidebar (or press Command-D), make sure Include Assets is selected, and click Save.

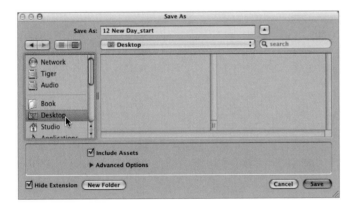

The whole project is saved on the desktop, and a few progress indicators show the audio files being copied to the new project folder.

5   In the Finder, double-click the 12 New Day_start project folder to look at its contents.

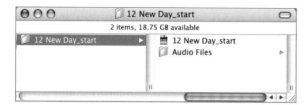

The project folder contains the 12 New Day_start project file and an Audio Files folder.

6   Leave the Finder window open, switch back to Logic, and look at the Arrange window's title bar.

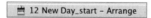

In the title bar, notice the plain Logic project icon in front of the project name. That plain icon indicates that the open project is identical to the one on the hard disk.

7   In the Arrange area, drag a region to move it by a few bars.

Now notice the Logic project icon. It is dimmed, indicating that the current project exists only in RAM and is different from the version on the hard disk.

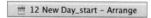

8   Choose File > Save (or press Command-S).

Your project is saved to the hard disk and the icon returns to its previous state to indicate that the versions onscreen and on the hard disk are identical.

9   Switch to the Finder.

The project folder now includes a Project File Backups folder, which contains a backup of the project file. That backup corresponds to the previously saved version of the project file, which was made before you last saved. In this case, the 12 New Day_start.00 file in the Project File Backups is the file you first saved in step 4, before moving the region, while 12 New Day_start (at the root of the project folder) is the new project file you saved in step 8, after moving the region.

Each time you save a project, the previously saved version is moved to the Project File Backups folder and assigned a sequential number. The Project File Backups folder contains up to ten saved versions of your project, numbered 00 through 09. The file numbered 00 is the most recent and 09 is the oldest. If you ever save your project by mistake, you can close the project and open an earlier backup.

Backing Up Project Files

Like any other computer file, a Logic project file can become corrupted. This usually results in unexpected behaviors when you work with a project, behaviors not present when you work with other project files.

When a project file is corrupt, there is very little you can do. You can start a new project and import the audio files, MIDI regions, channel strip settings, and other data from the corrupt project into the new project. Needless to say, the process can be long and tedious for complex projects.

You should save copies of your project file at regular intervals, or after you've made any significant changes. For example, if you save a copy every 20 minutes, and your project is corrupted, the worst that can happen is that you have to return to the previous version and will lose the past 20 minutes of work.

1   Choose File > Save As (or press Shift-Command-S).

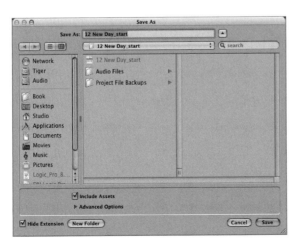

The Save As dialog opens and you can see the contents of the project folder. You don't have to change the location of the file you are about to save, it will be saved in the project folder.

2   Name the new project file **12 New Day_start 2**, and press Enter.

A copy of the project file is saved on the hard disk as *12 New Day_start 2*, and that is the version you are now working with. You can verify the name in the title bar of the Arrange window.

You will now save one more backup version of the project file.

3   Choose File > Save As (or press Shift-Command-S).

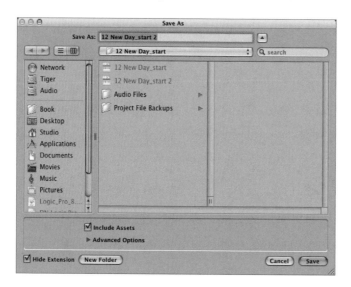

You can see the contents of the project folder, which now contains two project files: 12 New Day_start and 12 New Day_start 2.

4   Name the copy *12 New Day_start 3* and save it.

This saving technique ensures you have an earlier backup to go to in the case of project file corruption. It also offers an easy means to revert to a previous version of your project, should you decide that you are no longer happy with the artistic direction you have taken in the last saved version(s).

Backing Up Projects Folders to External Devices

Until now, you saved your project file to the hard disk and made backup copies inside the project folder. But one day your hard disk will die, and you can't know when that day will be. It could be the very first day you use the hard disk, or it could be years from now.

To protect yourself against human error or hard disk failure, you have to back up the entire project folder to another hard disk. An easy solution is to purchase an external hard disk dedicated to backing up your project folders. You can also back up to another computer's hard disk over a network, or even to online storage (such as a .Mac account). Having a backup in a remote location adds protection in case of burglary or fire.

When your project folder contains only one project file, you can choose File > Save As, make sure Include Assets is selected and choose a location on your external hard disk. However, if you use the technique described in the previous exercise, your project folder will have several project files, and a Save As won't work. In that case, use the Finder to copy the whole project folder to the new location.

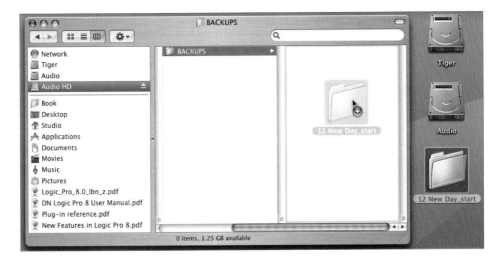

Solving Audio and MIDI Routing Problems

A music production system built around Logic can quickly grow into a complex network of interconnected devices. When a problem occurs, finding its cause can become a high-tech scavenger hunt.

Troubleshooting requires one part logical reasoning and one part experimentation. When troubleshooting a signal chain comprising several devices, you can systematically bypass each device in turn, or substitute one device for another, to find the culprit. By carefully examining which device combinations work and which don't, you can often isolate the offending device.

Whether the problem is due to human error (such as an improper setup) or component failure (such as a bad connection), the techniques to identify the point of failure are the same.

Restoring Your Audio Output

The greatest frustration of working with music equipment occurs when the equipment does not produce any sound. When troubleshooting the solution, you can easily rule out your audio interface and monitoring system by making sure that Logic can play Apple Loops from the Loop Browser.

1   If the Media area is not visible, in the Toolbar, click the Media button.

2   Click the Loops tab.

3   Click any category button.

4   Select the first loop in the Search Results list.

The loop icon turns into a speaker, and its signal is displayed in the Inspector on the Out 1-2 channel strip's level meter.

If the loop icon doesn't change when you click it, and no signal is displayed on the Out 1-2 channel strip, check your audio driver settings.

5 In the Toolbar, click the Preferences button, and choose Audio from the pop-up menu.

Make sure the Enabled checkbox is selected and the correct audio interface is chosen in the Device menu. If both settings are correct, try to initialize the Core Audio driver.

6 If the settings that you checked in step 5 appear to be correct, deselect Enabled.

The audio driver is disabled

7 Select Enabled again, and click Apply Changes.

After a moment, a progress indicator appears, showing the initialization progress of the Core Audio engine.

If the loop icon still doesn't change when you click it, try bypassing your audio interface as described in the next section, "Bypassing Your Audio Interface."

When a signal appears on the Out 1-2 channel strip, you know Logic is producing sound. If you still can't hear the sound, you should suspect the monitoring chain (drivers, audio interface, cables, monitors, and headphones).

Any level meter on your interface, mixer, or even speakers can help you determine where the signal is being lost. Plugging headphones into your audio interface can help determine if the problem occurs between the computer and the audio interface (no sound in the headphones), or between the audio interface and the monitors (sound in the headphones but not in the monitors).

A few things to check:

▶   If you are using your Mac's built-in audio interface, click the speaker icon on the right side of the main menu bar and make sure the volume slider is up.

▶   Make sure you have installed the latest audio interface drivers.

▶   If the audio interface has additional software installed, open that software and make sure that the signal routing is correct and no volume fader handle is down or mute button is on.

▶   Check the audio interface's manual for a reset procedure.

▶   Check the fuse or temporary protection on the monitors.

▶   Check all cables between the computer, the audio interface, and the monitors.

Bypassing Your Audio Interface

Many audio problems and data errors (such as sample rate errors, or audio and MIDI synchronization errors) can be traced to the audio interface and its drivers. The easiest way to determine if the audio interface is at fault is to bypass it and use the Mac's built-in interface and speakers.

1   From the main menu, choose Logic Pro > Preferences > Audio; or, in the Toolbar, click the Preferences button and choose Audio from the pop-up menu.

2   In the Devices menu, choose Built-in Audio (or Built-in Output).

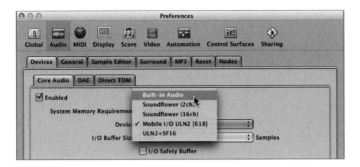

3 Click Apply Changes.

4 In the Apple menu, choose System Preferences.

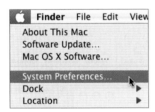

5 In the Hardware area, click the Sound button.

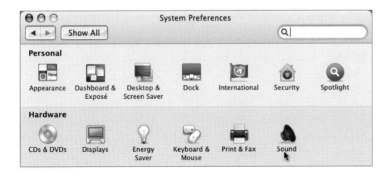

TIP ▶ To quickly access your Mac's Sound preferences, skip steps 4 and 5 and, while holding down Option, press any of the speaker keys (Volume Up, Volume Down, or Mute).

6   Click the Output button.

7   Select "Internal speakers."

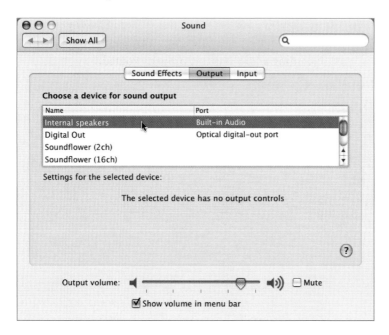

8   Make sure the Output volume slider is positioned toward the right and Mute is deselected.

If the problem goes away when you're using the Mac's built-in interface, then you can suspect your audio interface or your speakers. After you've made sure the speakers work, check the audio interface's manufacturer's website to be sure you're using the most current drivers for your system. Check the audio interface manual for a way to implement a reset procedure. If all else fails, contact the manufacturer to get help troubleshooting the audio interface and its accompanying software.

Checking Audio Input

If no sound is produced when you're recording or monitoring an audio source in Logic, you should first make sure you are getting sound out, as described in the previous exercises. In other words, before troubleshooting your microphones, make sure your speakers work!

If your interface has input meters, make sure the meters display a level when the artists perform. If they don't, the problem lies ahead of Logic's inputs. Try replacing the instrument or microphone, switch to another cable, or use the built-in audio interface.

If your interface does display an input level and you still can't hear incoming sound in Logic, chances are you are dealing with human error. Check that your audio interface settings are correct and your incoming audio signal is properly routed.

First look at the channel strip. Does the level meter display a signal? If it doesn't, you might be attempting to monitor the wrong device or the wrong input on the correct device.

1   In Logic, don't close the current project and choose > New, or press Command-N.

2   Click the Empty Project template button.

3   Create a new mono audio track and select Record Enabled.

    A Save As dialog opens.

4   Name your project and save it to the desktop.

5   In the Toolbar, click the Preferences button and choose Audio from the pop-up menu.

6   Make sure the correct device is chosen.

7   Make sure Software Monitoring is selected and close the preference window.

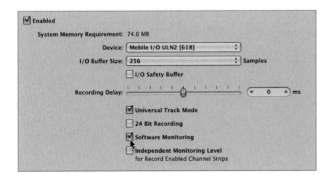

> **NOTE ▶** Some audio interfaces offer near-zero latency monitoring, usually accessible through the software accompanying the interface. Other configurations use a hardware mixer to route live instruments directly to the headphones or monitors. In those situations, Software Monitoring should be deselected so that Logic no longer routes incoming audio to its outputs.

8 On the audio channel strip, make sure the correct input from the Input menu is chosen.

Sometimes audio interfaces don't label inputs in the same way as Logic, and what appears to be Input 1 on the audio interface could be labeled Input 3 in Logic. In that case, you can use the driver labels.

9 Open the Mixer, and choose Options > I/O Labels.

The I/O Labels window opens.

10 For all input channels, select the options in the Provided by Driver column.

NOTE ▶ The number of channels and their labels depend on the audio device you use. Some drivers do not provide labels. You can select the User labels and enter your own custom labels.

11 In the audio channel strip, check the Input menu again, this time looking at the driver labels.

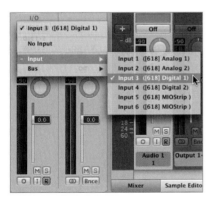

12 Make sure the Record Enable button is turned on in the channel strip.

If the record-enabled channel strip displays a signal and the Out 1-2 channel strip still doesn't display a signal, you need to check for proper routing of the signal.

13 Make sure the output of the channel strip is set to Out 1-2.

14 Make sure the Level fader is up.

15 Make sure the Mute button is not on.

16 Make sure the Mute button is not blinking.

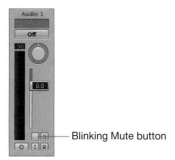

Blinking Mute button

A blinking Mute button indicates that the channel strip is temporarily muted, even though its Mute button is not on. This situation happens when another channel strip is soloed.

TIP ▶ When you realize that one or more tracks are soloed, it can be cumbersome to open the Mixer and unsolo them all, especially in larger sessions featuring many tracks. Instead, click to turn on the Solo button of the current channel strip, then Option-click that same Solo button again. This will take all tracks out of Solo mode.

17 Close the project, and don't save it. You should see the 12 New Day_start Arrange window again.

Once the Out 1-2 channel strip meters display a signal, you should hear that signal through your monitors. If you don't, take another look at "Restoring Your Audio Output" in this lesson.

Getting MIDI Out

When trying to play MIDI regions on external MIDI instrument tracks, first make sure the track is assigned to the correct MIDI instrument, as explained in the Appendix "Using External MIDI Devices."

When troubleshooting MIDI Out routing, it is important to isolate the MIDI Out signal routing from the audio routing of your MIDI device. If the MIDI device has a MIDI input activity monitor, you can check it to verify that the MIDI device is receiving the MIDI data sent by Logic. You can also plug a headphone directly into the MIDI device to verify that the device properly responds to the MIDI events it receives. If it does, then use the techniques described in the previous exercises to check the audio input routing (from the MIDI device into Logic), and the audio output routing (from Logic to your speakers).

The MIDI Activity (In/Out) display in the Transport bar is a great tool to troubleshoot MIDI problems. It displays incoming (upper line) and outgoing (lower line) MIDI events in real time.

If you do not see any outgoing MIDI activity in the display, check for muting at the track, region, and note levels.

1   Make sure the Mute button in track 6 is off, and start playback.

You still can't see any activity in the Transport bar's MIDI Out display.

2   With the Mute tool chosen, click the MIDI region on track 6 (or select it and press M), and start playback.

The MIDI Out display still doesn't show any outgoing MIDI activity.

3   Double-click the MIDI region.

MIDI notes are displayed in the Piano Roll Editor, but they are dimmed, indicating they are muted.

4   Using the Mute tool, click the notes (or select them and press M), and start playback.

The notes are unmuted, and the MIDI Out display shows activity.

If Logic's MIDI Out display shows note events and you still can't hear anything, then the problem lies somewhere else. Check your MIDI routing, as explained in Lesson 4. To temporarily bypass all audio routing, plug your headphones directly into the receiving MIDI device's headphone output. Make sure you have installed the latest drivers for your MIDI interface or MIDI device.

> **MORE INFO ▶** To monitor all incoming and outgoing MIDI events at the computer level, you can use a free third-party utility, MIDI Monitor, available from Snoize (http://www.snoize.com/MIDIMonitor/).

Getting MIDI In

In Logic, all incoming MIDI events are routed by default to the record-enabled MIDI or software instrument track. Incoming MIDI events are also shown in the Transport bar in the MIDI In display.

If no MIDI activity is displayed when you play a MIDI controller, check all the MIDI devices in the chain *before* Logic.

1   Check your MIDI controller's MIDI output activity display, if present.

2   Check your MIDI interface's MIDI input activity display, if present.

3   Power cycle the MIDI controller. Turn it off, and then turn it on.

4   Power cycle the MIDI interface.

5   Disconnect and reconnect the cable connecting the MIDI device or MIDI interface to your computer.

6   If you are using a USB MIDI device, try using another USB port on your computer.

7   Try unplugging other USB devices from your computer, aside from keyboard and mouse.

8   In the Toolbar, click the Preferences button, then choose MIDI from the pop-up menu.

9   Click Reset All MIDI Drivers in the General tab.

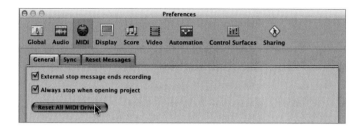

After these steps, if Logic still does not show any incoming MIDI activity when you play your MIDI controller, close the current project and open a factory template. If the template shows activity on the Transport bar's MIDI In display, then the problem lies with your project file. Reopen your project.

In Logic, the Environment contains all the objects you can assign to a track in the Arrange area, such as audio and instrument channel strips and external MIDI devices. It also contains several MIDI objects that control MIDI input and output.

When a MIDI input issue has been isolated to a specific project file, you need to check the default MIDI input cabling of objects in the Environment.

In this project file, the default cabling was broken. Now, you will fix it.

10 Select the Piano track (track 3) and click the record enable button to put the software instrument in live mode.

11 Play a few notes on your MIDI controller.

In the Transport bar, the MIDI In display does not show any activity, and you can't hear the piano.

12 Choose Window > Environment (or press Command-8).

The Environment window opens. A Layer menu at the upper left allows you to view different layers or sections of the Environment. The Click & Ports layer is where incoming MIDI is connected to Logic's sequencer input.

13 Next to the Layer menu, click the arrow button and choose Click & Ports.

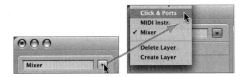

The Click & Ports layer appears. A default Click & Ports layer should show a Physical Input object. The SUM output of the Physical Input is cabled into a keyboard named Input Notes. The keyboard is cabled to a monitor named Input View. That monitor is cabled into the Sequencer Input. Make sure those objects are properly connected. If a cable is missing, cable the objects according to the picture.

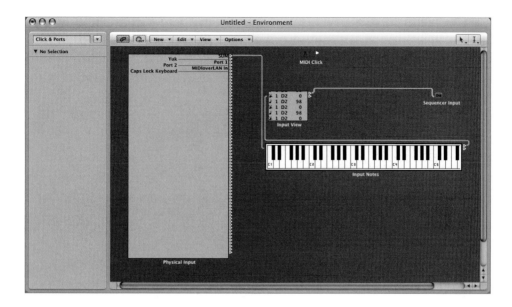

In this project file, you can see a cable is missing between the Input View object and the Sequencer Input object. Now, you will reconnect the two objects. To cable objects, click the output triangle at the top right of the source object, and drag the connector to the destination object.

14 Hold down the Input View output triangle and drag the cable onto the Sequencer Input object.

Output triangle

When the proper default cabling is restored, incoming MIDI events should be displayed in the Transport bar on the MIDI Activity display, and you can hear the piano when playing notes on your MIDI controller.

   MIDI In display

Optimizing Hardware Performance

To get the most performance out of your system, you need to understand how Logic uses and balances hardware resources.

The computer consists of three main components:

▶   Random access memory, or RAM

▶   The hard disk

▶   The CPU

The hard disk stores the applications and files. When the computer starts, OS X is loaded from the hard disk into RAM. When an application is opened, it is also loaded into RAM. Then the CPU can process the files as requested by an application.

When a Logic project is opened, the project file is loaded into RAM along with all the samples (including impulse responses used by Space Designer), Apple Loops, audio files set to follow tempo, and plug-ins used in the project. The amount of RAM influences the number of Apple Loops, samples, and audio files set to follow tempo that can be used in a project.

When playback starts, the audio files and samples used by the project are streamed from the hard disk. The hard disk influences how fast the computer starts, how fast applications are opened, and how many simultaneous audio tracks and samples can be played or recorded.

> **NOTE ▶** By default, the EXS24 mkII sampler loads only the attack section of longer samples. When those samples are played, the rest of the sample is then streamed from the hard disk, and each sample also uses hard disk bandwidth.

The CPU influences the amount of processing power Logic can use in real time while playing back a project. All plug-in and summing calculations require real-time processing. Certain plug-ins (like Guitar Amp Pro or Space Designer) require a lot of processing, while others (like Channel EQ) require very little.

When any of the three main components overload, Logic will stop, or display an alert message, or both. Logic doesn't always know precisely why the problem arises but usually tries to point you toward the source.

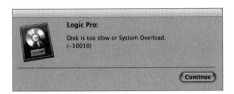

Other times, Logic will alert you to a problem without giving you any hint as to the source. For example, a loss of synchronization between audio and MIDI can be triggered by many events, including too much stress being placed on the hard drive or the CPU.

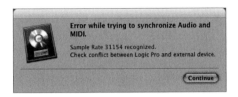

When you have a problem, or feel Logic's performance is sluggish, monitor the CPU and HD (hard drive) meters in the Transport bar. Once you know which component is responsible, you can take the necessary measures to fix or work around the issue.

Optimizing CPU Resources

When the CPU meter goes into the red, it indicates that you are reaching the limits of the computer's processing power. Effects and software instrument plug-ins all use processing power, some more than others. With a little experience, you will get a sense of which plug-ins need the most processing power. Try to locate the more demanding channel strips on the Mixer, and freeze their corresponding tracks. Freezing a track bounces it to an audio file, thereby eliminating all the real-time CPU calculations needed by the software instrument and effects plug-ins on that track.

When all the calculations required by a project cannot be processed in real time, the CPU overloads and you usually get the following message:

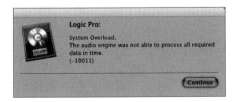

When you get this alert or another indication that you might be reaching the limits of the CPU, look at the CPU load meter.

If the meter goes into the red, it's time to freeze some tracks.

1   Control-click a track header and choose Configure Track Header from the pop-up menu.

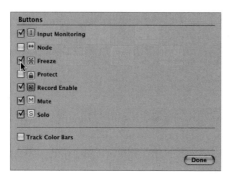

The Track Configuration dialog drops down from the Arrange area title bar, showing the elements you can choose to display in the track headers.

2   Select the Freeze button.

The track headers display the Freeze button.

3   Click Done, or press Enter.

4   Click the Freeze buttons for the tracks you want to bounce to an audio file.

The buttons turn green, indicating those tracks will be frozen.

When deciding which tracks to freeze, find the tracks that include the most CPU-intensive plug-ins and that you don't intend to tweak any further, at least for now. Plug-in settings cannot be modified on a frozen track.

5   Adjust the position of the project end marker to bar 22.

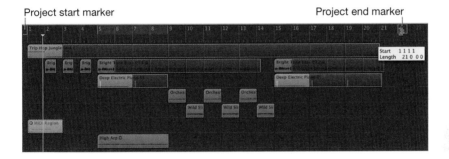

The project end marker is in the Bar ruler. When freezing, Logic bounces individual tracks between the project start and end markers. If your project end marker is located beyond the actual end of the project, you are wasting precious time bouncing silence!

NOTE ▶ Logic bounces freeze files in 32-bit floating point, which is the internal resolution of its audio engine. The audio quality of the freeze file is exactly the same as the unfrozen track.

6   Press the Spacebar.

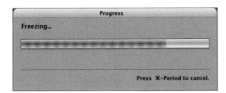

Logic starts the freezing process and displays a progress indicator. Wait until the process ends.

7 Start playback.

The CPU load meter should now be at a lower level. Note that the HD load meter will reach a little higher, since Logic now has to stream the freeze files from the hard disk. When a track is frozen you can't edit the regions on that track, and you can't change the plug-in settings on its channel strip. If you need to access a track's plug-ins or regions, click its freeze button to unfreeze it.

TIP ▸ When no signal is routed to a channel strip, the plug-ins on that channel strip have nothing to process and do not use any CPU cycles. You can temporarily relieve the CPU by muting all the regions on a few tracks.

Optimizing Hard Disk Bandwidth Usage

When the HD load meter goes into the red, you are reaching your hard disk's bandwidth limit. This happens when you're trying to record or play back too many tracks simultaneously or streaming too many samples.

As you approach your hard disk's bandwidth limit, you will notice that Logic responds slower to your commands, especially play and record commands, sometimes giving you the colored pinwheel wait cursor. When you're trying to stream more data than the disk can handle, you get the following alert message:

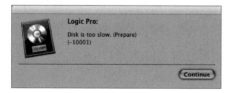

In that case you have to reduce the data streamed from the hard disk. Unfreeze some tracks, especially if the CPU meter is low. If you really need to freeze some CPU-demanding tracks, consider bouncing them individually to 16-bit audio files: those files will be half the size of the corresponding 32-bit floating point freeze files.

If that's not enough, you need to submix sections of the arrangement. For example, you could mix down all the backup vocal tracks into one stereo audio file.

When you don't want to compromise flexibility by submixing tracks, and if you have enough RAM installed on your system, you can force Logic to load an audio region into RAM using the Follow Tempo option. Remember that the Follow Tempo option is available only for audio recorded in the current project. Here is an example of how to use Follow Tempo to load an audio region into RAM.

1   On the last track, select the High Arp audio region.

2   Click to select the Follow Tempo checkbox in the Region Parameter box.

The double-arrow follow tempo icon appears next to the region name.

3   Adjust the tempo to a new tempo.

Logic briefly displays a progress indicator while loading the audio region in RAM.

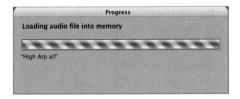

If the song contains tempo changes, you won't be able to change the tempo. In that case, open the Tempo track and choose a new tempo alternative.

4 Revert to the original tempo and play back the song.

> **MORE INFO ▶** To monitor the CPU, hard disk, and RAM activity in real time with more detail and precision, choose Applications > Utilities > Activity Monitor.

Addressing Unexpected Behaviors

While issues related to signal routing and hardware limitations can be easy to identify, sometimes you may experience unexpected behaviors for no apparent reason. It can be hard to trace the exact cause of those problems; however, you can try a few safe and fast methods that will solve most of them.

First Steps

When facing unexpected behaviors, the first step you should take is to return the system to its normal condition or initial state.

▶ Restart Logic, or

▶ Restart the computer

Initializing Preferences

A common cause of application error is corrupt preferences files. When an application opens, its preferences file is loaded into RAM. When you quit the application, the preferences file is saved to the hard disk. If the application quits unexpectedly, or the computer crashes, an application may not properly write the preferences file to the hard disk, resulting in a corrupted preferences file. This often results in unexpected application behaviors.

Keep in mind that after initializing your preferences, you will have to reset them manually.

1 From the main menu, choose Logic Pro > Preferences > Initialize All Except Key Commands.

A confirmation alert appears.

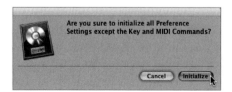

2 Click Initialize.

> **NOTE ►** You can also delete the preferences files manually from the Finder. Your main preferences file is ~/Library/Preferences/com.apple.logic.pro.plist and your control surface preferences file is ~/Library/Preferences/com.apple.logic.pro.cs. (Logic Express preferences are named com.apple.logic.express.plist and com.apple. logic.express.cs.)

To avoid manually resetting your preferences every time you troubleshoot, you should make a backup of your preferences file. Locate the file ~/Library/Preferences/com.apple .logic.pro.plist, and copy it to another drive or storage device.

Restoring Preferences

If you have a backup preferences file, and you suspect the current one might be corrupt, you can replace your current file with the backup.

1 Quit Logic.

2 Locate your backup preferences file, and drag it to ~/Library/Preferences/.

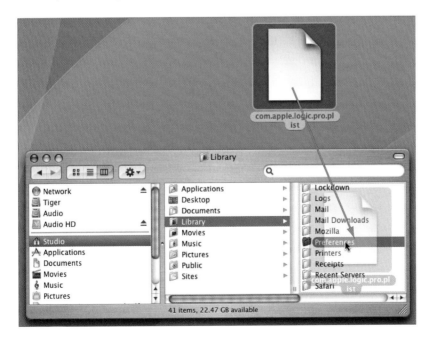

A dialog appears asking you if you want to replace the current file with your backup.

3   Click Replace.

4   Open Logic again.

Project File Corruption

When a project file is corrupted, you can experience unexpected behaviors, and some functions can stop working altogether.

When experiencing unexpected behaviors even after restarting and initializing the preferences, open a brand-new template and try to reproduce the problem. If after experimenting for a while you notice a particular problem or behavior occurs only in a specific project file, chances are the file is corrupt.

Although you won't be able to repair the file, identifying project corruption can help you decide on what direction to take: revert to an earlier backup, rebuild the project by importing the audio and MIDI regions in a new template, or attempt to finish the project with the limited functionality.

Monitoring Problems

Input/output buffers were explained in Lesson 2 "Recording Audio." The smaller their size, the more pressure on the CPU. This generally results in clicks and pops in the monitoring, or in extreme cases a complete loss of monitoring. If you experience monitoring problems, increase the I/O buffer size.

Disabling Audio Drivers at Startup

When Logic freezes at startup, the problem usually lies with the Core Audio engine. Often an incompatible or corrupted third-party plug-in contained in a template or song that opens at startup is the cause of freezing. You can disable the audio drivers at startup by holding down Control immediately after clicking Logic in your Dock. A dialog will open, allowing you to open Logic without launching the Core Audio engine. You can then look at the template or song, uninstantiate any suspicious third-party plug-ins, and re-enable the Core Audio devices in your Audio Preferences window.

When a problem occurs, it can be difficult to decide where to start. In this lesson you learned typical troubleshooting steps you can take depending on the issue at hand. As you gain more experience and a better understanding of how your system works, you will get faster at diagnosing issues you may have when you work in Logic and finding a solution to fix them.

Lesson Review

1. When are automatic backups created, and where are they saved?
2. Describe an easy way to have Logic produce an audio signal in Logic when trouble-shooting audio output.
3. When you are reaching the limits of your CPU, how can you quickly reduce the load on it?
4. How can you avoid reaching the limits of your hard disk's bandwidth?
5. When a project file isn't receiving incoming MIDI events, even though other project files are, what should you do?
6. How can you determine if your audio interface is causing a playback problem?

Answers

1. Each time you save a project file, Logic moves the previously saved project file into the Project File Backups folder inside the project folder.
2. Preview an Apple Loops file from the Loops Browser.
3. Freeze CPU-intensive tracks.
4. Unfreeze tracks, submix several tracks together, or load audio regions into RAM using Follow Tempo.
5. Open that project file's Environment window, and check for proper default Click & Ports layer cabling.
6. Bypass the audio interface by playing a project through your Mac's built-in audio interface. If the project plays properly, the problem probably lies in the interface.

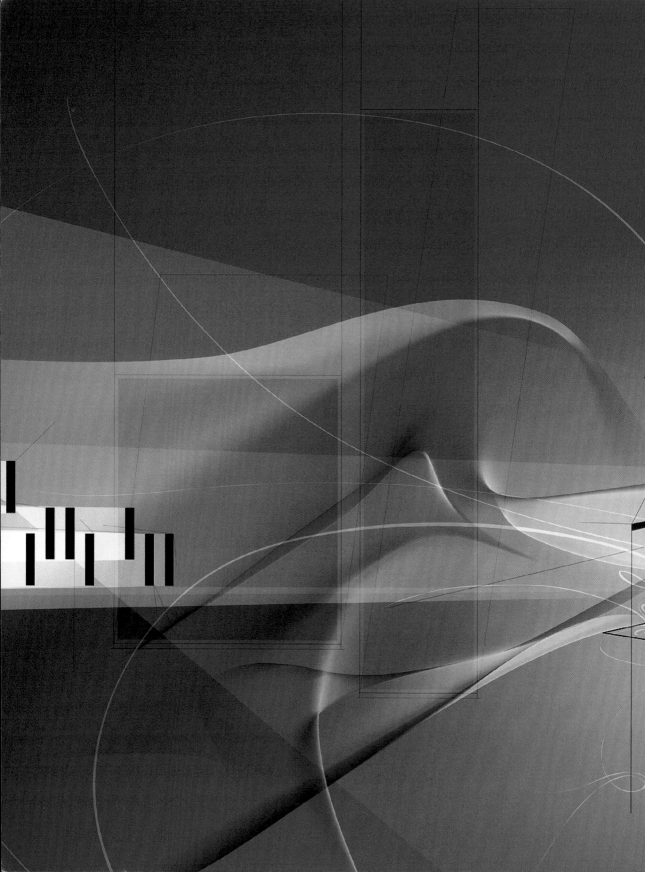

Using External MIDI Devices

Although Logic comes with a wide array of software instruments and supports third-party Audio Unit software instruments, sometimes you may want to use Logic to trigger a hardware synthesizer or sampler, or even a software instrument in another software application.

In the following exercises, you will set up hardware instruments so you can access them from Logic, and use external MIDI tracks to route the MIDI events to an MIDI instrument outside Logic. You can then record on external MIDI tracks with the same techniques you used to record on software instrument tracks. An external MIDI track can be routed to a hardware MIDI device, a ReWire application (such as Ableton Live or Propellerhead Software's Reason), or to any other MIDI-compatible application on your computer or network.

Configuring MIDI Hardware

Logic can access any device configured in Audio MIDI Setup, a Mac OS X configuration tool. Audio MIDI Setup automatically detects USB or FireWire MIDI devices connected directly to the computer, provided the necessary drivers have been properly installed. The MIDI synthesizers connected to that MIDI interface would not be detected, however. Setting up those synths in Audio MIDI Setup will allow you to access them by name in Logic, so you don't have to remember which device is connected to which port on the MIDI interface.

For the purpose of this exercise, you will set up two external synthesizers in Audio MIDI Setup, a Korg Triton and a Yamaha Motif.

1   Open a Finder window.

The Finder is the active application, and its name is displayed to the right of the Apple in the main menu bar.

2   Choose Go > Utilities (or press Command-Shift-U).

The Utilities folder opens.

3   Double-click Audio MIDI Setup.

The Audio MIDI Setup utility opens.

4   At the top of the Audio MIDI Setup window, click the MIDI Devices button.

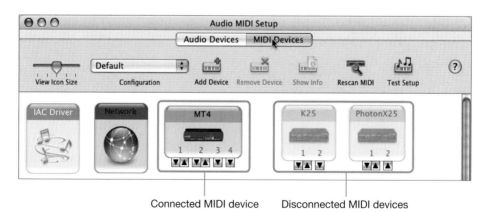

Connected MIDI device   Disconnected MIDI devices

You should see an IAC Driver button, a Network button, and buttons for MIDI devices connected directly to your computer.

NOTE ▶ If a device is connected to your computer but does not appear in Audio MIDI Setup, make sure you properly install the most recent driver for that device.

NOTE ▶ You can double-click the Network button to create network MIDI ports. Network MIDI ports are virtual MIDI cables that allow you to connect applications over a wired or wireless network. Existing network MIDI ports are displayed in Logic's Library when an external MIDI track is selected.

You can double-click the IAC Driver button to create Inter-Application Communication buses. IAC buses are virtual MIDI cables that allow you to connect applications on your computer. Existing IAC buses are displayed in Logic's Library when an external MIDI track is selected.

5   Click the Add Device button.

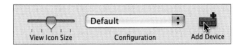

A new external device is created.

6   Click the Add Device button again.

A second new external device is created.

7   Double-click the first new device.

A Properties floating window appears.

8   In the Device Name field, enter *Triton*.

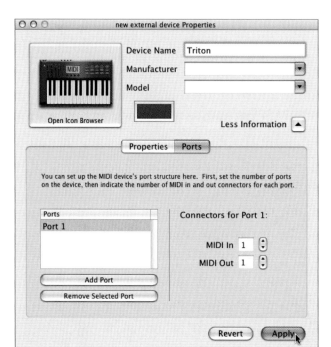

9   Click Apply.

The device is renamed.

10   In the Audio MIDI Setup window, click the second device.

The Properties window displays the properties of the selected device.

11   In the Device Name field, enter *Motif.*

12   Click Apply and close the Properties window.

Now you need to identify the physical connections between the MIDI interface and the synthesizers in Audio MIDI Setup. Since Logic routes all incoming MIDI events to the record-enabled track, you only need to route outgoing MIDI events. For this exercise, let's assume you have an MT4 MIDI interface with the following physical MIDI connections:

▶   MT4 MIDI Out port 1 connects to the Triton MIDI In port.

▶   MT4 MIDI Out port 2 connects to the Motif MIDI In port.

You will now enter these connections in Audio MIDI Setup.

13   Click the MIDI Out 1 port of the MT4 interface and drag the cable to the MIDI In port of the Triton.

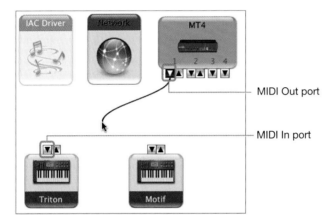

14   Click the MIDI Out 2 port of the MT4 interface and connect it to the MIDI In port of the Motif.

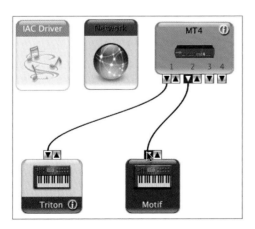

15 Choose Audio MIDI Setup > Quit Audio MIDI Setup (or press Command-Q).

Now Audio MIDI Setup knows which MIDI Out port is connected to which device, and Logic's Library will display *Triton* and *Motif* instead of MT4 Port 1 and MT4 Port 2.

> **MORE INFO ▶** If you want to record or monitor the audio outputs from the hardware synthesizers in Logic, you also need to connect the synthesizers' audio outputs to audio inputs on your audio inteIrface. In Logic, record-enable an audio track to record or monitor those audio inputs (make sure you have chosen the desired setting in the input slot of the I/O section on the audio track's channel strip).

Routing External MIDI Tracks

When using external MIDI tracks, you use the Library to route the MIDI events on the track. All the devices set up in Audio MIDI Setup are displayed in the Library (including IAC buses and network MIDI ports). All the ReWire applications installed on your computer are also displayed in the Library.

In the next exercise, you will use the Library to choose a destination for an external MIDI track.

1 Open a new Empty Project template, and in the New Tracks dialog, leave 1 in the Number field, select External MIDI as the Type, select the Open Library checkbox and click Create.

A new external MIDI track is created.

The Library opens and displays available MIDI destinations for the external MIDI track (the available destinations depend on your studio setup).

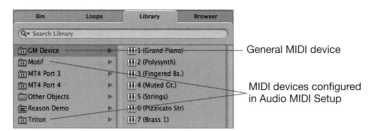

General MIDI device

MIDI devices configured in Audio MIDI Setup

▶ The GM (General MIDI) device is a multi-timbral instrument that always sends to all existing MIDI Out ports. A *multi-timbral* instrument is one that can respond to more than one MIDI channel at a time to play several sounds (more commonly called patches or program) simultaneously. A single MIDI port can transmit 16 MIDI channels simultaneously, and each MIDI channel can play one program. The 16 MIDI channels of the GM device are displayed in the right column.

▶   The Motif and Triton MIDI synthesizers you configured in Audio MIDI Setup are displayed in the list of available MIDI destinations.

▶   All ReWire applications on your computer are displayed in the Library. You can double-click a ReWire application in the left column to open it, and all available ReWire instruments will be displayed in the right column.

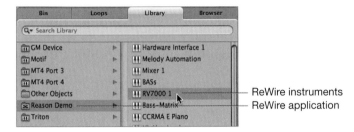

You will now assign the selected track to MIDI channel 1 of the Motif synthesizer.

MORE INFO ▶   If you do not have an external MIDI synthesizer or sampler, in the next step choose GM Device instead of Motif, then follow along with the steps, but keep in mind since no external instrument is connected you won't hear any sound.

2   In the Library, click Motif.

3   In the right column, click Channel 1.

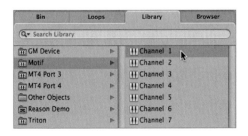

The track is assigned to MIDI channel 1 of the Motif. Any MIDI events on that track will be routed to that destination. While the track is record-enabled, any incoming MIDI events will be routed to the track, and from the track to MIDI channel 1 of the Motif.

The track header displays the name of the instrument, the MIDI channel number, and the interface's MIDI port name. You may need to zoom vertically to see all that information.

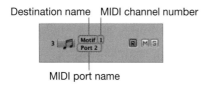

In the Inspector, the Arrange channel strip appears unlike the audio and software instrument channel strips. Since the external MIDI channel strip generates MIDI events, it does not have processing plug-in inserts or audio routing settings.

External MIDI channel strip

The volume fader and the knobs on the external MIDI channel strip send MIDI continuous controller events to the external MIDI instrument, allowing you to remotely control the external instrument's volume, pan position, reverberation, and chorus of the program on that MIDI channel.

Choosing a Program Remotely

Logic allows you to remotely choose a program or patch on your external MIDI device. This avoids interrupting your workflow to choose the program on the MIDI device itself and also allows you to save the programs used on each track in your project.

1   On the track header, double-click the track name.

The Motif's Multi Instrument window appears.

NOTE ▶ The GM Device Multi Instrument window contains the General MIDI program names.

2   Click a program name.

The corresponding program-change MIDI event is sent to the external MIDI instrument. (You can see the program-change event on the Transport bar's MIDI Out display.) When you play your MIDI keyboard, you can hear the new sound.

 — Program change event

Most instruments have more than 128 programs. To access additional programs, you need to switch to another bank of programs.

3   Click the Bank menu, and choose 1.

An alert message appears asking if you want to initialize the bank.

4   Click Initialize.

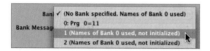

Choosing a bank in the Bank menu sends a bank select MIDI event to the external MIDI instrument, instructing it to switch to the new bank. If your instrument does not react to the bank select event, try choosing another type of bank select event for that instrument in the Bank Message menu (right below the Bank menu).

You can name all the programs for your instruments and save the project as a template so that you can choose programs by name, rather than by number.

5   Double-click the first program number.

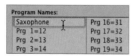

A text field appears.

6   Type a name for the first program, and press Enter.

The text field focus moves to the second program, ready to be renamed.

TIP You could repeat this process until you've named all the programs in all the banks, but that could take a while! To save time, search a website devoted to Logic users for a Logic template where the desired hardware instruments have already been configured.

If you can't find a Logic template, look online for an electronic voice list, usually in PDF format (sometimes part of the electronic manual). Start your search by searching the instrument manufacturer's website. Copy and paste the list of program names for your MIDI device into a text editor (such as Apple TextEdit) and edit it so that you have a list of 128 names, one name per line. Select all 128 names and choose Edit > Copy. In Logic, at the upper right of the Multi Instrument window, click Options and choose Paste All Names. Repeat the process for each program bank.

When you are done entering program names for all the instruments, save that project as a template. Program names are saved in the project file, not as a general preference; so, unless you save the project, all your program names will be lost.

7   Choose File > Save As Template.

A Save As dialog appears and the location is already set to the Project Templates folder. All you need to do is name your template.

8   Name and save your template.

Your new template is available in the Templates dialog that appears when choosing File > New, in the My Templates collection folder.

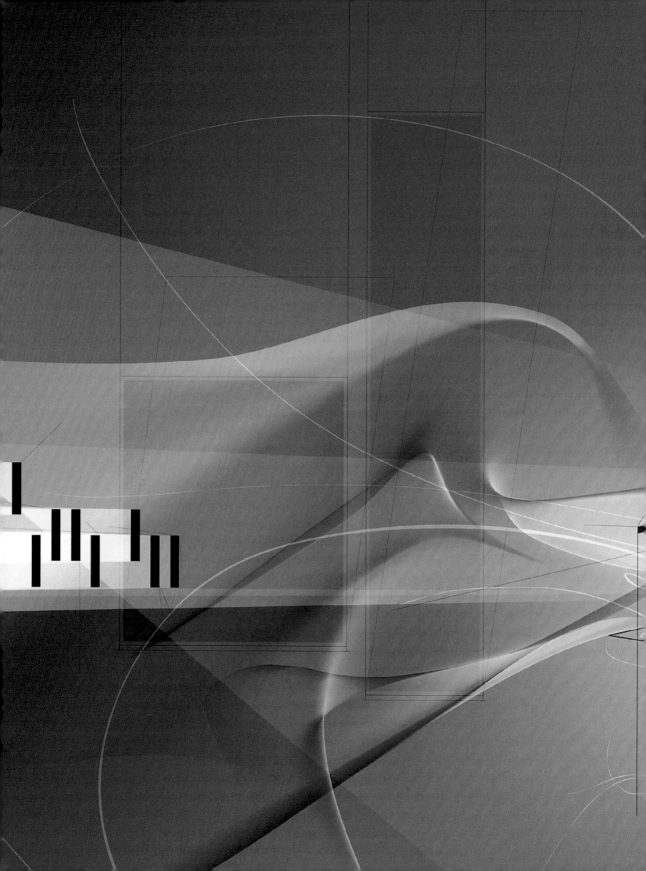

Appendix B
Keyboard Shortcuts

Transport Controls

Key Command	Action
Spacebar	Play/stop
Enter	Play
Shift-Enter	Move playhead to start of selected region or event and begin playback
0	Stop (or return to beginning when stopped)
0-0	Stop recording or playback and go to beginning
Control-0	Stop recording or playback and go to last play position
Return	Move playhead to beginning of project
Shift-Return	Move playhead to start of first selected region or event in active window
/ (on main keypad)	Open Go To Position dialog
Control-Enter	Play from left window edge
. (decimal point on numeric keypad)	Pause playback

Transport Controls (continued)

Key Command	Action
< (left angle bracket)	Rewind
> (right angle bracket)	Forward
Shift-<	Fast Rewind
Shift->	Fast Forward
* (on numeric keypad)	Record
Shift-* (on numeric keypad)	Toggle record (for punching on the fly)
Control-* (on numeric keypad)	Capture as recording

Zooming

Key Command	Action
Control–Down Arrow	Zoom in vertically
Control–Up Arrow	Zoom out vertically
Control–Right Arrow	Zoom in horizontally
Control–Left Arrow	Zoom out horizontally
Control-Option-Z	Zoom to fit selection vertically and horizontally, and store navigation snapshot
Control-Z	Navigation: Back (zoom out)
Control-Option-drag	Zoom tool

Tools

Key Command	Action
Esc	Opens Tool menu at Pointer position
Esc-Esc	Make Pointer tool the default (left-click) tool
Control–Option–any tool	Turn current tool into Zoom tool
Option–drag Pointer tool	Copy
Shift–Pencil tool	Import audio file at clicked location
Control–Shift–drag Crossfade tool	Adjust the crossfade curve
Option–click Crossfade tool	Delete crossfade
Option–resize	Time stretch region when resizing
Control–click	Opens shortcut menu
Shift-Option-drag	Adjusts parameter to same value

Channel Strip, Track, and Region Operations

Key Command	Action
Command-S	Save
Command-Z	Undo
Shift-Command-Z	Redo
Option-Command-N	Create new tracks
Command-A	Select all
Shift-Command-A	Deselect all

Channel Strip, Track, and Region Operations (continued)

Key Command	Action
L	Toggle looping of selected region
Command-R	Repeat regions/events
K	Convert loop to a real copy of selected original region
Control-C	Crop regions outside marquee selection
Control-= (equal sign)	Set locators by regions/events (Standard)
Control-' (apostrophe)	Set locators by regions/events (MacBook)
Command-F	Pack selected regions into a folder
Command-U	Unpack regions from folder
Command-T	Match project tempo to that of selected audio region, using cycle length
Shift-Option-N	Assign name of selected track to its regions
S	Toggle Solo mode for selected regions
Option-S	Lock the Solo status of selected regions
M	Mute/unmute selected notes, regions, or folders
Control-M	Mute/unmute selected Arrange area track
Command-click Track Mute button	Mute/unmute all tracks
Option-click fader, knob, parameter	Reset to default, or centered, value
Option-click Insert/ Instrument/Send slot	Bypass plug-in or send
Shift-]	Load next channel strip setting
Shift-[	Load previous channel strip setting

Channel Strip, Track, and Region Operations (continued)

Key Command	Action
Command-G	Toggle group clutch
Shift-U	Select unused (Audio Bin)
Option-Command-S	Save selection as new audio file (Sample Editor)

Views

Key Command	Action
B	Show/hide Audio Bin
E	Show/hide Event List
G	Show/hide global tracks
I	Show/hide Inspector
P	Show/hide Piano Roll Editor
N	Show/hide Score Editor
X	Show/hide Mixer
Y	Show/hide Hyper Editor
V	Show/hide all open plug-in windows
Z	Auto track zoom
Double-click MIDI region (in Arrange area)	Open default editor
Option-C	Open Color palette
Option-G	Open Configure Global Tracks dialog
Option-K	Open Key Commands window
Command-K	Open controller assignment window

Views (continued)

Key Command	Action
Option-P	Open Audio project settings
Option-V	Open Video project settings
Option-Y	Open Synchronization project settings
Option-Z	Open Undo History window
Option-*	Open Recording project settings (Option-R on laptop)
Option-Command-O	Open QuickTime movie
Option-Command-W	Close active project
Command-1	Open Arrange window
Command-2	Open Mixer
Command-3	Open Score Editor
Command-4	Open Transform window
Command-5	Open Hyper Editor
Command-6	Open Piano Roll Editor
Command-8	Open Environment window
Tab	Cycle key focus forward through Arrange window areas
Shift-Tab	Cycle key focus backward through Arrange window areas
Control-H	Hide current track and select next track
Shift-Control-H	Unhide (show) all tracks
Control-X	Open Strip Silence window
Shift-L	Lock/unlock current screenset
Caps Lock	Use computer keyboard as virtual MIDI keyboard

Automation

Key Command	Action
A	Show/hide track automation
Shift–drag Pointer tool	Select nodes while dragging around them in automation track
Control–Option–Pointer tool	Adjust curves in automation track
Option-A	Open Automation preferences
Control-Option-Command-A	Toggle Automation Quick Access
Shift-Control-Command-O	Turn automation mode off for all tracks
Shift-Control-Command-R	Set automation mode to Read for all tracks
Shift-Control-Command-T	Set automation mode to Touch for all tracks
Shift-Control-Command-L	Set automation mode to Latch for all tracks
Control-Command-Backspace	Delete currently visible automation data of current track
Shift-Control-Command-Backspace	Delete all automation data of current track

Finder

Key Command	Action
Command-Tab	Switch to next application
Shift-Command-Tab	Switch to previous application
Command-H	Hide active application
Option-Command-H	Hide other applications

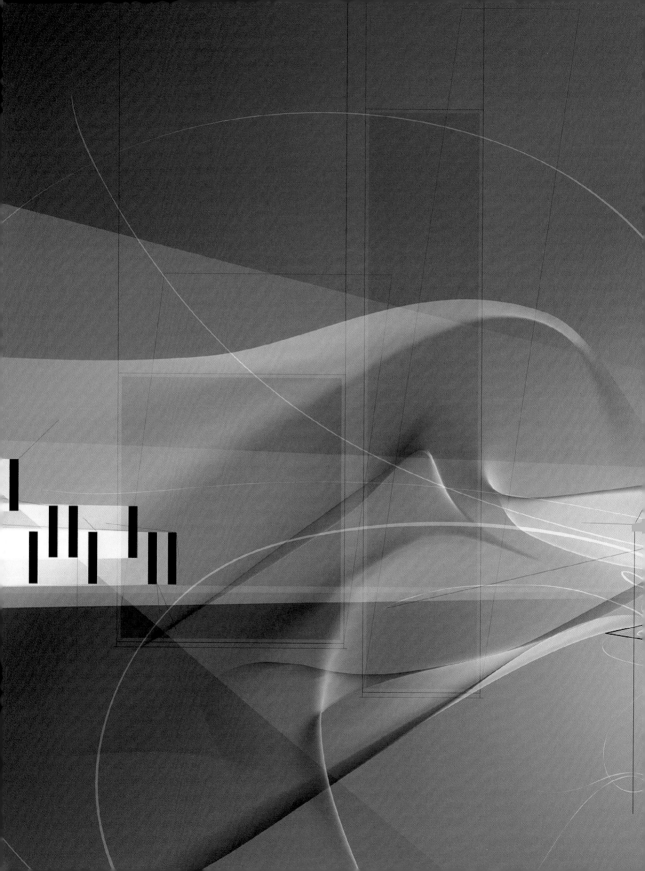

Glossary

5.1 A common surround sound format, typically comprising five full-frequency speakers, which are fed by five independent channels, plus one dedicated low-frequency subwoofer.

#

aftertouch MIDI data type generated by pressure on keys after they have been struck. Aftertouch is also known as pressure.

A

AIFF Audio Interchange File Format. A cross-platform file format supported by a large number of digital video and audio editing applications. AIFF audio can use a variety of bit depths, but the two most common are 16 bit and 24 bit.

alias A region in the Arrange area that mirrors a MIDI region someplace else. You cannot edit an alias, only a real region, but any change to the region will be reflected in the alias. To create an alias, Shift-Option-drag the original MIDI region to a new location.

anchor A temporal reference point, or the point that Logic Pro uses to snap a region to the Arrange area's time grid. In the Audio Bin window and Sample Editor, the anchor is represented by a small triangle under the starting point of a region.

Apple Loops An audio file format in which recurring rhythmic musical elements or elements suitable for repetition are recorded. Apple Loops have tags that allow Logic to perform time stretching and pitch shifting. These tags also allow you to locate files by instrument, genre, or mood in the Loop Browser.

arming Enabling a track to be recorded.

Arrange area The primary working space of the application, where audio and MIDI regions are edited and moved to create a project.

Arrange window The primary working window of the application. It shows the Arrange area (see above) and can incorporate all other working areas and editors.

Audio Bin A window, or a tab in the Media area, used to add audio files from your hard disk to your project. You can use the Audio Bin to manage the project's audio files.

audio file Any digital audio recording stored on your hard disk. The default storage format for audio files in Logic Pro is AIFF, but you can store audio files in the CAF, Sound Designer II and WAV formats as well.

audio interface A device that provides audio inputs and outputs to your computer.

audio region An area of an audio file registered in the Audio Bin for use in the project. It can be placed on audio tracks in the Arrange area, just as a MIDI region can be placed on MIDI tracks. Audio regions are pointers to portions of audio files.

audio track A track in the Arrange area used for the playback, recording, and editing of audio regions.

automation The ability to record, edit, and play back the movements of all knobs and switches, including volume faders and pan, EQ, and aux send controls.

Automation Quick Access A Logic Pro feature that assigns a slider or knob on your hardware MIDI controller keyboard to modify track automation data.

aux An auxiliary channel strip, either mono or stereo, in the Mixer.

B

bar A measure of music, containing a specified number of beats, that establishes the rhythmic structure of the composition.

Bar ruler The timeline that runs the length of the project, divided into bars, beats, and even finer divisions. It contains the playhead, the cycle and auto-punch areas, and markers. It is found at the top of the Arrange area, Piano Roll Editor, Hyper Editor, and Score Editor.

bit depth The resolution (number of 0s and 1s) of a digital audio sample, which influences the dynamic range of a digital audio recording.

bounce To combine several tracks of audio into one file.

bus A virtual audio cable to route audio between channel strips, for processing or submixing tasks.

bypass To temporarily deactivate a plug-in.

C

Caps Lock Keyboard A small MIDI controller on your screen, activated by pressing the Caps Lock key on your computer keyboard.

Catch A mode that continuously updates the contents of a window to show the position of the playhead. The Catch button shows a man running.

CD Audio Short for Compact Disc–Audio; the current standard for stereo music CDs is a 44.1 kHz sampling rate and a 16-bit depth.

channel A path used to transport a signal.

channel strip A virtual representation of a channel strip on a mixing console. Each channel strip contains a number of controls, such as Solo and Mute buttons, a volume fader, a pan/balance knob, Input and Output slots, Send slots, and Insert slots.

channel strip settings A combination of plug-ins and their settings that make a certain sound.

clip To feed too much signal through a channel, producing a distorted sound. Audio channel strips have a clip detector.

continuous control number (cc#) The number assigned by the MIDI specification regarding audio events or software functions such as volume, modulation, or sustain.

Core Audio The standardized audio driver for a computer running Mac OS X 10.2 or higher. Allows the connection of all audio interfaces that are Core Audio compatible.

Core MIDI The standardized MIDI driver for a computer running Mac OS X 10.2 or higher. Allows the connection of all MIDI devices that are Core MIDI compatible.

Crossfade tool One of the tools in the Arrange area Tool menu. The tool creates a cross-fade when you drag across a section where two audio regions meet. You can also drag the tool over the beginning or end of a region to create a fade-in or fade-out, respectively.

cross-fade To bring the volume of one audio file up while simultaneously lowering the volume of another file in a smooth transition.

Cycle mode A mode in Logic Pro in which you can repeat a section of a project. To turn on Cycle mode, click the Cycle button in the Transport bar or click the top part of the Bar rule (on the gray locators stripe). Two locators define a cycle region.

D

dB Short for decibels, a measurement that relates the relative change in the volume of audio.

digital audio workstation (DAW) A computer that records, mixes, and produces audio files.

Digital Factory A suite of digital signal processors in the Sample Editor. It can time compress or time stretch an audio region, change its pitch, add groove or swing to a machinelike audio loop, or alter its sampling rate. The Digital Factory functions are destructive, permanently changing the source audio file.

digital signal processing (DSP) In Logic Pro, the mathematical process of manipulating digital information to modify sound. An example is the Insert slot of a channel strip, which assigns DSP effects such as dynamic range compression and delay to a channel's sound.

dithering A process of reducing an audio signal from a higher-bit resolution to a lower one.

driver A software program that allows your computer to communicate with another piece of hardware.

editor In Logic Pro, one of a multitude of editors to help you compose music. All of them alter the raw input in some way. The primary MIDI editors are the Piano Roll, Hyper and Score editors, and the Event List. You can edit audio regions in the Arrange area, Audio Bin window, and Sample Editor.

E

Environment A window that graphically reflects the relationship between hardware devices outside your computer and virtual devices within your computer.

Environment layer A place to organize the objects in the Environment for easy access. As a general rule, objects of the same type are usually placed on the same layer.

Eraser tool A tool for deleting items. When you click a selected item, all other currently selected items are also deleted.

event A MIDI message. The main events in Logic Pro are note, control-change, pitch bend, aftertouch, and SysEx events. MIDI events can be edited in a number of ways.

Event List A list of events and regions that gives you access to all recorded event data. Thus, you can directly manipulate events and regions and make precise alterations.

fader Generally thought of as a volume control found on audio channels.

F

Finger tool A tool that looks like a hand with an extended index finger. The selection tool changes from the Pointer tool to the Finger tool to enable you to manipulate events or change window parameters. Different mouse and key commands activate the Finger tool in different windows.

floating A term that describes a window that's always visible on your desktop.

folder A container in Logic Pro's Arrange area for MIDI regions, audio regions, or other folders.

Freeze function A function that bounces a track and its plug-ins into an audio file and then plays back that audio file instead of the original one, saving your computer's processing power.

G

General MIDI (GM) A specification designed to increase compatibility between MIDI devices. A musical sequence generated by a GM instrument should trigger the same sounds on any other GM synthesizer or sound module.

global Tempo track A track in which you can view and edit all the tempo changes of a project. The track displays tempo changes as nodes.

global Video track A track displaying frames of a QuickTime movie as "thumbnails" that are perfectly synchronized with the music, making it ideal for film scoring. Cuts in the movie can be automatically detected and marked.

Glue tool A dedicated tool for merging regions or events.

grid Vertical lines used to map the positions of measures, beats, and sub-beats in various editors.

H

Hand tool A tool that appears when you click and hold an event or region with the Pointer tool. It is used to move regions or events in the editors.

headroom Refers to the available dynamic range before clipping, or distortion, occurs.

help tag A small yellow text window that appears when the mouse cursor is placed over an interface element, indicating its name, value, or other information.

Hyper Draw A function that lets you create and edit MIDI CC automation in a region by graphically inserting a set of points or nodes, which are automatically connected.

Hyper Editor A MIDI editor, used mainly for creating and editing drum sequences and control-change data.

hyper set A layer in the Hyper Editor containing a user-defined collection of MIDI events.

I

input filtering Preventing MIDI information such as pitch bend or aftertouch events from reaching a track. The Input Filter tab is in the MIDI Project Settings window.

Insert slot A slot on channel strips where you can insert an audio processing plug-in.

Inspector The pane at the left edge of the Arrange area and editors containing the Parameter boxes and Arrange channel strips of the selected track.

instrument object An object in Logic Pro's Environment that represents a physical or virtual device that reacts to MIDI information.

I/O buffer size How big a bite a computer tries to chew at one time when working with audio. Larger buffers give you more CPU power, but also more latency when monitoring record-enabled tracks. The buffer size is set in the Audio Hardware & Drivers preferences.

K

key command An instruction to Logic Pro that triggers an action, done by pressing a key or a combination of keys. All of Logic Pro's main functions can be activated by key commands.

L

latency The delay between, say, playing your keyboard and hearing the sound. One factor contributing to latency is the I/O buffer size.

Link mode A mode that determines the relationship of one window to another. Clicking the Link button toggles the Link mode.

local menu bar The place where the functions of the currently active window can be found.

locators The two positions defining the edges of the cycle area. The locators are displayed in the Transport bar, directly to the right of the playhead position.

Loop A region parameter allowing a region to repeat.

M

marker Used for indicating and quickly moving to sections of your project.

Marquee tool A crosshair-shaped tool in the Arrange area with which you can select and edit regions, or even portions of regions.

menu bar The bar extending along the top of the computer screen that gives options for global functions like opening windows and saving and loading projects. The local menu bars in the individual editing windows provide access to most of Logic Pro's functions.

metronome In Logic Pro, a component that produces a sound measuring the beat. It can be set with a button in the Transport bar.

MIDI Musical Instrument Digital Interface. It's an industry standard that allows devices like synthesizers and computers to communicate with each other. It controls a musical note's pitch, length, and volume, among other characteristics.

MIDI channel A conduit for MIDI data. MIDI data flows through MIDI ports in channels, and up to 16 MIDI channels can pass through each port at the same time.

MIDI region Data container for MIDI events, shown in the Arrange area as a named horizontal beam. It does not contain sounds, but rather contains MIDI events that tell a synthesizer how to produce sounds. In earlier Logic versions MIDI regions were called sequences.

Mixer A virtual mixing console used to position Logic Pro's tracks. It mirrors the number and order of tracks in the Arrange area. In the Mixer you can also change a channel strip's volume or panorama (pan) position, insert DSP effects, or mute and solo channels.

mixing The process of shaping the overall sound of a project by adjusting the volume levels and pan positions, adding EQ and other effects, and using automation to dynamically alter aspects of the project.

MP3 A digital coding standard used to compress audio files and distribute them over the Internet.

multi instrument An object in the Environment that represents a multi-timbral device.

multi-timbral Describes an instrument or other device that can use several MIDI channels simultaneously.

mute To silence the output of a region or track.

Mute tool A tool that stops a region or event from playing by clicking it.

nodes Dots in Hyper Draw and automation tracks that mark the positions where data manipulation begins or ends. Occasionally referred to as points.

N

nondestructive Said of an audio editor that does not change the source audio files in the course of editing.

object In Logic Pro, a general term that refers to the graphical representations of elements in the Environment. Each connection between Logic Pro and the studio's MIDI devices is represented by an object, and objects can be used to create and process MIDI and audio data.

O

Object Parameter box A box that displays the properties of an object in the Environment.

output channel strip Channel strip type in the Mixer that controls the output level and pan or balance for each physical output of your audio interface.

PCM Pulse-code modulated audio. This is simply uncompressed digital audio, including AIFF, WAV, and SDII files.

P

Pencil tool A tool used to draw various types of information in an editor.

Piano Roll Editor The main MIDI editor in Logic Pro. It displays note events as horizontal beams. Events can be cut, copied, moved, and resized in a similar fashion to regions in the Arrange area.

playhead A vertical white line in the Arrange area and in other horizontal time-based windows that indicates where you are in a project. In Play mode the project begins playing from the playhead position. You can position the playhead with the mouse, by clicking the Bar ruler, or by entering bar numbers in a dialog.

plug-in A small software application that adds functions to a main program (in this case, Logic Pro). Logic Pro's plug-ins are typically audio effects processors.

Pointer tool The default selection tool, shaped like an arrow. It is in every window's toolbox.

preferences User settings that are applied to all Logic Pro projects.

programs Synthesizer sounds.

proxy movie A low-resolution and tightly compressed version of a high-resolution movie that places less strain on your computer as you score.

punch in, punch out A technique that allows you to interrupt playback and record audio as the sound is playing. It can be automated in Logic Pro.

Q

quantize To correct the position of notes so that they conform to a specific time grid.

QuickTime Apple's cross-platform standard for digitized media. You can run QuickTime movies in a Logic Pro window or on a global Video track, in sync with the project. Whenever you move the playhead, the video follows, and vice versa.

R

region A rectangular beam that represents a container for audio or MIDI data. Regions can be found in the tracks of the Arrange area. There are three types: audio regions, MIDI regions, and folders.

Region Parameter box A pane in the upper-left corner of the Arrange window, used to nondestructively set the individual regions' playback parameters, including quantization, transposition, velocity, and delay. These parameters do not alter the stored data. Rather, they affect how the events are played back.

Replace mode An operating state you can activate in the Transport bar. The Replace button is next to the Cycle and Autodrop buttons. In Replace mode, newly recorded information takes the place of the old information.

S

sample accurate Describes editors (such as the Sample Editor or Arrange area) that display or allow you to edit individual samples in an audio region.

Sample Editor An editor in Logic Pro where stereo or mono audio files are destructively cut, reversed, shortened, changed in gain, and processed in a number of other ways. The Sample Editor allows sample-accurate editing of an audio file.

sampling rate Refers to the number of times per second a digital audio file is sampled. When audio comes in through your sound card, analog-to-digital converters sample the signal's voltage level. Logic Pro can record and edit audio at sampling rates ranging from 44.1 kHz (44,100 times per second) to 192 kHz.

Scissors tool A tool with which you divide regions. It offers different options for dividing audio regions from those for MIDI regions.

Score Editor A MIDI editor that displays notes in standard musical notation.

screenset An onscreen layout of windows that you can save. Each window retains its position, size, and zoom settings.

Scroll in Play A function similar to the Catch function, but instead of the playhead playing across the Arrange area's regions, the regions scroll past a stationary playhead, as a tape would.

scrubbing Moving the pointer back and forth (in a scrubbing motion) while playing back an audio region to locate a specific section.

send An output on an audio channel that splits a portion of a channel's sound and sends it through a bus to another audio channel strip.

sequencer A computer application that allows you to record both digital audio and MIDI data and blend the sounds together in a software mixing console.

Shuffle A drag mode that causes a region to shuffle up to the region immediately to its left or right, depending on the Shuffle mode selected. This ensures that one region plays smoothly into the next with no drop in the track's audio.

SMPTE Society of Motion Picture and Television Engineers. These folks set up a synchronization system that divides time into hours, minutes, seconds, frames, and subframes.

software instrument The software counterpart to a hardware sampler or synthesizer module, or an acoustic sound source such as a drum kit or guitar. The sounds generated by software instruments are calculated by the computer CPU and played via the audio interface outputs. Often called soft synths or soft samplers.

solo A way to temporarily allow you to hear one or more selected tracks, events, or regions without hearing others that aren't soloed.

Solo tool A tool that enables you to listen to selected events or regions by themselves (click and hold the event or region to do so).

Standard MIDI file A common file type that almost any MIDI sequencer can read. In Logic Pro you can export selected MIDI regions as Standard MIDI files.

step-input To record notes one step at a time in a MIDI region.

synthesizer A hardware or software device used to generate sounds. Logic Pro features several software synthesizers, including the EVOC 20 PolySynth, EFM1, ES E ES M, ES P, ES1, ES2, EVB3, EVD6, and EVP88.

SysEx System Exclusive data.

T

template An project file that is preconfigured with a set of Arrange area tracks designed for a specific purpose such as mastering, 24-track recording, or surround mixing.

tempo The speed at which a piece of music is played, measured in beats per minute. You can create and edit tempo changes in the global Tempo track.

Text tool A tool for naming audio and MIDI regions.

time signature Two numerals separated by a slash that appear at the beginning of a project. Common time signatures are 4/4 and 2/4. The first number denotes the number of notes in a measure, or bar. The second number denotes a unit of time for each beat. With a 2/4 signature, each bar has two beats and each beat is a quarter note long.

time stretch To change the length of an audio region without changing its pitch. You can do this in the Arrange area or Sample Editor.

Toolbar The top of the Arrange window features the Toolbar, which is used to access or hide certain onscreen areas, such as the Media or Lists area or the Inspector. It also contains a number of buttons for key functions. You may freely customize the Toolbar to meet your needs.

Tool menu Available in the local menu bar of a window, the Tool menus contain tools for editing, zooming, cropping, and otherwise manipulating items in the window.

track A row in the Arrange area that contains a collection of MIDI or audio regions that can be played back. Each track has a specified destination where the data will go.

track automation Used for programming control changes that are not necessarily tied to a specific region, such as a volume fade or a cutoff sweep. The track automation system allows you to quickly find and automate any plug-in parameter. It has its own recording modes, which function independently of Logic Pro's other recording features.

track list A list to the left of the Arrange area that displays the channel strips assigned to various tracks as well as the track Mute, Solo, and other buttons.

Transform window An editor used to select and modify various aspects of MIDI events according to user-defined parameters.

Transport bar An area at the bottom of the Arrange window that holds buttons used to control Logic Pro's playback and recording functions. Several buttons (Record, Pause, Play, Stop, Rewind, Forward) work the same way as the control buttons on a cassette deck or recordable audio CD player.

velocity The speed at which a MIDI note is struck.

V

virtual instrument A software element that mimics a traditional hardware sound module.

W

WAV, WAVE The primary audio file format used by Windows-compatible computers. In Logic Pro, all recorded and bounced WAV files are in Broadcast Wave format.

waveform A visual representation of an audio signal.

Z

zero crossing A point in an audio file where the waveform crosses the zero amplitude axis. If you cut an audio file at a zero crossing, there will be no click at the cut point.

zoom An action that enlarges (zooms in on) or reduces (zooms out from) a viewing area in any window.

Zoom tool A tool that enables you to zoom in on any part of the display. Pressing Control-Option while selecting a part of the window section enlarges the area.

Index

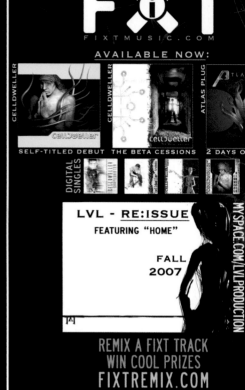